Fly Tyer

The Master's Fly Box

America's Best Anglers Share Their Favorite Trout Flies

David Klausmeyer

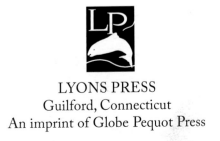

LYONS PRESS
Guilford, Connecticut
An imprint of Globe Pequot Press

Copyright © 2012 by David Klausmeyer

Lyons Press is an imprint of Globe Pequot Press.

Interior photos by David Klausmeyer unless otherwise credited.

Text design: Lisa Reneson
Layout artist: Sue Murray
Project editor: David Legere

Library of Congress Cataloging-in-Publication Data is available on file.

ISBN 978-0-7627-6396-2

Printed in USA

10 9 8 7 6 5 4 3 2 1

Contents

Introduction 5
Tell Me about Yourself

Chapter 1 7
Al and Gretchen Beatty: Our Favorite Husband-and-Wife Fly-Tying Team

Chapter 2 13
Don Bastian and His Classy Wet Flies

Chapter 3 21
Brian Chan: Sage of the Kamloops

Chapter 4 31
Charlie Craven Keeps It Simple

Chapter 5 40
George Daniel: No Bull, No Bravado—Just Pure Fly Fishing

Chapter 6 49
Pat Dorsey Is Always Fishing

Chapter 7 56
John Gierach: Fly Fishing's Best-Selling Author Is Also a Hell of a Fly Tyer

Chapter 8 64
Aaron Jasper: Leading Fly Fishing into the Future

Chapter 9 75
Craig Mathews and Blue Ribbon Flies

Chapter 10 84
Mike Mercer: "I Still Love to Tie and Fish"

Chapter 11 97
Kevin McKay and the New Age of Fly Fishing

Contents

Chapter 12 107
Harry Murray of the Beautiful Blue Ridge

Chapter 13 116
Dennis Potter and the River House Fly Company

Chapter 14 125
Al Ritt and Rocky Mountain National Park

Chapter 15 135
Fishing the Canadian Prairies with Philip Rowley

Chapter 16 146
Scott Sanchez: A Wyoming Favorite

Chapter 17 156
Lisa Savard and New Hampshire's Upper Connecticut River

Chapter 18 165
Eric Stroup: An Innovative Tyer with a Growing Reputation

Chapter 19 174
Mike Valla: Preserving the Catskill Traditions

Chapter 20 182
Vince Wilcox: "Fly Fishing and Tying Are Just in the Blood"

Chapter 21 191
Davy Wotton: From Wales to the White River

Index 198

About the Author 208

Introduction

Tell Me about Yourself

For several years I have been experimenting with a new way to write about fly fishing and tying. It's based on a very simple premise: Find good anglers and fly tyers, and get them to talk about themselves. It's a lot of fun to do, and the folks I profile say it is a painless experience. It's also a great way to gather a lot of valuable information from experts about how to tie flies and fish and to tell a more complete story. The process works like this:

Once I've identified my quarry, I contact that person to see if he or she would consent to being profiled. (I've been turned down only once, but many others have contacted me first and asked to be profiled.) The subject sends a batch of his or her favorite flies for photography and hopefully includes the matching pattern recipes. Sometimes I write the recipes for the person, and if I can't identify an ingredient or a logical substitute (or both), I can ask the subject for help. Once the flies arrive, and I know the person is committed, I schedule an appointment for a telephone interview.

The interview generally takes about an hour—maybe a little more. When we chat, a tape recorder catches what we say so I don't have to slow down the pace of the conversation to take notes. I've also discovered that some people feel freer to talk over the telephone rather than face to face with a tape recorder or note pad sitting between us.

I ask my subjects how they got into fly fishing and tying. I ask them to describe where they fish. I ask them about their favorite flies and how they use them. I get them talking about pattern design and any unusual fishing techniques they've developed. One topic naturally flows into another, and by the time we're done I feel as though I've spent a day on their favorite water with them: I know what will be hatching, what patterns I will select, and how I will use them.

After the phone call I rewind the tape and transcribe what was said. I remove or tone down any expletives and then maybe rearrange some blocks of conversation. I also whittle down the overall length of the text to the essentials to make it fit the allotted space of a typical magazine article; remember, I have to leave room for photos of the flies and the accompanying recipes. (In book form, of course, those pesky expletives are less of a problem, and there is more room to include fuller interviews and more flies.)

This method sounds so obvious, yet it has been overlooked by other fly-fishing writers. I play more the role of a reporter than an author. It's an excellent way to learn about fly tying and fishing from the best in the game, and it gives all of us an opportunity to meet other talented, passionate anglers.

Those articles appeared in *Fly Tyer* magazine. They were often in the *Fly Tyer* Profile or First Wraps sections of the magazine, but sometimes they appeared as features; how they were used usually depended upon how much space I needed to tell a story. I am gratified that so many readers responded favorably to those pieces.

The Master's Fly Box

The Master's Fly Box is an outgrowth of this experiment in fly-fishing journalism. For this book I have selected anglers from both the United States and Canada. Some are on the cutting edge of new fly design; others are recognized masters at tying the most elegant and historic patterns. Some are working guides; others are just passionate anglers. Some are fly-fishing household names with wide followings; others, I believe, have a good shot at becoming well known beyond their local waters. All are first-rate, interesting people who are making major contributions to the sport of fly fishing and the craft of tying flies.

I would like to thank all of these gentlemen—and two gentlewomen—for their time and important contributions to this project.

Chapter 1

Al and Gretchen Beatty:
Our Favorite Husband-and-Wife Fly-Tying Team

Al and Gretchen Beatty each have been tying flies for almost half a century. Gretchen says she learned to tie flies when she was about eleven or twelve years old, and Al says, "I bought a fly-tying kit when I was fourteen, and I sold my first fly a month later. I've been a commercial fly tyer, to one degree or another, ever since."

Today Al and Gretchen have retired from jobs in the real world, and they spend a great deal of time filling orders for their beautiful flies from their home in Boise, Idaho. In their system, one person starts a batch of flies—perhaps tying the tails and bodies to the hooks—and the other adds the wings and collars. This method allows them to vastly increase their production. In addition to commercial fly tying, the Beattys have vast experience guiding and running a fly-tying business. Al has also served as a national officer for the Federation of Fly Fishers and as editor of that organization's magazine. The Beattys are in high demand to give fly-tying demonstrations and lead classes.

The Beattys are regular contributors to *Fly Tyer* magazine, and it was a particular pleasure to include them in this book. Al and Gretchen's articles often feature some of their favorite professional fly-tying tips, and I've included a lot of their ideas in my own tying.

You've always talked about your tag-team approach to tying fly. How does it work?

"Weeks might go by, and neither of us will tie a complete fly. Say we're filling an order for Humpies. I'll

COURTESY OF AL AND GRETCHEN BEATTY

Gray Wulff
Hook: 1X-long dry-fly hook, sizes 20 to 8.
Thread: Black 6/0 (140 denier).
Tail: Deer-body hair.
Wing: Deer-body hair.
Body: Gray dry-fly dubbing.
Hackle: Blue dun or grizzly.

Parachute Adams (Western Style)
Hook: 1X-long dry-fly hook, sizes 22 to 10.
Thread: Gray 6/0 (140 denier).
Tail: Moose-body hair.
Wing: Calf-body or tail hair.
Body: Gray muskrat.
Hackle: Brown and grizzly mixed.

Double Magic Royal Double Wing
Hook: 3X-long dry-fly hook, sizes 20 to 6.
Thread: Black 6/0 (140 denier).
Tail: Green Antron.
Tip: Red floss.
Rear wing: Brown deer hair.
Body: Peacock herl and lime green Antron
    Touch Dubbing.
Body hackle: Brown, clipped on the top
    and bottom.
Front wing: White calf tail.
Hackle: Brown.

put on the tail clump and the wing clump, and I'll pass it on to Gretchen. She'll stand and divide the wings and sort the hackles and put them on. Each of us basically ties our part."

It sounds like a great way to speed up production.
"As a team we'll tie a lot of flies. We find that we can get really fast if we just tie our parts. Each of us has fewer materials on our benches, so we can easily find what we need, and you get really fast concentrating on fewer steps."

How many flies a year do you tie?
"A few years ago was our high year. How many flies did we tie that year, Gretchen?" Al asked. "Twelve hundred dozen?"
    "Yes, that's about right."
    "Now we're lucky to do three or four hundred dozen," Al continued. "We're writing a lot more for *Fly Tyer*, and frankly on some days writing about tying flies is nicer than doing it. But we still do our commercial tying. It helps us maintain our skills for when we do demonstrations or teach classes."

What are your home waters for fishing?
"Let's start right here in town. The Boise River is a blue-ribbon trout fishery. There are several forks to the Boise that are a little drive from town, but they also offer good fishing. And just over the border in Oregon we have some really good fishing; in some cases it's closer to go to Oregon to fish. Eastern Oregon has mountains that offer good trout fishing and some phenomenal steelhead fishing."

What's the fishing like on the Boise River?
"It depends upon which fork of the river you want to fish. It's open all year here in town. The South Fork has

a more limited season, but you can fish for whitefish all year long; if those pesky trout get on your hook, you just have to let them go."

The flies you sent are wonderful. I'm familiar with a lot of your patterns, but I've never seen the Bullethead Mayfly or Bullethead Caddisfly. These look like low-rising emerger imitations.

"Yes, both flies do ride low in the water. The major difference between them is that the wing on the Bullethead Mayfly stands more upright. The wings on both patterns are tied using squirrel-tail hair, but the heads are deer or elk hair."

When would you use these patterns during a hatch?

"You can use these flies during hatches, but actually, because of the way they're tied, they are all-day searching patterns. You can easily see the body on the Bullethead Caddisfly; it's spun and clipped deer hair. That body floats like corks. These flies also work well during stonefly hatches; just base everything on the color and size of what's happening on the river."

How do you tie the wing on the Bullethead Mayfly?

"When we tie on the squirrel-tail wing, we add a couple wraps here and there in the wing to get the different clumps of squirrel hair to stand up. It's actually three or four clumps of hair."

Do you use this technique when tying other flies?

"We also use this style of wing on some of our steamers. A regular squirrel-tail wing doesn't have any motion—it just lays flat along the top of the body. But if you tie the wing with the individual clumps standing up, it opens and closes when you draw the fly through the water. It gives the fly a very realistic swimming action."

Bullethead Mayfly
Hook: 1X-long dry-fly hook, sizes 20 to 12.
Thread: Gray 6/0 (140 denier) or a color
    to match the body.
Tail: Moose-body hair.
Wing: Fox- or gray squirrel-tail hair.
Body: Dry-fly dubbing, color to match the
    natural insect.
Head: Deer hair, spun and clipped to shape.

Bullethead Caddisfly
Hook: 1X-long dry-fly hook, sizes 22 to 8.
Thread: Color to match the body of the
    natural insect.
Tag: Tying thread.
Body: Deer hair, spun and clipped to
    shape.
Wing: Fox- or gray squirrel-tail hair.
Head: Deer hair, spun and clipped to shape.

Muddle Mayfly
Hook: 1X-long dry-fly hook, sizes 24 to 12.
Thread: Gray or a color to match the
    natural insect, size 6/0 (140 denier).
Tail: Moose-body hair.
Body: Gray dry-fly dubbing.
Wing: Grizzly hackles folded backward to
    form the wings.
Collar: Deer-hair tips.
Head: Deer hair, spun and clipped to shape.

H&L Variant
Hook: 1X-long dry-fly hook, sizes 20 to 12.
Thread: Black and white 6/0 (140 denier).
Tail: White calf-body hair.
Wing: White calf-body hair.
Body: Stripped and natural peacock herl.
Hackle: Brown.

Wonder Wings are another ingenious style of tying you use to tie good-looking imitations. To tie Wonder Wings, you clip sections of hackles and pull the fibers backward toward the hook. You use Wonder Wings on your Muddle Mayfly and Scuddle Muddle. Are they hard to make?

"Wonder Wings take a little more time to tie, but they are very nice. And just like with a parachute-style pattern, a fly with Wonder Wings lands upright almost every single time."

What's the history of the pattern called the H&L Variant?

"The H&L Variant was originally a Western fly developed in the 1930s. Dan Bailey was at least one of the guys who claimed credit for that pattern. It was called the Hair Wing Variant at the time. Dwight Eisenhower, who, of course, was a fly fisherman, really liked it. Well, part of his campaign slogan used the words 'House and Lot,' and that phrase was applied to the name of the fly. It's an incredible pattern, and we really like fishing it in cutthroat country because those fish are such suckers for it. We'll tie a Renegade to it and fish them in tandem; the Renegade is a couple of sizes smaller than the H&L."

And the body is stripped peacock herl, right?

"It's half stripped peacock and half regular peacock."

The Scuddle Muddle is new to me. Tell me about this pattern.

"It's a wet or dry sort of pattern, depending upon which fly you're looking at. It's actually an emerger imitation. You can tie and fish it to mimic just about everything. I sent a large fly for you to photograph, but we normally use it in sizes 22 to 14."

Is that true of just the Scuddle Muddle, or does it apply to all of the flies you fish?

"I think that applies to most of the flies we fish; we normally start out using about a size 14 and eventually work our way down to size 22. With something like the Scuddle Muddle, we stop tying the flared deer-hair head on about size 18 hooks."

It's incredible that you tie these sorts of flies with split-hair wings and all the other features on such small hooks.

"Well, go into any fly shop, and you'll find Trudes, Humpies, and Wulffs in sizes 18 and 20. When guiding, I'd always start the day with a size 10 Royal Wulff and a dropper for one client and a size 10 Humpy with another dropper for the other client. We'd see if the fish were interested. If we didn't catch a fish, I started changing patterns and sizes. The Trude has always been an all-around good pattern because you can fish it as a dry fly, and when it starts to drag, you can jerk it under the surface and fish it as a wet fly."

You sent only dry flies and emergers. Would you say that you fish mostly surface patterns?

"We probably use half dry flies and half subsurface patterns. It depends upon the body of water."

Come to think of it, most of the articles you've written for **Fly Tyer** *magazine that feature patterns have been about dry flies.*

"We have a whole gob of wet flies and nymphs that we also fish. But I'll tell you something: It's pretty hard screwing up wrapping peacock herl on a hook when tying a nymph, but tying and dividing hair wings on a dry fly is something people struggle with. I think that's why we spend so much time talking and writing about hair-wing dry flies: So many tyers want to learn how to do it."

You're very well known for your fly-tying classes and demonstrations. Tell me a little about them.

"We do quite a few classes and demonstrations at clubs and fly shops. They can take a lot of different

Scuddle Muddle
Hook: Curved-shank emerger hook, sizes 18 to 12.
Thread: Black or a color to match the natural insect, size 6/0 (140 denier).
Body: Green dry-fly dubbing or a color to match the natural insect.
Rib: Extra-fine black wire.
Wing: Grizzly hackles folded backward to form wings and tips of deer hair.

Royal Wulff
Hook: 1X-long dry-fly hook, sizes 18 to 6.
Thread: Black 6/0 (140 denier).
Tail: Deer-body hair.
Wing: White calf-body hair.
Body: Peacock herl and red floss.
Hackle: Brown.

forms. Sometimes we're asked to spend an entire day tying one style of fly, such as Humpies: how to make the bodies and tie the hair wings. We had one interesting experience in Texas where the club set up a video theater, and we just demonstrated fly tying all day: I'd tie for an hour, and then Gretchen would tie. We shared a lot of tips and tricks, and they had vises set up, and people were following along; whichever one of us wasn't tying could help the members of the audience. That was a fun class, and we helped a lot of people learn to tie better flies."

The people I've met in Texas are very enthusiastic about fly fishing and tying.

"They damn sure are. That was a great day. But then, almost any day you tie flies or go fly fishing is a good day."

Royal Trude
Hook: 1X-long dry-fly hook, sizes 18 to 6.
Thread: Black 6/0 (140 denier).
Tail: Deer-body hair.
Wing: White calf-body hair.
Body: Peacock herl and red floss.
Hackle: Brown.

Royal Humpy
Hook: 1X-long dry-fly hook, sizes 20 to 8.
Thread: Red 6/0 (140 denier).
Tail: Moose-body hair.
Body: Tying thread and elk hair for the hump.
Wing: Calf-tail or body hair.
Hackle: Brown.

Regular Humpy
Hook: 1X-long dry-fly hook, sizes 18 to 8.
Thread: Your choice of color.
Tail: Moose-body hair.
Body: Tying thread and elk hair for the hump.
Wing: Elk-body hair.
Hackle: Grizzly and brown, mixed.

Chapter 2

Don Bastian
and His Classy Wet Flies

You must be wondering: Why is an entire chapter devoted to classic wet flies? Shouldn't a book about flies and fly tying contain only new patterns? Is anyone even interested in patterns that were developed one hundred or more years ago?

The answers to those questions are "because," "no," and "yes."

I'm including Don Bastian, a recognized authority on tying classic wet flies, because these patterns are drop-dead gorgeous. They add class to the large collection of flies we are studying. And classic wet flies still catch fish; he even recommended many of these patterns to his clients when he served as a professional guide.

No, I don't think we should concentrate on only new patterns. I see a lot of new flies: Some are obviously winners, and some, I am sad to say, are obviously bogus. I'm thrilled when I discover a new pattern that catches trout, but I get just as excited—tempered with a tinge of nostalgia—whenever I catch fish using old favorite flies.

And, yes, there is still a great deal of interest in these patterns. I've watched Don tie flies at major fly-fishing shows, and there is always a ring of admirers surrounding his table. I once saw a young man—he couldn't have been twenty years old—ask the most particular and insightful questions about proportions and materials handling, and he eagerly recorded Don's answers in his notebook. And when Don appears at the L. L. Bean Spring Fishing Expo, his large display of framed flies is one of the most popular attractions at that major event.

COURTESY OF DON BASTIAN

Governor
Hook: Regular wet-fly hook, sizes 16 to 10.
Thread: Black 8/0 (70 denier).
Tip: Scarlet floss.
Body: Peacock herl.
Hackle: Brown.
Wing: Dark brown mottled turkey.

Black Gnat
Hook: Regular wet-fly hook, sizes 16 to 10.
Thread: Black 8/0 (70 denier).
Tip: Silver tinsel.
Body: Black chenille.
Hackle: Black.
Wing: Slate.

Red Squirrel Picket Pin
Hook: Regular wet-fly hook, sizes 16 to 10.
Thread: Black 8/0 (70 denier).
Tail: Brown hackle tips or fibers.
Rib: Silver or gold wire.
Hackle: Brown tied palmer is original,
   but a brown throat or beard hackle is
   more durable for fishing.
Body: Silver tinsel.
Wing: Red squirrel tail.
Head: Peacock herl.

Don is from Cogan Station, Pennsylvania, in the heart of some of the best fly fishing in the East. With so much excellent fishing available, it was only natural that he took up fly tying.

"I've been tying since I was twelve years old," he said at the beginning of our interview. "It's coming up on forty-six—forty-seven years this spring."

In addition to fishing for yourself, you've been a professional guide. Do you still guide?

"I guided for sixteen years. I sort of started going in a different direction with what I like to do, but I'm thinking of getting back into it."

Where is Cogan Station?

"It's very near Williamsport, so it is in Lycoming County, which I guess is the north-central part of the state. We're about an hour from the New York border."

What are your home waters?

"There's a lot of good wild trout fishing, and there are some stocked populations as well. The Pennsylvania Fish Commission has a statewide program that assessed our waters to find wild, sustainable populations of trout, and they took these best streams off the stocking list. So, within an hour's drive of my home, you have Spring Creek, Big Fishing Creek, and Penn's Creek, which would be on anybody's list of the top-ten streams in the state.

"Closer to home, more in the mountains of Lycoming County, there are three major freestone streams. For example, Big Pine Creek is as big as the Beaverkill River. Ten miles farther east there is Lycoming Creek, and eight miles farther than that is Loyalsock Creek. All three of these are very large. Big Pine Creek is sixty or seventy miles long. Loyalsock Creek is forty miles long, and Lycoming Creek is also about forty miles long. And all three streams have tributaries that offer more fishing. All of this water contains both stocked and wild brown and brook trout."

Is all of this accessible?

"Pretty much. There's a combination of private and public land, and, of course, some of it requires a little bit of walking to get to, but there is a lot of access to fishing. I've said to a lot of people that you could spend an entire hour fishing within an hour of Williamsport and not visit the same place twice. Pennsylvania has about five thousand miles of what they call 'approved trout water,' which is water that is open to the public; it's more than that if you include private water."

How long have you been fishing?

"My brother and I have been fishing since we could walk; I don't ever remember not fishing. My dad tied flies and fished before we were born, but he eventually gave it up. I don't know why, and I never thought to ask. But one day when I was about twelve, we were at a farm pond that had bass and bluegills. My brother was catching fish with worms and a bobber using a fly rod and reel, and we asked our dad how to fly fish. He didn't argue a bit: He just rerigged the rod to cast flies. He quickly taught us how to cast and use the hand-twist retrieve, and we staring catching bluegills on flies. When we got back to this old farmhouse, I asked him if he had any books on fly fishing, and he pulled out a ninth-edition printing of *Trout*, by Ray Bergman. The first thing I did was look at the pictures.

"My dad also gave us a copy of E. C. Gregg's book, *How to Tie Flies*, which was dated 1940. He then taught us everything he knew about fly tying, and he gave us all his stuff. Between my dad's instructions and all the information from those two books, that's how I learned to tie. It was a full ten years before I saw anyone else tie a fly."

Black and Silver
Hook: Regular wet-fly hook, sizes 16 to 10.
Thread: Black 8/0 (70 denier).
Tail: Golden pheasant tippet.
Body: Silver tinsel.
Hackle: Black.
Wing: Black.

Royal Coachman
Hook: Regular wet-fly hook, sizes 16 to 10.
Thread: Black 8/0 (70 denier).
Tip: Gold tinsel.
Tail: Golden pheasant tippet.
Body: Peacock herl and red floss.
Hackle: Dark reddish brown.
Wing: White.

Yellow Sally
Hook: Regular wet-fly hook, sizes 16 to 10.
Thread: Black 8/0 (70 denier).
Tip: Gold tinsel.
Tail: Yellow quill sections.
Body: Yellow floss.
Rib: Gold tinsel.
Hackle: Yellow.
Wing: Yellow.

Parmachene Belle
Hook: Regular wet-fly hook, sizes 16 to 10.
Thread: Black 8/0 (70 denier).
Tip: Silver tinsel (optional).
Tail: White and scarlet, married.
Butt: Black ostrich herl.
Rib: Silver tinsel.
Body: Yellow wool or rabbit dubbing.
Hackle: White and scarlet mixed.
Wing: White with scarlet stripe, married.

When did you first see a real master fly tyer at work?

"That was at a banquet in 1974. It might have been Ed Shenk or Vince Marinaro or Charlie Fox—one of those guys. We went to those events, and they had these celebrity tyers. After my dad, the first person I would have seen tie a fly would have been one of these fellows, but I can't remember who it was."

What were the first flies you tied and fished?

"The first flies I fished were the Royal Coachman and Yellow Sally. I sent you a Parmachene Belle because that was the first fly I tied that had married wings; that was in about 1975. But it wasn't until the mid-1990s that I got really interested in the Bergman flies and started tying older flies. I do tie a lot of other things—nymphs, dry flies, Woolly Buggers, and everything else—but for years I fished the Grizzly King, Professor, Coachmen of all varieties, Scarlet Ibis, and so on."

Do these flies still catch fish?

"They absolutely do catch fish. I could go on for a couple of hours telling stories about how these patterns work all over the United States. You met my niece, Emily. She spent three and a half months out west fishing the Bitterroot, the Flathead, and I don't know where else, using gaudy wet flies that no one uses anymore. And other fellows had a phenomenal day on the Big Horn fishing bright yellow-winged patterns like the Richardson. I think that pattern is originally from your neck of the woods in Maine."

Do you still use these flies when you fish?

"I often use them. A few years ago Emily was visiting over Memorial Day weekend. One day I had some stuff to do, but she wanted to go fishing. I told her to go up over the hill to Lycoming Creek about two miles away. So, she went in there, and there were three other guys already fishing, but they were having no luck. She, on the other hand, caught seventeen trout. Emily was using a black-and-olive Woolly Bugger as the point fly with either an Alexandria, a Yellow Sally, or a Parmachene Belle as the dropper. She caught thirteen of those fish on the wet flies."

What's the most difficult part of tying classic wet flies?

"Setting quill wings. I get more questions about this than anything else. I also get a lot of questions about obtaining good duck quills for making the wings. Finding good wing quills used to be a problem; the material supply houses said no one bought them, so many discontinued selling them. Then, just about three years ago, one of the major wholesalers reintroduced dyed colors because there was a new demand for them. There seems to be more interest in tying these classic patterns, and tyers are demanding these materials."

Do you tie the wings using duck or goose feathers?

"Both, actually. I think most of the original patterns were tied using either duck or goose-wing quills. If you stop and think about it, goose shoulder feathers are large enough to tie up size 3/0 and 5/0 flies, and it makes no sense to use these long-fibered feathers to make small wet flies. To tie a wing, you need only half an inch or less of the quill, so duck feathers are fine.

"I also looked at a lot of old, historic flies. I have an old sheepskin fly wallet—it's falling apart—that is full of snelled patterns, and it is obvious that the wings are nothing more than sections clipped from mallard quills. They also used a lot starling, snipe, and similar feathers to tie even smaller flies."

Do you tie on the wings using what is called the "pinch wrap"?

"I do use a pinch wrap, and I use no soft wraps. Once I gain control of the wings and I know they are in the correct position, the first wrap is tight. Each subsequent wrap is also tight. You're concerned with

Quill and Yellow
Hook: Regular wet-fly hook, sizes 16 to 10.
Thread: Black 8/0 (70 denier).
Tail: Brown hackle fibers.
Body: Stripped peacock quill and front yellow floss.
Hackle: Brown.
Wing: Slate.

Blue Dun
Hook: Regular wet-fly hook, sizes 16 to 10.
Thread: Black 8/0 (70 denier).
Tail: Dark dun hackle fibers.
Body: Blue-gray rabbit fur.
Hackle: Dark dun.
Wing: Slate or blue gray.

two things when tying the wings on wet flies: the quality of the material and the thread tension."

You've also been a commercial fly tyer. How did that experience help you become a better fly tyer?

"I've said for a long time that people need to develop good tying habits. I tied for twenty-five years, and then I started tying commercially. I learned more in that first year of commercial tying than I did in the first twenty-five. One of things that became important was using correct proportions. Let's say you tie a dozen or even five dozen Hare's-Ear Nymphs: The proportions of the tails, bodies, and ribs should all be identical. I find a lot of beginning tyers become overwhelmed, and they want to jump into this creative, freeform mode. I tell them to pick a handful of patterns and learn to do those well. Tie them until you can make five or six dozen that all look alike. Too many guys want to tie two or three of some pattern, and then they want to go on to something else. They never learn good tying habits, and they never progress. By staying with a few flies, you learn better material-handling skills and develop a sense for correct proportions."

I believe you've tied all of the flies that were in Ray Bergman's famous book, Trout. That seems like a Herculean task. What was it like?

"Yes, I've done it a couple of times. I didn't frame the first set; it was for a collector's-type book titled *Forgotten Flies*. Next, I did a framed set for a restaurant that has an outdoors theme; part of the building is re-created like an old Adirondack sporting lodge. The flies fit right in.

"There are 440 wet flies in *Trout*, but I also include the flies from Bergman's first book, *Just Fishing*, and different patterns from *With Fly, Plug, and Bait*, which was his last book, published in 1947. And then there was a new plate of flies included in the second edition of *Trout*, which was published in 1952; from that I

Gold-Ribbed Hare's Ear
Hook: Regular wet-fly hook, sizes 16 to 10.
Thread: Black 8/0 (70 denier).
Tip: Gold tinsel.
Tail: Brown hackle fibers.
Rib: Gold tinsel.
Body: Rabbit dubbing.
Hackle: Formed by long fibers of rabbit fur picked out from body.
Wing: Slate or dark slate.

picked just the wet flies, not the nymphs and streamers.
So, there are 483 flies in the entire set."

Mary Orvis Marbury's book, Favorite Flies, *is often
considered a major reference for understanding the evolution
of American fly tying up to the beginning of the twentieth
century. What can we learn from that volume?*
"It's interesting to note that *Favorite Flies*, which was
published in 1892, contains color plates showing about
three hundred flies. Bergman's book actually contains
more than six hundred total flies, so Bergman's was
the largest collection of illustrated fishing flies, and all
the pattern names and recipes are listed in the back.
Marbury's book contains no formal pattern recipes.
I know of two Bergman patterns—one is a wet fly,
and one is a dry fly—that call for condor quill on the
bodies. And some call for jungle cock. But none of the
Bergman flies call for bustard.

"Now, if you go back to the Marbury book, it's
not that uncommon to find bustard and similar exotic
feathers on her flies. I think the Migratory Bird Act of
1918 had a significant impact on fly tying. For example,
up until that time, wood ducks were one of the most
heavily hunted ducks in the eastern United States,
and they were almost wiped out. They were protected
under that law, and you couldn't hunt them until 1959.
So, Bergman's recipes called for Mandarin or barred
Mandarin instead of wood duck. Now we're back to
using wood-duck feathers. I assume the Migratory
Bird Act had the same effect on using other feathers
to tie flies, so you see a difference between the flies in
Favorite Flies and *Trout*."

If someone wants to tie the flies in **Trout,** *how accurate are
the pattern recipes?*
"I've found 54 flies of the original 440 where there's
a discrepancy between the painted flies in the
illustrations and the written recipes. Dr. Edgar Burke,
who painted the illustrations, was very detail-oriented.

He actually had samples of birds and ducks in his studio because he was a noted waterfowl artist; his paintings and prints still command high prices. According to the Bergman family, the flies in *Trout* were painted from actual samples, so bearing that in mind and knowing his attention to detail, I think the illustrations are probably accurate. But this is a debate you'll see on websites dedicated to classic flies: What's correct—the illustrations or the recipes? I lean toward believing the illustrations because sometimes you'll find a fly that has a component that is not listed in the recipe."

Do you still tie the complete set of flies?

"Yes, I do. I've replicated the flies in Plate One about eight times, and I have a customer in my hometown who has the first three plates, and another customer in Massachusetts who has the first five. Overall, I have tied the entire set three times. I also tie and sell single and small groups of flies for collectors. I've probably tied three or four hundred Parmachene Belle and Trout Fins—you know, the popular patterns."

Is there still an interest in fishing with these sorts of flies?

"There's absolutely an interest. I still get a lot of old-timers who say, 'That's the stuff that we used, and you don't see anybody use it anymore. But I still use them, and they still work.'

"There are actually a couple of advantages to these flies if you're interested in learning about the classics. The materials are fairly common and inexpensive; on the other hand, if you try to get into classic salmon flies, you have to spend a lot of money to acquire the authentic materials. This makes classic wet flies more accessible for people. And you can fish with these flies and feel good about it; not too many people want to fish with a fly that costs a lot of time and money to tie."

Trout Fin
Hook: Regular wet-fly hook, sizes 16 to 10.
Thread: Black 8/0 (70 denier).
Tip: White floss.
Body: Orange floss.
Rib: White floss.
Hackle: Orange.
Wing: Black, white, and orange, married.

Chapter 3

Brian Chan:
Sage of the Kamloops

British Columbia's Kamloops region is legendary for its fine trout ponds and lakes. But beyond the size and plentiful numbers of the trout, the skill level of the local anglers is what I admire the most. These anglers might rely on science when creating their patterns, but I always walk away with the feeling that they have turned fly fishing into a high form of art.

Brian Chan seems to be a modest man, and I think he might blush when I say this, but I often think of him as one of the fishing priests of the Kamloops. I have admired his writing for many years, and I apply many of his principles to the stillwater fishing I do in Maine. This chapter came about out of greed: I was aching for a reason to contact Brian and ask about his flies and fishing methods. I had several little problems I was trying to solve, and I knew he would have the answers. This project provided the perfect cover to see if he would consent to an interview.

What I encountered was one of the leading minds in both fisheries management and fly fishing.

"I spent thirty years working for the provincial government as a fisheries biologist," Brian said. "My specialty was recreational trout fisheries, in particular managing the still waters in the southern interior region of British Columbia."

Okay, I had a lot of questions about how to fish ponds and lakes. First, however, we talked about the terrific opportunities for fly fishing in the Kamloops area. I also learned a lot about how recreational fishing can actually enhance our coldwater fisheries.

"In my mind, these waters offer opportunities for really world-class fishing," Brian continued. "It's

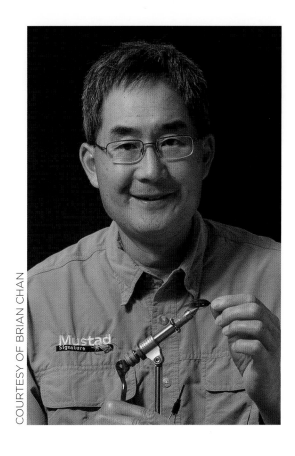

unbelievable how many trout lakes we have. In the last five years of my career, I was asked to join a new group called the Freshwater Fisheries Society of British Columbia. This group was formed about seven years ago to take over the provincial stocking program. This removed the stocking program from the government and placed it into a nonprofit society and changed the funding model. Under the new system, a certain percentage of the fishing license you buy goes to the society to pay for fish stocking. This has worked out very well.

"Now, since stocking was going to be paid for through license sales, you have to make sure you're selling licenses to survive. So, the society asked me to create a recreational-fishing marketing program. Like many jurisdictions in North America, the sale of fishing licenses has declined. We engaged in a very aggressive ten-year marketing plan, and we've been pretty successful. We're in the fourth year of our plan, and we've seen an increase every season."

British Columbia is famous for its coldwater fisheries. But beyond the enjoyment of fishing, Brian says that this resource has an important economic impact on the province.

"British Columbia has more than twenty thousand lakes, and the society stocks less than 850. But these 850 stocked lakes support more than half of the total recreational fishing that occurs in the province. These lakes are very important to the economic health of the province; they provide employment for lodges, guides, campground owners, and many more people. And when managed properly, these lakes are totally renewable resources."

What species of fish do you stock?

"We stock rainbow trout, Kokanee, a small amount of steelhead, cutthroat, and eastern brook trout. And we have a very aggressive sterile-stocking program; this is how we get our really big trophy trout. These fish live longer, and they get much bigger."

How many lakes are in the Kamloops region?

"In an area measuring thirty-six-thousand square miles, which is a very small part of this huge province, there are about a thousand lakes. We stock two hundred fifty to three hundred of these lakes. This is the interior, dry-belt region, with total annual precipitation averaging less than fourteen inches, including both rain and spring runoff. We have very hot, dry, sagebrush summers and cold winters. These are landlocked lakes that are nutrient rich. They are shallow, have lots of calcium, and the fish grow very quickly."

What is the source of water for these lakes?

"Some are spring fed; others have ephemeral flowing inlets and outlets. Some have little more than spring runoff filling them as the snow melts. This has become an issue in recent years because with global climate change, we're seeing less snow pack, and some of our lakes have suffered through years of low water.

"We're also having issues with mountain pine beetles, which have killed all of our lodgepole pines. The insects were always there, but there was a population explosion due to the warmer winters; the severe cold kept the beetles in check. The pine trees held the moisture back in the ground, but without the vegetation, the water runs off very quickly. This has also led to a change in the basic chemistry of the water. These are the challenges, but on the positive side we still have a lot of great fishing for large numbers of really outstanding trout."

Did these lakes naturally have fish?

"No. Many of these lakes were created during the last period of glaciation. Many of these lakes were made when the glaciers receded and created depressions

Stillwater Caddis Pupa
Hook: Mustad Signature R73, sizes 14 to 10.
Thread: Dark brown 8/0 (70 denier).
Rib: Stillwater Solutions *Chaoborus* green Midge Stretch Floss.
Body: Stillwater Solutions dark olive Soft Blend.
Throat: Peacock Angel Hair.
Legs: Dark brown pheasant-rump fibers.
Head: Peacock herl.

that filled with water. The majority of these lakes had no fish. In the early 1900s the provincial and federal governments had a small stocking program, and ranchers also stocked many lakes. That's what created many of these wonderful fisheries."

What is the source of fish used for stocking?

"Rainbow trout were native in some of the larger lakes. These were used to stock the fishless lakes. Even today more than 90 percent of the rainbow trout stocked in British Columbia come from wild adult fish. You don't have large numbers of brood stock living in our hatcheries. Each spring we go out and take eggs from trout living in lakes that have never been stocked; this is how we stock 'wild' trout. This is very unique in North America. This is the Pennask Lake strain of fish. These are strong-fighting trout that love to jump."

How large are the fish you stock?

"We stock yearling trout or fall fry trout that are six months old. A yearling is about two and a half inches long. In many lakes, if a yearling is stocked in May, it is twelve inches long by October. By May of the following spring, it weighs more than two pounds, and May of the third year, it's over three pounds."

Is the fishing readily accessible?

"Yes, 99 percent of the lakes are accessible by road. Some you need a pickup truck to drive to, and others might require four-wheel drive. There are a handful of lakes that are walk-in, but there's a lot of logging in this area, and the extensive road network has opened up a lot of waters. There are also a lot of 'wild' lakes that are walk-in and do not get stocked; these contain nothing but wild trout. They're at higher elevations, and because they are totally wild, you will get fluctuations in these fisheries; sometimes they're just full of smaller trout."

What is the basic source of forage for the trout?

"They are insectivores. They live in a monocultural environment with no competing coarse fish. They eat only insects, which make up the basis of our world-class fishery."

The lakes and ponds in the Kamloops are known to contain large trout. How big do they get?

"If you sterilize a Pennask rainbow trout, it can live to nine or ten years of age, and in the right lake with the right regulations—fly fishing only and catch-and-release—it can reach in excess of sixteen or seventeen pounds."

How long is your fishing season? When does it begin, and when does it end?

"The ice is coming off our lakes and ponds by early April. Prime time to catch the hatches is from early May through early July. It gets very warm from late July through August. We then have really superb late-season fishing from late September through October and into November. In late season you're fishing imitations of the bread-and-butter food sources such as leeches and scuds."

What are the most common forms of insects in these lakes?

"Chironomids are the largest source of food for these trout, then it's mayflies, damselflies, dragonflies, and caddisflies, in that order."

I've read a lot about fishing chironomid imitations in your area. Explain these methods.

"The majority of chironomid emergences occur in water that is five to twenty-five feet deep. At these depths, you can be very effective fishing with a floating line and a long leader. You can fish with or without a strike indicator. Ideally, set your indicator so that the fly hangs

Stillwater Caddis Emerger
Hook: Mustad Signature R43 or 94831, sizes 14 to 10.
Thread: Dark brown 8/0 (70 denier).
Tail: White Zelon.
Rib: Stillwater Solutions *Chaoborus* green Midge Stretch Floss.
Body: Stillwater Solutions dark olive Soft Blend.
Shellback: Whitetail deer-body hair.
Hackle: Dark brown.

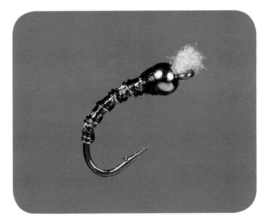

Black Holographic Chironomid Pupa
Hook: Mustad Signature C49S, sizes 16 to 12.
Bead: 7/64-inch black bead.
Thread: Black 8/0 (70 denier).
Rib: Black and red Ultra Wire.
Body: Black Holographic Flashabou.
Gills: Stillwater Solutions White Midge Gill.

within about twelve inches of the bottom. The trout like to eat chironomids closer to the bottom rather than the surface because our lakes are so clear, and the greater depth offers them more security from predators like ospreys and loons.

"Another option is to fish chironomid imitations without a strike indicator. Select a tapered leader that is at least 25 percent longer than the depth of the water you are fishing; if you're fishing in twelve feet of water, for example, you'd want to use a fourteen- or fifteen-foot-long leader. Tie your fly to the end of the 4X or 5X fluorocarbon tippet, and cast downwind. Wait a minute and a half to allow the fly to sink and then slowly—painfully slowly—retrieve the fly. You want to slowly retrieve the fly horizontally through the water within a foot of the bottom of the lake. Even though real chironomid pupae rise vertically through the water to the surface, you're presenting the fly in the strike zone, and the fish will hit it.

"We call this method 'fishing naked.' We also use it to fish mayfly nymphs, caddis pupae, damselfly nymphs, shrimps, and leeches. However, using a floating line and strike indicator allows you to suspend your fly at a very precise depth. Trout can be very focused on the depth at which they're feeding on chironomid pupae, and although it's often impossible to determine the exact depth at which the fish are feeding, it is safe to say that they do the majority of their feeding within twelve to eighteen inches of the bottom. It takes the fish less energy to slowly cruise along at a constant depth, sucking in the pupae, and they're safer near the bottom."

What if I don't get any strikes when fishing a chironomid imitation? What should I do next?

"If you're getting no strikes, move up in the water column in six-inch increments. You should have the right fly on because you can see the pupae near the surface;

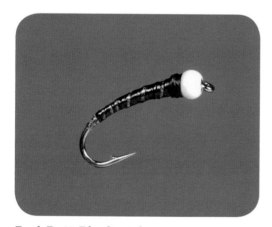

**Red-Butt Black and
Red Chironomid Pupa**
Hook: Mustad Signature C49S, sizes 18 to 10.
Thread: Black 8/0 (70 denier).
Butt: Fine red holographic tinsel.
Body: Stillwater Solutions black Midge Flex.
Rib: Small or fine red copper wire.
Bead: Super white metal bead.

just match the insects you see in the surface film. Continue raising your fly until you start catching fish."

Can you use multifly rigs in British Columbia?
"We can use only one fly at a time in British Columbia."

So you can't use droppers.
"No, we can't use droppers. This really affects your ability to determine the depth at which the fish are feeding. We could use droppers until around the mid- to late 1980s, then the regulations were changed to say that you can fish with only one fly at a time. On the other hand, if you're in a boat, you can fish with two rods at a time. This allows you to set two flies at different depths to more easily find out where the fish are feeding. When I'm fishing in other jurisdictions, however, I'll use two or three flies at a time to discover both depth and color preference.

"Now, here's a neat trick when fishing deep. I like to use a small swivel about eighteen to twenty inches above the fly. The swivel does three things. First, it adds a bit of weight to get the fly down quicker. Second, if it's a windy, choppy day, and I'm fishing with a strike indicator, I use a slightly larger swivel to help prevent the indicator and fly from bouncing. And third, you can use different colors of swivels to help discover what color of insect the fish are keying in on. There are days when you'll get strikes but not hook fish because they're hitting the swivel. That's an indication that you need to change flies to match the color of the swivel."

What's your favorite color of chironomid?
"If I could use only one color of chironomid, it would have a black body and red wire rib; that's the go-to color. The most common chironomids have black or maroon-black bodies. Tie those flies in a variety of sizes."

Chan's Chironomid
Hook: Mustad Signature R73, sizes 16 to 12.
Bead: Copper.
Thread: Dark brown 8/0 (70 denier).
Butt: Red holographic tinsel.
Body: Three fibers from the center tail of a cock ring-necked pheasant.
Rib: Red holographic tinsel.
Thorax: Peacock herl.
Gills: Stillwater Solutions Midge Gill.

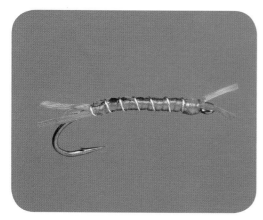

Rubber-Legged Bloodworm

Hook: Mustad Signature S82-3906B, size 14 or 12.

Thread: Red 8/0 (70 denier).

Tail: Stillwater Solutions red Midge Stretch Floss.

Rib: Silver Ultra Wire.

Body: Stillwater Solutions red Midge Stretch Floss.

Shellback: Red holographic tinsel.

Front legs: Stillwater Solutions red Midge Stretch Floss.

Lady McConnell

Hook: Mustad Signature R50 or 94840, sizes 16 to 12.

Thread: Black 8/0 (70 denier).

Tail: White Zelon and grizzly hackle tip.

Shellback: Deer hair.

Body: Black Antron.

Hackle: Grizzly.

How large should I tie them?

"We have some very large chironomids. We regularly tie pupae imitations on size 10, 3X-long hooks. We call them 'bombers.' And some tyers use really large, 2X-long hooks."

What's the smallest chironomids I should make?

"We tie them down to sizes 18 and 16."

Let's talk about some of your other flies. You sent a very interesting collection. Let's start with the Rubber-Legged Bloodworm. How do you fish this pattern?

"Fish the Rubber-Legged Bloodworm using the same techniques I described for fishing chironomid pupae: Hang it under a strike indicator or fish it naked with a floating line and long leader."

I've never fished in the Kamloops, but even I have heard of the Lady McConnell.

"I developed the Lady McConnell in the early 1980s. I use that pattern when the fish are feeding on adult chironomids. The tail is meant to imitate a trailing shuck."

You also sent a Booby. It seems out of place among the other imitations. How do you fish it?

"The Booby is a very interesting pattern; there's nothing in the water that looks like it. We fish the Booby when we can see the fish. Remember, many of our lakes are very clear and have marl bottoms. This marl is calcium that precipitates out of the water to form a yellowy-white bottom; it looks a lot like sand. You'll see the fish when they're cruising on the marl. They can be very picky because they're usually looking for scuds, bloodworms, or shrimp. When fishing a Booby—black, orange, lime green, olive, or even white— use the fastest-sinking line you can get, and a three-foot-long leader ending with a 3X tippet. Tie the fly on using a loop knot so that it will swivel. When you see a cruising trout or pod of trout, cast twenty-five to thirty feet ahead of the fish to give the line ample time to sink into the marl; the foam eyes will keep the Booby suspended above the marl. Next, when the fish comes within ten to twelve feet of the fly, start stripping in line very quickly; use fast, three-inch-long strips. The Booby will dart down and pop back up. The fish will either jump all over it, or they will turn and flee. The most aggressive fish will often chase it right to the boat and then eat it. I've found that 80 to 90 percent of the trout you catch with the Booby are males; they're just more aggressive than the females. And the best color is probably bright orange, and there's certainly nothing in our lakes that is bright orange.

"The other way to fish the Booby is to anchor in deeper water, allow your line to fully sink, and then quickly strip it up through the water column. The fish will sometimes pound it."

The Ruby-Eyed Leech looks like it has a lot of natural swimming motion. How do you fish this fly?
"The Ruby Leech is another of my go-to patterns. It's a deadly, all-around leech imitation. You can fish it using a sinking line or a floating line with a long sinking leader, but it's also extremely effective under a strike indicator. The most effective way to fish a leech imitation with an indicator is to use a leader long enough so that the fly hangs about a foot from the bottom, and then cast slightly into the wind. Let the fly wind-drift naturally back to you; just pick up the slack line. It's the most natural drift to imitate the swimming action of a leech."

You sent a nice imitation of a water boatman. Are these insects important to your fishing?
"Yes, they are, especially in the spring and fall. Water boatman breathe air; even under the ice, they'll find

Las Vegas Booby Leech
Hook: Mustad Signature R73-9671, size 8.
Thread: Black 6/0 (140 denier).
Tail: Black marabou and black holographic Flashabou.
Body: Peacock green Crystal Chenille.
Eyes: White Rainy's Boobie Round Eyes.

Ruby-Eyed Leech
Hook: Mustad Signature R73 or 9671, size 10 or 8.
Bead: Silver-lined maroon glass bead behind a 1/8-inch copper cone.
Thread: Black 8/0 (70 denier).
Tail: Red/black mohair dubbing.
Body: Red/black mohair dubbing brush using small red copper wire as the core.

Stillwater Boatman
Hook: Mustad Signature S82 or 3906B, size 14.
Thread: Dark brown 8/0 (70 denier).
Shellback: Stillwater Solutions dark red-brown Midge Flex.
Body: Yellow Uni-Stretch.
Legs: Rusty brown dyed goose biots.
Note: Coat the shellback with head cement or Zap-a-Gap.

pockets between the ice and the surface of the water. When the ice comes off the lake, the boatman are the only insects available to the trout, and this is a good springtime fly. However, the fall is the best time to fish a water boatman imitation. That's when the boatman and their cousins, the backswimmers, go on mating flights. A swarm will rise into the air from one lake, fly to another lake, and dive to lay eggs. This occurs from mid- to late September after a heavy frost. The insects are momentarily stunned when they hit the water, and the trout feed on them."

This is only a portion of the conversation I had with Brian Chan. We talked for a very long time about fishing in the Kamloops, about tying flies, fisheries management, and much more. I was extremely impressed by his breadth of knowledge and the freedom with which he shared it.

I think Brian answered most of my questions. I realize now that I've been retrieving most of my flies too fast. I probably haven't been fishing deep enough. And he was emphatic that I should try chironomid imitations more often: "Don't think twice about it," he said. "Your Maine lakes and ponds are full of chironomids, and the fish feed on them."

Sound advice. All sound advice.

Chapter 4

**Charlie Craven
Keeps It Simple**

You haven't heard of Colorado's Charlie Craven? Then you will.

Charlie has a fast-growing reputation among serious trout fishers. He's a regular contributor to *Fly Fisherman* magazine. He wrote a great fly-tying book aimed at beginners, and as of this writing was composing a companion volume showcasing how to make many of his favorite personal flies. His shop, Charlie's Fly Box, is so well respected in the fly-fishing industry that he was awarded *American Angler* magazine's Retailer of the Year Award in 2009. And his patterns are some of the most popular in the Umpqua Feather Merchants' fly catalog; you'll find his patterns for sale in fly shops across the country.

Charlie got his start in fly tying like many of us: His parents gave him a fly-tying kit. Sometimes the interest in fly tying and fishing sticks, and it becomes a lifelong hobby; sometimes it doesn't, and it is soon forgotten. For a few folks, fly fishing becomes a consuming passion and a lifelong pursuit. Charlie Craven falls into this last group, and we're all the better for it.

The flies accompanying this article are only a few of his original creations; he has designed many dozens of original fish-catching flies.

"After you received that fly-tying kit, what did you do then?" I asked Charlie. "How did you learn to tie flies?"

"I got a fly-tying kit from my parents when I was eight years old, and it took off from there," he replied. "I never took a class or anything like that. I grew up in Northglenn, just north of Denver. I've always been

© CHARLIE CRAVEN

Go to Hell Variant
Hook: Tiemco TMC100SP-BL, sizes 18 to 10.
Thread: Chartreuse 8/0 (70 denier).
Tail: White calf tail.
Tag: Pearl Mirage Tinsel.
Abdomen: Tying thread.
Thorax: Black peacock Ice Dub.
Wing: White calf tail.
Hackle: Brown and grizzly.

in this area; it's where I learned to fish and tie flies. Of course, I now live in Arvada—that's where the shop is—but I'm just fifteen miles from where I grew up."

I understand that you were once a commercial fly tyer.
"Yes, I was a commercial tyer for a solid ten or twelve years. And I guess you could say that I'm still a commercial tyer, but I don't do it to fill the bins in the shop."

What are your shop's home waters?
"I guess you'd say it's the South Platte River. That's where I used to guide, but I really don't fish there all that much anymore. There was a big fire up there ten years ago, and it really changed the river. It's coming back, but it's very different. Now I fish the Eagle and the Colorado Rivers a ton. I'm not picky about where I fish, but I probably go to those places more than most other rivers."

We were once talking about the fly fishing in your area, and you said that the interest in fishing still waters was increasing.
"Stillwater fishing has really taken off around here. There are even guys who only fish lakes because they contain some really big fish."

Do you think a lot of anglers are looking for less-crowded water? Is that part of what's driving the interest in trout ponds and lakes?
"Yes, I think it started that way; people were looking for solitude. But Denver and Colorado Springs have really grown, and I don't want this to come out wrong, but it's hard to have a lake entirely to yourself. A lot of anglers are enjoying them, but the secret is out on them."

What species of trout are in these lakes?
"The lakes contain rainbow and brown trout. There are some very nice browns, but there are also very huge rainbows."

How large do the fish get?
"Every year somebody catches a twelve-pound fish on a fly rod, and some guys will catch ten five-pound fish in one day. And sometimes you'll catch a total of a hundred trout in a day. When you time everything right, the fishing can be really good.

"That's why I sent those chironomid patterns. They've become very important for fishing around here."

The folks at Umpqua Feather Merchants are raving about your Jumbo Juju Chironomid. They say stillwater anglers have fallen in love with this fly.
"Yes, it's become a big hit—much bigger than I expected. I think it's doing particularly well because there aren't a lot of chironomid-specific patterns out here. There are upsized midge patterns but not a lot specifically designed to imitate a chironomid.

"When Umpqua picked that fly up for their catalog, they said that they didn't sell many chironomids, and I said the reason was that they didn't *have* many chironomids. This fly just fills that niche, and now there are some other chironomid patterns out there, too."

What's the body on this fly?
"The body on the Jumbo Juju is Super Hair: three strands of one color and one strand of a second color, all wrapped together. I then coat the body with either epoxy, Clear Cure Goo, or something like that. The thorax is black dubbing, and the wing case is a strip of Thin Skin with a strip of flash. The Thin Skin prevents

Jumbo Juju Chironomid
Hook: Tiemco TMC2302, sizes 16 to 10.
Bead: Spirit River Hot Bead, pearl white.
Weight: Lead wire.
Thread: White 8/0 (70 denier) for tying the abdomen; black 8/0 (70 denier) for tying the thorax.
Abdomen: Orange or red Super Hair.
Rib: Brown Super Hair.
Thorax: Olive brown, black, or peacock Ice Dubbing.
Wing case: Black Thin Skin.
Coating: Five-minute epoxy or Loon UV Knot Sense.

the epoxy on the wing case from wicking into the dubbing. The Thin Skin hardly shows on the finished fly, but it is important."

Where in the water column do you fish this fly?

"All depths. I was talking to a guy last year who fished it two inches below his strike indicator, and he was catching fish. But the whole thing with fishing still waters is that you have to get the fly to where the fish are; that might be fifteen deep, or it might be just under the surface. That's the challenge of fishing lakes: In a river you move around and fish to different pieces of structure; in a lake you move up and down the water column until you find the trout."

One of the limiting factors to succeeding at stillwater fishing is patience: waiting for your fly to sink to the proper depth.

"I couldn't agree more. I know some of these guys will cast out and let their flies set for twenty minutes. Lake fishing is great fun if you're catching fish, but if that indicator isn't doing something every two minutes, I have to do something else."

Let's talk about your river patterns. I'll bet the foam-bodied Charlie Boy Hopper will float all day.

"The Charlie Boy Hopper is one of my favorite patterns. For what it ended up being, that fly went through a lot of variations, but I couldn't be happier with the final results. You tie a fly that's pretty basic, and you start fishing it. Then you add some pieces and continue testing it. And then you start subtracting things. Very often you end up where you started: with a very basic fly."

When do you fish the Charlie Boy Hopper?

"I use the Charlie Boy Hopper from summer through late fall. A lot of the rivers have a lot of grasshoppers on the banks, but I'll also fish it with a couple of

Charlie Boy Hopper
Hook: Tiemco TMC100SP-BL, size 10 or 8.
Thread: Tan 3/0 Monocord.
Body: Tan foam.
Legs: Brown round rubber legs.
Wing: Deer hair.

droppers and use it as an indicator. And it's also a very good stonefly imitation."

Baby Boy Hopper
Hook: Tiemco TMC100SP-BL, size 10.
Thread: Chartreuse 3/0 Monocord.
Body: Chartreuse foam.
Legs: Chartreuse round rubber legs.
Wing: Deer hair.

The Baby Boy Hopper looks like a scaled-down the Charlie Boy Hopper. It's a cool little fly.

"The Baby Boy Hopper is essentially the same as the Charlie Boy Hopper. I wanted to tie a smaller version of the Charlie Boy, but as you work down in hook size, the foam fills the hook gap. You could switch to thinner foam, but then you'd lose a lot of buoyancy. The solution was tying it on a short-shank hook that maintained the hook gap of the larger fly. Now I can tie this pattern in small sizes to imitate crickets and similar smaller insects. Umpqua Feather Merchants offers this fly in black, chartreuse, olive, and tan."

How many of your patterns does Umpqua Feather Merchants sell?

"I have about twenty flies with Umpqua Feather Merchants. They're only ten miles from here. It's nice having them so close, and working with them has been great. It's really easy to ramble back and forth about making changes in this or that pattern."

The Mugly Caddis is really different. What's the story behind this fly?

"The Mugly Caddis is out of my normal realm. I typically tie very clean, neat patterns, but that one is more ragged. There's a funny story to that one.

"There was a guy on the Henrys Fork River who had a very poorly tied Elk-Hair Caddis. It was really chewed up; it had hardly any wing left, and it was just falling apart. But he was the only guy on the river catching fish. So, it prompted me to tie a more ragged-looking imitation. It's worked very well as an adult caddis, but I also fish it as an emerging and a diving caddis. That rabbit's-foot fur and shaggy dubbing trap a lot of air bubbles. Another cool thing is that it's

Mugly Caddis
Hook: Tiemco TMC100SP-BL, sizes 20 to 12.
Thread: Tan 6/0 (140 denier).
Abdomen: Whitlock SLF Blend Dubbing, color of your choice.
Underwing: Natural mallard CDC.
Overwing: Natural cow elk-body hair.
Thorax: Whitlock SLF Blend Dubbing, color of your choice.

Craven's Soft-Hackle Emerger
Hook: Tiemco TMC101, sizes 22 to 16.
Thread: Gray 8/0 (70 denier).
Tails: Medium dun Betts Tailing Fibers.
Abdomen: Gray beaver or muskrat
    dubbing.
Wing: White Umpqua Fluoro Fiber.
Hackle: Medium dun hen-neck hackle.
Thorax: Gray beaver or muskrat dubbing.

Caddistrophic Pupa
Hook: Tiemco TMC2487, sizes 18 to 12.
Bead: Black tungsten.
Abdomen: Cream dubbing.
Back: Brown Flexi Floss.
Rib: Chartreuse wire.
Wing: Gray CDC.
Antennae: Fluoro Fiber.
Wing pads: Black Flexi Floss.
Thorax: Peacock UV Ice Dub.

buoyant enough that you can pull it under and let it pop back to the surface right in front of the fish."

I suspect you can tie this fly to match a wide variety of real caddisflies.
"Yes, you can easily tie that pattern in a variety of colors and sizes to match just about any caddisfly on the river, but brown and olive are my favorite colors."

The Mugly Caddis is obviously a very simple fly to tie. One thing I've noticed is that the guides are sending simple, basic patterns; they're typically not using anything overly fancy.
"I'm a huge fly tyer, and I don't have a problem spending a lot of time tying my patterns. It's fun to make complicated patterns, but when you really boil it down, adding more parts decreases the effectiveness of a fly. In most cases, a simpler pattern catches more fish."

But your Caddistrophic Pupa seems more realistic.
"That's another one that is an improvement on another pattern. That fly is built around a collar of cul de canard. The first time I saw CDC on nymph, it didn't make sense to me. But when you fish a CDC nymph and see what it looks like when it gets wet, you'll see that the material flows and looks very lively. The first thing I thought of was to use the material to tie a caddis pupa."

How did you tie the body of the Caddistrophic Pupa?
"The body is just dubbing, and the back strap is a piece of Flexi Floss."

And this fly has a small bead head.
"Yes, a tungsten bead. I use tungsten beads on all of my bead-head patterns because they're heavier and keep the flies down better."

What did you use to tie the antennae?
"Fluoro Fiber is perfect for making the antennae on caddis pupae."

This is just a great fly; I'm definitely going to tie some of these.
"Yes, it's a shaggy, snotty-looking thing; it's ragged, just like a real caddis pupa."

At the other end of the spectrum, the Hellfire Variant is a more traditional-looking fly.
"For sure. It has a more standard-looking attractor profile."

So you use this pattern as an attractor.
"Yes, I do. The whole idea is that the white wings and tail show up so that you can see the fly on the water. Fish this fly wherever you might use a Royal Wulff. I was simply trying to come up with something that no one else was tying. There aren't a lot of lime-colored dry flies out there. I just wanted something different so that you could fish something different from the other guy in the boat."

The Mole Fly looks incredibly simple to make.
"The Mole Fly is in fact one of the simplest flies ever created. But honest to God, if I could have one fly to fish to trout rising to Baetis, it would be the Mole Fly."

Obviously the body is mole hair.
"No, it's not. The body is actually beaver dubbing, and the CDC wing allows the fly to hang in the surface film. I prefer using natural dubbing on this fly because synthetic dubbing would have a greater tendency to float. That fly came about a long, long time ago and is a great Baetis emerger imitation. And any novice can tie this fly."

A lot of beginners would think that this fly is too simple to catch fish.
"You're absolutely right: I run into that problem every day. A lot of people think that a fly has to be complicated to work. Most fishers don't think the Mole Fly will catch fish, but they always come back and buy more."

Charlie's Mole Fly
Hook: Tiemco TMC2487, sizes 24 to 18.
Thread: Gray 8/0 (70 denier).
Wing: Mallard CDC.
Body: Brown beaver dubbing.

Charlie's Mysis
Hook: Tiemco TMC9300, size 18.
Thread: White 8/0 (70 denier).
Abdomen: White Egg Yarn.
Thorax: White Egg Yarn cut and mixed
    into dubbing.
Eyes: Small black round rubber legs.

Two-Bit Hooker
Hook: Tiemco TMC921, sizes 18 to 14.
Beads: Two 1.5-millimeter copper beads.
Thread: Brown 14/0 or 10/0.
Tail: Mottled brown India hen-back
    feathers fibers.
Abdomen: Tying thread.
Rib: Black 14/0 tying thread.
Wing case: Opal Mirage tinsel.
Thorax: Rusty brown Super Fine Dry Fly
    Dubbing.
Legs: Mottled brown India hen-back
    feathers fibers.
Coating: Five-minute epoxy.

Charlie's Mysis is another interesting fly. Do you have a lot of **mysis** *shrimp in your waters?*
"Yes, that is a *mysis* shrimp imitation. I don't know how widespread *mysis* shrimp are anywhere else in the world, but they're common in Colorado. Our state wildlife division actually stocked them in our reservoirs as a source of food for the fish, and they get washed into the tailwaters below the dams. Most of them die when they enter the rivers due to the change in water pressure, but they remain alive for a while. The trout in the tailwaters feed on these shrimp; that's why this pattern works so well.

"That's another one of those supersimple flies. The entire thing is white Egg Yarn and black rubber legs for the eyes."

How do you fish it?
"I typically cast it down and across stream. One thing I've noticed is that the shrimp are constantly facing into the current. I tie it facing forward, with the tail dangling out the back on purpose; a *mysis* shrimp is more like a krill than a scud. It's long and skinny, sort of like a damsel nymph."

This pattern is tied with no weight.
"The shrimp are typically not very far under the surface, so I add just a small split shot to the leader just to keep the line taunt. I use this pattern to sight-fish to the trout on shallow-water flats."

The Two-Bit Hooker is a fun fly.
"I'm really excited about that fly; it's been a really big hit. It's one of my newer patterns, and I'm pretty damn excited about it. That's another pattern that took way longer to come up with than you first might think. I wanted a fly that has a slim profile but a lot of weight. I achieved that by using two beads. I make it in red, black, olive—a bunch of colors."

If you like fishing a Copper John, you'd like the Two-Bit Hooker.

"Exactly. It sinks very quickly, and it has a slimmer profile."

We concluded our conversation talking about Charlie's Jujubaetis. This pattern has gained widespread popularity wherever Baetis mayflies are common.

"The Jujubaetis is my most popular fly; that pattern has been a hit everywhere. It's just a tiny nymph imitation. There's also a PMD version, and a red one is coming out. But the plain Jujubaetis has worked very well; it's just a small, dark, accurate-looking mayfly nymph. And it's an incredibly durable fly."

Throughout our journey, we will encounter tyers who rely on tried-and-true favorite patterns, and we will meet tyers who push the envelope of pattern design to develop fresh flies. Charlie Cravens falls into the second camp. Using an economy of materials—sometimes only two or three ingredients—he fashions fish-catching imitations of common trout foods. Charlie continually emphasizes movement and general shape when designing his patterns; he shies away from embellishing his flies with too many parts. And, as his flies prove, keeping it simple is the best way to create a fish-catching pattern.

———————————

Craven's Jujubaetis
Hook: Tiemco TMC2488, sizes 22 to 16.
Thread: White 10/0 for tying the abdomen; black 14/0 for tying the thorax.
Tail: Brown Hungarian partridge.
Abdomen: Two strands of dark brown and one strand of black Super Hair, wrapped at the same time.
Flashback: Opal Mirage tinsel.
Thorax: Black tying thread.
Wing case: Gray Fluoro Fiber.
Legs: Butt ends of the wing case.
Coating: Loon UV Knot Sense.

Blue Poison Tung
Hook: Tiemco TMC2487, sizes 20 to 16.
Bead: Silver tungsten bead.
Thread: Gray 8/0 (70 denier).
Rib: Blue Ultra Wire.
Thorax: Blue/gray Hareton Dubbing.

Chapter 5

George Daniel:
No Bull, No Bravado—Just Pure Fly Fishing

COURTESY OF GEORGE DANIEL

I rise in defense of competitive fly fishing.

Yes, I know having a contest to see who can catch the most or the largest fish seems to run counter to the spirit of fly fishing, and I've heard all the objections.

They say that fly fishing is the quiet sport. It's the contemplative sport. It is supposed to be a refuge from the ills of everyday life, especially all those things—from conducting business to attracting a mate—that have an element of competition to them. Fly fishing is supposed to soothe our souls and relax our minds, and we are supposed to leave the water with renewed spirits.

Oh, give me a break.

Listen to the chatter at your local fly-fishing club, or pop into the tavern next to one of the major fly-fishing shows. There's an endless competition for bragging rights about who catches the most fish or the largest fish and who fishes in the most exotic destinations. As the evening wears on and more glasses are emptied, the fish always become more plentiful and get larger. Braggarts and fishing stories—they go together. And it's all a form of competition.

But a braggart puts no skin in the game. He has nothing to lose.

A competitive fly fisherman, however, puts his reputation and ego on the line with each cast. Very few outside the world of competitive fly fishing know who wins or loses these events—it gets almost no coverage in the United States—but *they* know. And perhaps that's the hardest thing: wanting to succeed in front of the people you respect the most.

George Daniel: No Bull, No Bravado—Just Pure Fly Fishing

I've met several members of the team that represents the United States at the World Fly Fishing Championships, and they're always quite modest when describing their abilities and accomplishments. But isn't that the way it is with truly talented people? I suspect if the braggart could win a competitive fly-fishing tournament—hell, if he could just qualify to make the team—he'd be the first in line to try. Wouldn't those be some bragging rights?

George Daniel seems like a modest man. I met him one evening at The Fly Fishing Show in Somerset, New Jersey. We shared a couple of beers and hamburgers (actually, I think I drank the beer—he had Pepsi), and he made some mention that he had a little experience in competitive fly fishing. It wasn't more than a passing comment. We spent most of the night talking about nymph fishing, the latest tackle, and all the things that interest fly fishers. Later I was told that he was one of the leading members of Team USA and that he serves as a coach to the American youth team. It turns out that George is a very busy man who is carving out a life in fly fishing.

"I work at the TCO Fly Shop in State College, Pennsylvania," he said at the beginning of our interview. "That's my day job. But I also have two small children, I'm involved with Team USA in the World Fly Fishing Championships, and I'm a coach of the American youth fly-fishing team. Oh, I also forgot: Right now I'm writing a book about European nymph-fishing methods. My plate is pretty full."

Tell me about your involvement with competitive fly fishing.

"I started at the Fly Fishing Masters. That was one of the first nationally televised fly-fishing competitions on the Outdoor Channel. There were a couple of parts. There were casting obstacles in which you'd score points based on accuracy and distance. From there you'd move into the fishing portion. I participated in those events in 2003 and 2004. I was pretty successful."

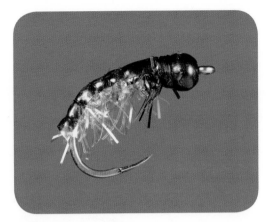

GD's Czech Catnip
Hook: Tiemco TMC2499 SP-BL, sizes 10 to 6.
Bead: Black tungsten.
Thread: Black 6/0 (140 denier).
Body: UV olive Micro Polar Chenille.
Thorax: UV black Micro Polar Chenille.
Wing case: Mottled oak olive Thin Skin.
Rib: 3X monofilament.

Hard-Bod Sow Bug
Hook: Tiemco TMC3679, sizes 18 to 12.
Thread: Tan 6/0 (140 denier).
Weight: .025 lead wire, wrapped on the hook and flattened.
Body: Scud olive gray Micro Polar Chenille.
Back: Loon UV Fly Finish.

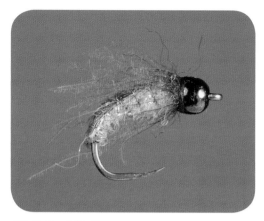

CDC Caddis Pupa
Hook: Tiemco TMC2499 SP-BL, sizes 18 to 12.
Bead: Black tungsten or brass.
Thread: Brown 6/0 (140 denier).
Abdomen: Chartreuse Ice Dub.
Thorax: Peacock Ice Dub.
Overwing: Pheasant-tail fibers.
Collar: Dark brown CDC.
Rib: 5X Monofilament.

Crystal Killer
Hook: Knapek Streamer Hook, sizes 10 to 6.
Bead: Black tungsten or brass.
Thread: Red 6/0 (140 denier).
Tail: Pheasant-tail fibers.
Body: Red Crystal Chenille.
Hackle: Coachman brown saddle hackle.

Eventually George participated on the official team that represents the United States at the World Fly Fishing Championships. That sounds simple, but it is not: George first had to try out for the team, and he wasn't a shoo-in.

"The team has been in existence since the early 1980s, but for the longest time it was just a good old boys club. But in May 2005, they opened it up to let the public try to become part of the team. The tryouts were held in Bend, Oregon. A friend told me about it, and while I'd never been on an airplane before, I bought a ticket the moment I heard about it. About thirty anglers tried out, and I placed third. I didn't make the actual traveling team that competed overseas, but it qualified me to become part of a fifteen-man roster at that time."

How did you feel about not making the traveling team?

"I didn't get upset; I just stuck it out. Throughout the next year, there were qualifying events across the country. I participated in three of the qualifiers and won a medal in two of them. That earned me a spot on the 2006 World Fly Fishing Team that went to Portugal; that was probably my best competition because I ranked fifth out of 115 anglers. That was also the second-highest finish ever in North American history up to that point. I competed with the U.S. fly-fishing team until just last year, when I officially retired from competition. I competed in five world championships."

In which countries did you compete?

"Portugal, Finland, New Zealand, Scotland, and Poland."

I had no idea you were so involved with competitive fly fishing.

"Absolutely. And then, from a national standpoint, I traveled across the country to qualifying events. Of the three national championships, I was the national champion in two out of the three events in which I competed. I guess you could say that I had a pretty successful record as a competitive angler."

Let's talk about the nature of competing. For instance, all waters have their own unique characteristics, insect hatches, and so forth. Do you arrive early to fish and practice before the competition begins?

"That's a great question. It really depends upon the venue. In Portugal, for example, they don't have a lot of really good trout water, at least not in the area where we were. All the best water had already been identified for the competition, and you're not allowed to fish the competition area sixty days before the event. That left us with what was basically a bunch of frog water. We got there two weeks before the championships, and our guide told us that we'd made a mistake in coming. He said we could fish and practice, but we wouldn't be catching trout. After that, there were a couple of other countries where we decided we wouldn't arrive early to practice; when that happened, we'd just arrive two or three days early and try to get as much information as we could from local experts and guides."

But there were times when you did arrive early to practice and learn the local water?

"New Zealand and Scotland were different stories: There was a lot of water for practice. In 2008 the world champions were held in March in New Zealand, so we made a scouting trip in January. Luckily for me, I spent six or seven weeks in New Zealand that year, so I have no complaints there."

Relying on your experiences as a competitive angler, here's a question we'd all like answered. If you're visiting water for the first time, and you don't really know what to expect, what flies do you select first?

"That's another great question. One of the common themes behind the mind-set of a competitive angler

William's Biot Nymph
Hook: Knapek Nymph Hook, size 14.
Bead: Black tungsten.
Thread: Dark brown 6/0 (140 denier).
Tail: Brown partridge.
Abdomen: Mahogany brown turkey quill.
Thorax: Dark brown SLF Squirrel Dubbing.

PT Cruncher
Hook: Knapek Nymph, sizes 16 to 10.
Thread: Black 6/0 (140 denier).
Tail: Pheasant-tail fibers.
Abdomen: Pheasant-tail fibers.
Rib: Small copper Ultra Wire.
Thorax: UV chartreuse Micro Polar Chenille.
Collar: Brown hen hackle.

TCO's Tan Adult Caddis
Hook: Tiemco TMC2487, sizes 18 to 12.
Abdomen: Yellow tan TCO's East Coast Dubbing.
Thorax: Gray caddis TCO's East Coast Dubbing.
Wing: Medium dun CDC.

Egan's Iron Lotus
Hook: Tiemco TMC3679 SP BL, sizes 18 to 12.
Bead: Gold tungsten.
Thread: Red 8/0 (70 denier).
Body: Olive dun 6/0 (140 denier).
Rib: White 6/0 (140 denier).
Thorax: Dark olive SLF Squirrel Dubbing.
Tail: Medium pardo coq de Leon.
Wing case: Black Thin Skin.
Coating: Sally Hanson's Hard as Nails Polish.

is using patterns that are very suggestive: Hare's-Ears, Pheasant-Tails, and maybe some basic caddisfly larvae. You might fish with no more than a dozen different patterns. These flies don't imitate anything specific; they are neutral and suggest a wide variety of common forage.

"The French competitors all had flies they called 'Frenchies.' A Frenchie is nothing more than a tail of coq de Leon fibers, pheasant-tail fibers for the body, a bead head, and a hot spot right behind the bead. Those are very simple patterns that can suggest a lot of small aquatic insects."

Your pattern called the Iron Lotus is an example of a very basic, suggestive type of fly.

"Exactly. Lance Egan of Utah came up with that. It's a pattern that I've used to catch fish everywhere in the United States, and I've used it to catch fish overseas. No matter where I go in the future, it's one of the flies I'll take with me; it's one of my confidence patterns.

"Every competitive angler has his baker's-dozen of flies, or maybe just half a dozen flies, that they have confidence in. They'll use these flies anywhere in the world."

Do most of the competitive anglers use nymphs?

"They do the majority of the time. As you know, most of a trout's diet consists of nymphs. But there are times when, such as on this one river in Poland, that there's so much water that it is tough to use nymphs. Nothing on that river was defined; it was one wide blast of flowing water. In this situation, you'd go into searching mode. That's where a lot of guys did well using streamer patterns and really long casts to cover as much water as they could.

"Another example was fishing for grayling in Europe. Grayling can be suckers for dry flies, so a lot of times a single dry fly works best. But for the majority of the time, most of the anglers use nymphs."

We're hearing more about what are called "European nymph-fishing methods." I think they've become popularized because of competitive fly fishing. Are many of the competitors really using these new methods?

"Yes—absolutely. But a lot of it has to do with the rules for the world championships. According to rules, all of the weight must be built into the fly; you cannot add split shot to your leader. As a result, all of the guys are using weighted flies, and they are relying on these newer methods of fishing."

Do any of the competitors use strike indicators?

"No, manufactured strike indicators are prohibited from the competition. They consider strike indicators almost unethical. A dry fly is the only strike indicator you can use."

You're also one of the coaches of the American youth fly-fishing team, correct?

"Yes. I was asked to take on head coaching responsibilities of the United States Youth Fly Fishing Team. I took the kids to Portugal, and then we went to the Czech Republic. But what with expenses and my own family responsibilities, it became too much, and I had to resign. But it was another great experience. Then I was asked to coach the adult team, and I have agreed to do that. I've also agreed to help with the youth team—run clinics and the like."

What's it like to coach the kids? How do they respond?

"The kids are amazing. A lot of the adults think that they know it all, and they're just not open to new ideas and concepts. But with these young kids, it's just amazing how willing they are to learn. You tell them

Pisco's Caddis Pupa
Hook: Tiemco TMC2499 SP-BL, size 12.
Thread: Dark brown 6/0 (140 denier).
Body: Dark olive SLF Squirrel Dubbing.
Rib: Extra-small copper Ultra Wire.
Underwing: Medium dun CDC.
Overwing: Natural deer hair.
Collar: Dark brown SLF Squirrel Dubbing.
Eyes: Melted monofilament.

and show them something, and within minutes they're replicating whatever you demonstrate. These kids, who are between the ages of fourteen and eighteen, are doing more with a fly rod, and catching more fish, than I was when I was in my twenties.

"A part of this is due to the new sources of information. With the Internet and things like YouTube, there's just so much information out there. I really think anglers are going to get better as the years go on."

Do the kids also tie flies?

"Yes, that's one of the prerequisites to being on a team. When you go overseas, you just never know what you'll encounter, and you have to be ready to make flies to match the insects and conditions you find. For instance, when we went to Portugal, we discovered ants all over the riverbanks. There were going to be some rainstorms, and our guide told us that we would have to tie some ant patterns and be ready for when the ants got washed into the water."

Do all of the adult competitors also tie?

"Absolutely. There was one American who won a medal who did not tie, but he was an exception to the rule."

How is the camaraderie among the members of the different teams? Is there a friendly atmosphere?

"It's excellent. But it's also excellent here at the U.S. championships. Of course, everyone is tight-lipped going into these events, but after the competition, you'll see a table with ten different nationalities, and everyone is swapping stories and sharing flies. I don't really go to these competitions to compete or battle other anglers but to learn and form friendships. I just wish more people could grasp the idea and see the benefits that the competitive fly-fishing world brings to all of us."

I know you hear the objections to competitive fly fishing. How do you respond?

"Well, of course, fly fishing is a quiet, contemplative sport, but so is golf, and no one objects to golf tournaments. No one is forcing anyone to compete, but it's just like with any other sport: Once you start competing, your mind starts working in ways to develop strategies to become more efficient. Look at the people who watch *Bass Masters* on Saturday morning. Most of the viewers will never become competitive bass fishermen, but they watch because tournament anglers are on the cutting edge of fishing techniques, and they want to learn from them. That's really no different with competitive fly fishing."

I agree with you. The development of new nymphs and the growing use of hot spots on flies are largely the result of competitive fly fishing.

"Look, if you're happy fishing with the same patterns—over and over—then that's just fine. But I'll tell you, the people I love talking with are the ones who are open to new ideas and concepts about how to fish and catch trout. This is how you learn and grow and continue getting the most enjoyment out of your fishing."

I also think some tackle development is being driven by competitive fly fishing. For example, all of the new extra-long nymph-fishing rods we're seeing are the result of manufacturers responding to the needs of competitive anglers, and average fishermen are seeing the benefits in this new tackle.

"Competitive fly fishing is certainly pushing the envelope of fly and tackle design. What's wrong with that? In the end, we'll all become better anglers."

As I said at the beginning, I learned very little about George Daniel's accomplishments in competitive fly fishing that first evening we met. I was assured, however, that he was someone I needed to know better. George seemed interesting and friendly—I could tell that he would be a good subject for an interview—and so I asked him to participate in this project. Later, as we talked on the phone, with the tape recorder silently catching our conversation, I was surprised to learn of his success in competitive fly fishing; he revealed none of this at our first meeting.

In order to succeed, competitive fly fishers constantly look for new and better ways to catch fish. They develop fresh flies and fishing methods. No bull. No bravado. Just pure fly fishing. We can benefit from their efforts, and I am willing to learn.

———————

Chapter 6

Pat Dorsey
Is Always Fishing

Colorado's Pat Dorsey lives a great life. Not only does he live in a state that contains some of this nation's best trout rivers, but also he spends most of his time on the water.

Pat is co-owner of a great fly shop called Blue Quill Angler in Evergreen. In addition to manning the shop, he spends as much time as he can guiding. From his vast fishing experiences, he designs flies to meet the local fishing conditions.

I started by asking Pat to describe his home waters.

"Our home waters are predominantly the South Platte River, the Blue River, the Colorado River, and the Williams Fork River. Those are our predominant rivers for guiding."

What is your fishing season?

"We have four-season fisheries on just about all of these waters. They're tailwaters, so we can fish them throughout the year, even during the winter."

Do the dams on those rivers release the water from the bottom? Do the rivers maintain fairly constant temperatures?

"Yes, for the most part those are bottom-release dams, and the rivers maintain fairly steady temperatures. We have a lot of fishing within one to two hours of the shop, so we always have some fishing going on, even under the harshest weather conditions."

COURTESY OF PAT DORSEY

Puterbaugh Caddis
Hook: Tiemco YMC100, sizes 19 to 12.
Thread: Black 8/0 (70 denier).
Abdomen: Black closed-cell foam.
Wing: Elk hair.
Hackle: Brown.

Top Secret Midge
Hook: Tiemco TMC2488, sizes 26 to 18.
Thread: Brown 8/0 (70 denier).
Abdomen: Tying thread.
Rib: White 6/0 (140 denier) tying thread.
Wing: Glamour Madera.
Thorax: Super Fine Dry Fly Dubbing, rust-
  brown.

Matthew's Olive Sparkle Dun
Hook: Tiemco TMC100, sizes 18 to 14.
Thread: Olive 8/0 (70 denier).
Tail: Olive Zelon.
Wing: Comparadun deer hair or fur.
Dubbing: Olive.

This is March, and we spoke just a couple of weeks ago. You were getting ready to guide that day.
"Yes, we have clients throughout the year. We're not one of those destination type of places, but we get a lot of businesspeople who visit Denver and want to go fishing. We're perfectly set up to work with those people. We don't do a tremendous amount of guiding during the winter, but we do some."

Are there any hatches during the winter?
"We have midge hatches, and the spring midge we have is a bigger variety. It's March, and our dry-fly fishing is just beginning to pick up."

Do these tailwaters suffer from spring runoff?
"It depends upon the river. Because the impoundments are for water storage, the water authorities allow the reservoirs to fill, and then the water will traditionally flow over the spillways. We'll see high water for a short period of time, but the rivers are still very fishable, and it's still good fishing."

When do you start seeing the major traditional hatches?
"We have midge hatches from November through March. On the Arkansas River, below Pueblo Dam, you'll also find blue-winged olives throughout the winter, which is very unusual.

"In early spring—the last of March and the first of April—we start seeing Baetis hatches. These will last from four to six weeks, and we'll have some pretty good dry-fly fishing to them. Unfortunately, we'll normally get high water around the first of May, and the dry-fly fishing deteriorates pretty quick."

As the water level drops and the fishing picks back up, what's the next hatch?

"We get some caddisflies. And then in June, we'll see some yellow sally and the big *Pteronarcys* stoneflies. As we get into early July, we'll get PMDs, in late July we have green drakes, and in August we have red quills.

"In late August and September we have Tricos. We have really good hatches on some of our tailwaters. And then the Baetis return in autumn, and then in November we're back to midges."

Do you fish with terrestrial imitations in August and September?

"Yes, we do: beetles, grasshoppers, and ants. We don't have cicadas, but we do have a fairly decent grasshopper season."

Let me ask you about a few of your flies. Your Mercury series of flies is particularly interesting. While you didn't send one, you even put a glass bead on the head of a cased caddis imitation.

"I probably should have sent a Mercury Cased Caddis, but I wanted to send what I consider to be my favorite guide flies. You have the patterns I wouldn't want to be without.

"With respect to the entire Mercury series, those flies revolve around silver-lined glass beads. I started trying to imitate the gas bubbles on emerging insects, and the name comes from the fact that the bead looks like a little thermometer filled with mercury. I developed a Mercury Midge, Mercury Baetis, Mercury PMD, and a lot more. But I needed a cased caddis, and I added the glass bead to the head, and it worked. I also tied

Dorsey's Hydropsyche
Hook: Tiemco TMC2457, size 18 or 16.
Thread: Black 6/0 (140 denier).
Head: Tungsten bead.
Tail: Brown Zelon.
Body: Olive dubbing.
Rib: D-Rib.
Wing case: Black Thin Skin.
Legs: Oliver Edwards Caddis Legs.

Amy's Ant
Hook: Tiemco TMC5263, sizes 8 to 4.
Thread: Brown 6/0 (140 denier).
Underbody: Tan foam.
Overbody: Brown foam.
Legs: Brown round rubber.
Hackle: Brown.
Body: Olive Crystal Chenille.
Wing: Light elk hair and rainbow Krystal Flash.
Thorax: Arizona peacock dubbing.

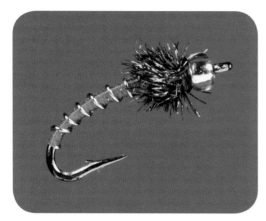

Mercury Blood Midge
Hook: Tiemco TMC200R, sizes 22 to 18.
Bead: Extra-small silver-lined glass bead.
Thread: Red 8/0 (70 denier).
Abdomen: Tying thread.
Rib: Fine or extra-fine gold wire.
Thorax: Peacock herl.

Dorsey's Medallion Midge
Hook: Tieco TMC101, sizes 24 to 18.
Thread: Dark brown 8/0 (70 denier).
Abdomen: Tying thread.
Rib: White 6/0 (140 denier) tying thread.
Thorax: Super Fine Dry Fly Dubbing, rust-
    brown.
Wing buds: Medallion Sheeting, medium
    dun.

a version with a tungsten bead that Umpqua Feather Merchants added to their catalog."

Do glass beads make that much of a difference?
"There's something about that bead that triggers fish to strike. And the UV dubbing that I use on a lot of my patterns adds more flash. I'm kind of a big proponent of flash. We have so many selective trout out here that adding a little dash of flash is a pretty good idea."

You sent a couple of midges. These flies must be important for where you are fishing.
"Midges are really important for our fishing. We have multiple hatches of midges 365 days a year. They're superimportant to our fishing success.

"The Top Secret Midge and the Medallion Midge are two of my best-selling flies with Umpqua Feather Merchants. And we sell a ton of midges here at the store."

Another small pattern you sent is the Sparkle Wing RS2.
"That's a really great fly. It's a mayfly emerger, and I tie it in a wide range of colors to imitate just about any type of mayfly. You can tie it in PMD, black, olive, gray, or whatever you need. I've probably caught more fish on a size 20 Sparkle Wing RS2 in Cheeseman Canyon than on any fly I tie or fish. It's the ultimate guide fly.

"A fellow named Bob Churchill came up with that pattern; it's obviously a takeoff on the original RS2. The RS2 is also a very important fly around here."

How do you fish it?
"All different ways. Sometimes I dead-drift it, and I vary the depth: Sometimes I dredge with it, other times I fish it higher in the water column, and sometimes I fish it in the film."

Using pearl braid for the wing is a great idea.

"It's a cool wing. It's easy to tie, and it's consistent. It's a lot easier than grabbing a bunch of marabou and trying to tie that to the hook."

You're using something called Glamour Madera for making the wings on some of your other flies. What's this material?

"That's an embroidery thread. It's an interesting material. With the introduction of the Top Secret Midge and the release of my book, *Tying & Fishing Tailwater Flies*, a lot of guys are asking about it. But it's not a fly-tying material; you'll find it at craft stores. But it makes great wings on flies."

You sent the UV Scud. Do you have a lot of scuds in your tailwaters?

"We have a lot of scuds out here. Scuds are especially important when the water is high because they get knocked loose and drift in the current. May and June are our best scud months, and they can offer some really good nymph fishing."

You sent on orange variety. Is this your favorite color?

"We fish tan, olive, and orange scud imitations, but I think I've caught more trout using the orange UV Scud. It's especially effective during the shoulder season. The aquatic insects changed a little because we had a big fire that actually affected the insects in the rivers, but the scuds have rebounded. We also had a downturn in the aquatic worms, but they've also come back."

Do you fish with a lot of worm imitations?

"Aquatic worm imitations can be deadly."

Sparkle Wing RS2
Hook: Tiemco TMC101, sizes 24 to 18.
Thread: Gray 8/0 (70 denier).
Tail: Gray hackle fibers.
Abdomen: Super Fine Dry Fly Dubbing, Adams gray.
Wing: Pearl braid.
Thorax: Super Fine Dry Fly Dubbing, Adams gray.

UV Scud (Orange)
Hook: Tiemco TMC2457, size 10.
Thread: Orange 6/0 (140 denier).
Tail and antennae: Orange Antron or Zelon.
Body: Shrimp pink UV Ice Dub.
Shellback: A strip clipped from a freezer bag.
Rib: 4X monofilament.

Dorsey's Golden Stonefly
Hook: Tiemco TMC300, sizes 10 to 4.
Thread: Brown 6/0 (140 denier).
Tail and antennae: Tan biots.
Underbody: Yellow yarn.
Abdomen: Woven brown and yellow D-Rib or tubing.
Thorax: Yellow Furry Foam.
Hackle: Ginger.
Wing case: Tan raffia.

Paper Tiger
Hook: Tiemco TMC300, sizes 10 to 4.
Thread: Brown 6/0 (140 denier).
Weight: 0.30-inch wire.
Tail and antennae: Black biots.
Underbody: Brown yarn.
Abdomen: Tyvek.
Legs: Pheasant-rump fibers.
Thorax: Brown yarn.
Wing case: Tyvek.

Let's talk about your stonefly imitations. Let's start with the Golden Stonefly. Is the abdomen woven?

"Yes, it's woven brown and yellow Larva Lace. You have to make an underbody of yellow floss because the yellow Larva Lace is fairly translucent, and the hook shank and any lead wire will show through. I tie that fly both weighted and unweighted. That pattern is a little more complicated to tie, but if you learn how to make a woven body, it looks really good. And rather than Larva Lace, you can use fly-tying tubing. It's a deadly fly."

I suspect you can use this pattern throughout the year.

"Absolutely. The real golden stone nymphs are always available to the trout, so you can always fish with that fly."

The Paper Tiger is another of your stonefly nymph patterns. What material do you use to make the body?

"The Paper Tiger has been around for many years. I started tying it about twenty-five years ago. It's constructed using Tyvek. The Paper Tiger is bombproof; you can't tear it up."

Did you originally design this pattern using Tyvek? I thought tying flies with Tyvek was a more recent development.

"Yes, I've always tied it with Tyvek. I actually think John Betts was using Tyvek before I started experimenting with it. It's been around a long time."

How long have you been designing flies?

"I've been designing my own patterns for a long time. Umpqua Feather Merchants has been selling my flies for only seven or eight years. But I've been goofing around with a lot of variations of flies for a lot of years.

"That was something that confused me when you contacted me. I didn't know if you wanted only flies that I designed or the flies that I fish. I sent you what I consider to be my guiding selection."

So, if someone came to visit you to fish, and he tied his own flies, these are the patterns you'd recommend.
"This would be a great starting point. These are the flies I always carry. Have these patterns in your fly box, and you'll have an excellent opportunity to catch fish."

————————————

Bead-Head Breadcrust
Hook: Tiemco TMC5262, sizes 18 to 12.
Thread: Black 6/0 (140 denier).
Underbody: Black yarn.
Body: Grouse tail feather. Clip the fibers very short.
Hackle: Grizzly hen.

Chapter 7

John Gierach: Fly Fishing's Best-Selling Author Is Also a Hell of a Fly Tyer

© VINCE ZOUNEK

Even though he says, "I'm not so sure about that," it's very possible that John Gierach is the best-selling author in the history of fly fishing.

Well, maybe Norman McLean's *A River Runs Through It* ended up selling more copies than any of John's books, but that's what happens when Brad Pitt is cast in the starring role for the movie version: A mostly forgotten book gets propelled to the forefront, and a new generation of readers discovers it. But for straight-up fly-fishing literature—books that find a market based solely from their merit, not from some form of Hollywood hype—nothing compares with the success of *Trout Bum*, *Where the Trout Are All as Long as Your Leg*, *At the Grave of the Unknown Fisherman*, or any of John's other collections of stories.

I once wrote that nothing in the history of publishing has depleted more bank accounts or wrecked more relationships than the title *Trout Bum*. When that book was published, it seemed like everyone I knew wanted to become one, and some are still trying. And the title—or at least the romantic notion—became so popular that the term *trout bum* became part of the fly-fishing lexicon.

But John Gierach isn't just a teller of stories. Don't dismiss him as a wit wearing a fly-fishing vest. His books *Fishing Small Streams*, *Favorite Flies*, and *Fishing Bamboo* blend John's charm with solid discussions of how to catch trout from water that is little more than a trickle, how to tie flies, and how to collect and care for fine handmade tackle.

John is a complete fly fisherman. He can see the humor in a technical sport, and he can make a technical sport more entertaining and enjoyable. In *A River Runs Through It*, McLean used fly fishing as a metaphor for life; for John life is a metaphor for fly fishing. He views daily existence from the perspective of a fly fisherman. Fly fishing is what he does. Fly fishing is who he is.

Did you know, for example, that many years ago John was a guide and professional fly tyer? It's true. (I think I discovered that tidbit reading *Trout Bum*.)

I thought that asking him to participate in this project was a long shot. He and I had met several times, but it was always just in passing. We have never fished together, and I don't think we have even shared a meal. It was always just handshake, a hello, a little small talk, and then a goodbye. Not much else.

Eventually I was privileged to publish a couple of his articles in *Fly Tyer* magazine, but we remained only acquaintances. I assumed he received a lot of requests and demands for his time, but I thought, "What the hell. I have his phone number, so ask him."

I was thrilled when he consented to an interview and sent a batch of flies.

When we started, and I turned on the tape recorder that was patched into the phone, I said that we might eventually talk about his flies. "What I really want to know," I told him, "is how you got into fly fishing and how you became a professional tyer. And I'd really like to know how you got into writing about fly fishing."

The phone went silent for a moment, and then he started telling me his story.

"Well, I got into professional fly tying in sort of a haphazard way. It was back when I was struggling as a writer. I did some professional tying to try and keep body and soul together. It was kind of like my guiding: I did enough of that to realize that it wasn't something I wanted to do. I don't know. The drudgery of tying professionally wasn't anything like the fun of tying for yourself. I suppose I wasn't suited for it. Oh, I suppose I could have arisen to the occasion, but I just wanted to be a writer."

Elk-Hair Caddis
Hook: Regular dry-fly hook, sizes 18 to 12.
Thread: Tan 8/0 (70 denier).
Body: Brown dubbing.
Hackle: Brown.
Wing: Elk or deer hair.

Parachute Caddis
Hook: Regular dry-fly hook, sizes 18 to 12.
Thread: Brown 8/0 (70 denier).
Body: Hare's-ear dubbing.
Hackle: Grizzly.
Wing: Elk or deer hair.

The only reason I even know about this is from reading one of your stories based on your days as a professional tyer. As I recall, you describe drinking a cup of coffee, and then you go from this to that diversion, knowing that at some point you are supposed to sit down and make a batch of flies. I don't remember how the story ended, but I don't think you ever got back to the vise.

"It's the repetition that gets to you. I mean, I can sit down and tie a dozen flies of a certain size for myself, but ask me to tie twenty dozen for someone else, and that's just hard."

Who were you tying for? Was it fly shops?
"I think it was. I just remember picking up some orders along the way. But that was thirty years ago."

How did you come to fly fishing?
"I was at loose ends when I came to Colorado in the late sixties. I was working for shares in a silver mine up in the mountains. I grew up in the Midwest and had never fly fished, but everybody out here was doing it, so I just tried it. I'm a self-taught fly fisherman, and it probably still shows. Now I'm a good caster, but I'm not stylish—I just get the job done. I'm not a pretty caster—I'm a good 'fishing' caster."

When did you decide to try your hand at writing?
"I always wanted to be a writer, and so I started writing about fly fishing. And, of course, I wasn't making a living at it. Oh God, I drove a garbage truck, and I tied flies and tried guiding, and I worked in a fly shop. I also installed insulation and was a roofer, but I didn't care for heights, so that didn't work out very well; when the foreman let me go, he said, 'It's okay, kid—it's not for everyone.'"

You actually worked at a silver mine?

"Yes, I did. It turned out, though, that it was a scam. The guy had sold several hundred percent worth of shares to investors, and he had just one real miner and a couple of hippies working the mine. We were bringing out just enough ore so that he could have assay reports that showed that it was a real mine. He just needed something to show potential investors. I never made a fucking penny at it."

How did you get into writing?

"I know my mother has some copies of a high school literary magazine where I was published. I've always been interested in writing and have always been fooling around with it. It's what I've always wanted to do. I was a poet for a while. I was publishing in these little literary magazines and hanging out with writers—and fishing. I remember reading *Fly Fisherman* magazine and thinking that I could write that sort of stuff. I'm not saying that it wasn't any good, but it's not *War and Peace*. I knew I could do this. So, I wrote a story and sold it, and it was like a month's wages. It might have been a whole seventy-five dollars, but it was the first time that I'd been paid for my writing. As you know, getting paid for your writing is really compelling, so I started pursuing that and working part-time jobs—and fishing. It just started ballooning from there."

It's a little-known fact, but you were one of the first contributors to **Fly Tyer** *magazine.*

"Yes, I did contribute to *Fly Tyer* in the 1970s. I would write for anybody, for almost any price. Soon after I discovered writing for the fishing magazines, I stumbled onto writers such as McGuane, Chatham, and some of those guys and realized that fishing writing could be done as well as any other type of writing; it's not a secondary sort of genre. It can be real literature. That is when I started getting really excited about it."

Hare's-Ear Parachute
Hook: Mustad 94831, sizes 14 to 12.
Thread: Tan 8/0 (70 denier).
Tail: Moose.
Body: Hare's-ear dubbing.
Rib: Brown thread.
Hackle: Dun.
Wing: Turkey T-base or a similar feather.

Pheasant-Tail Nymph
Hook: Regular wet-fly hook, sizes 16 to 12.
Thread: Brown 8/0 (70 denier).
Tail: Pheasant-tail fiber tips.
Abdomen: Pheasant-tail fibers.
Rib: Gold wire.
Thorax: Peacock herl.
Wing case: Turkey.

Flavilinea
Hook: Mustad 94831, size 14 or 16.
Thread: Brown 8/0 (70 denier).
Tail: Elk hair or a substitute.
Abdomen: Olive biot.
Thorax: Olive dubbing.
Wing: Dun hen-hackle tips.
Hackle: Dun.

Dave's Hopper
Hook: Mustad 94831, size 14 or 12.
Thread: Brown 3/0 (210 denier).
Tail: Red hackle fibers.
Body: Yellow polypropylene yarn.
Hackle: Brown.
Wing: Brown mottled turkey.
Legs: Pheasant fibers.
Head and collar: Deer hair.

How much of your writing is autobiographical?

"Most of it. Almost all of it is autobiographical—in a way. Ed Engle and I have taken many trips together. Sometimes we'll both write essays about the same trip. We'll both tell the truth in our essays—explaining what happened and what we saw—but you'd never know that we were describing the same trip. Everybody sees and feels something different. I don't make this stuff up; I'm not a fiction writer."

How long does it take for you to write a story or a book?

"People always ask me how long it takes to write a book. That's a hard question to answer. Do you count long walks thinking about it? What do you count as work time? Most days, when I'm home, and I am not off fishing or doing something else, I'll write. I always have something going on and stories in various drafts. But, yes: I usually work some every day when I'm home."

You use the word work, but I suspect you really don't consider it work, not in the conventional sense.

"No, I don't consider it work. I enjoy it."

In addition to your short stories, you write more technically oriented stories and books. I'm thinking of your book Fishing Bamboo. *You really love bamboo rods. Do you own many?*

"I've got a bunch, more than I need."

What are your favorites?

"My current favorite is a little seven-foot, nine-inch four-weight that was made by Walter Babb, Jim Babb's brother. I love that rod. I also have an old Leonard 39DF five-weight that I like. I also have a couple of really nice Mike Clark rods. Just the other day I was fishing on the South Platte with an eight-and-a-half-foot, five-weight rod that he made. This was the third rod he ever made for sale; that was in 1983, I think. It's just a wonderful rod."

You also wrote the book **Good Flies.** *I was the proofreader on that project.*
"Oh, were you?"

Nick Lyons was the editor, and I proofed the manuscript. That book certainly contains your voice and sense of style, yet there is plenty of technical discussion about fly design and selection. It seems to me that many readers are familiar with your more popular collections of short stories and miss some of these other wonderful books. But your writing is actually fairly broad.
"I like to think so."

What is the future for fly-fishing literature?
"I think the genre is very strong."

Did you know that at least one university is teaching an English course based on fly-fishing literature?
"No, I didn't know that. But, yes, I think the genre is alive and well. There are several young up-and-coming authors who are developing good reputations for their writing. There are a lot of people out there doing excellent work, and, of course, there's some stuff out there that could be good if it was done more carefully.

"It seems to me that there's an arm of it—for lack of a better term—that is serious literature. And then there's an arm that is just about fishing; it just talks about going fishing, and it is little more than a string of clichés. There's a market for that sort of writing, too. I suppose this describes the history of most forms of literature."

I believe your books are some of the most widely read in the history of fly-fishing literature. Are you surprised with their popularity?
"I don't know if they are or not. Nick Lyons once said that I was the highest-paid fishing writer in America,

Hare's-Ear Soft Hackle
Hook: Regular wet-fly hook, sizes 16 to 12.
Thread: Olive 8/0 (70 denier).
Body: Hare's-ear dubbing.
Rib: Copper wire.
Hackle: Mottled hen soft hackle.
Eyes: Black bead chain.
Head: Hare's-ear dubbing.

Olive Midge Emerger
Hook: Curved-shank nymph hook, size 18.
Thread: Olive 8/0 (70 denier).
Tail: Wood-duck or mallard flank fibers.
Abdomen: Olive biot.
Thorax: Olive hare's-ear dubbing.
Hackle: Mottled hen hackle.

Hare's-Ear Stonefly Nymph
Hook: Curved-shank nymph hook, size 14
   or 12.
Thread: Olive 8/0 (70 denier).
Tail: Brown biots.
Body: Hare's-ear dubbing.
Rib: Copper wire.
Back and wing case: Turkey.
Legs: Teal or wood-duck flank feather.

but I don't think that's true, either. I think people are just being nice.

"But, sure: Writers are always surprised when they are successful. You struggle along for so long, and then it starts to click a little bit. I'm just amazed that I can make a living doing this and go to a lodge someplace and write it off my taxes because it's supposed to be work. Stuff like that just astonishes me. I have an accountant who specializes in small businesses and sole proprietors like me, and he said that if his other clients saw what I can write off that they'd shit a brick.

"And there's something else that really surprises me. I'm a pretty reclusive guy, you know; I've never been interested in being one of the stars at these fly-fishing shows. But sometimes I'll go to a fly-fishing show, and I'm always shocked by the number of people who recognize me."

I also enjoyed your book Fishing Small Streams. *At the time, I was living in Knoxville, and I fished the streams in the Great Smoky Mountains. You really love fishing smaller waters, don't you?*
"I do, partly because that's where I started. But I also like the solitude. I was fishing the South Platte just the other day, and it was cold and windy—this is the middle of February—and there was a shitload of people down there. But the West has hundreds of thousands of miles of these little creeks that have decent fish, and you can have an entire creek to yourself if you're willing to sniff out an obscure one and do a little hiking and four-wheeling. You can be off by yourself forever.

"Now, don't get me wrong: I love big fish, and I go to great lengths to catch big fish. But I remember one time when I was in the Northwest Territories up on the Arctic Ocean catching big, beautiful sea-run char. It was August, and I was sitting in this little shack with an oil heater that looked like it came over on the Amundsen expedition, and I was thinking about how I was missing the fishing back home. It was prime time for the little creeks I consider my home waters—they were just at their best, and I was missing them."

That's a wonderful position: to live exactly where you want to be.

"Yes, it is. During the season, I'll get up in the morning and come down into my office to write for a couple of hours. Then I'll make a sandwich and Thermos of coffee and drive up and fish for the afternoon. In half an hour I can be on one of half a dozen nice creeks. Some days I fish hard, and some days I just tie on a fly and walk along the bank, just seeing what's going on. Some days it's all about fishing, but on other days it's all about taking the fly rod for a walk.

"I think it was Charlie Waterman who said, 'Sometimes writing about fishing is more fun than fishing.' That's one of my secret mottos. My actual professional motto came from Tom McGuane, who said, 'Whenever you feel like falling silent, do it.'"

Damselfly Nymph
Hook: Curved-shank swimming nymph hook, size 14 or 12.
Thread: Brown 8/0 (70 denier).
Tail: Mallard-flank fibers.
Body: Hare's-ear dubbing.
Rib: Copper wire.
Wing case: Turkey.
Legs: Teal or wood-duck flank feather.
Eyes: Black bead chain.
Head: Hare's-ear dubbing.

Chapter 8

Aaron Jasper:
Leading Fly Fishing into the Future

COURTESY OF AARON JASPER

One of the great things about editing a national fly-fishing magazine is discovering new talent. I've uncovered a few gems over the years. Some have dulled and fizzled over time, but others have grown into leading fly tyers and anglers.

After so many years, you develop a knack for recognizing the guys who will go the distance and develop good reputations in the sport. Aaron Jasper is one of the new diamonds you must know about. He is a great tyer, accomplished angler, and superb teacher. Aaron is coming on strong with a complete program—guide, author, and lecturer—and he has already released a fine fly-fishing instructional DVD. And he's maintaining a remarkably humble and friendly attitude.

Aaron specializes in the new European nymph-fishing methods and is in high demand among anglers who want to learn these methods. His enthusiasm is contagious, and it was a pleasure talking with him about his flies and fishing methods.

Aaron grew up in Paterson, New Jersey. He still lives in northern New Jersey, and his steady clientele pours out from New York City. But Aaron isn't new to fly fishing: He's been doing it almost his entire life.

"I learned to fish from my grandpa," Aaron said at the beginning of our interview. "I didn't have a choice. He had me start spin fishing when I was about four years old. He only fly fished, but he wanted me to fish with him. He had me pick up a fly rod when I was about six, and that's when I started fishing for trout. I was really young."

Further reflecting on his days fishing with his grandfather, Aaron continued, "We went everywhere to fish, from the Ramapo, which is a local stream, to the Catskills. We fished the Neversink and the Beaverkill a lot. We fished north-central Pennsylvania. All my grandpa wanted to do was fish. He was injured in World War II, and he didn't have to work much. He lived his life like a man who wanted to do whatever he wanted, and that was fishing—anytime, anywhere. He'd pick me up at school, and we'd go fishing. My grandpa was like my father. He had three daughters, so I was like his son."

[Rule of thumb: If you want to get a child excited about fishing, don't take him fly fishing. It's a difficult sport, and youngsters often don't have the patience required to learn the techniques and nuances. Besides, they're more interested in catching fish than worrying about the method of angling.]

"I really didn't like fly fishing when I was a kid," Aaron said, agreeing with my observation about children and fishing, "but he'd buy me ice cream on the way home, so I'd tolerate it. I guess I was about eight when I really started getting into it because I started catching a decent amount of fish."

265 Nymph
Hook: Tiemco TMC100 SPBL, sizes 20 to 12.
Bead: Silver tungsten bead to match the size of the hook.
Thread: Brown 8/0 (70 denier).
Tail: Brown hen-saddle hackle.
Body: A blend of dubbing—Davy Wotton SLF caddis brown (75 percent), Davy Wotton SLF orange silver midge (20 percent), and brown UV Ice Dub (5 percent).
Rib: Small black wire.
Wing case: Black Thin Skin.
Legs: Brown hen-saddle hackle.

When did you start tying flies?

"My grandpa tied very bad flies, so he taught me to tie for him. I would tie the flies, and he'd give me all the rejects. If I lost the two flies out of the ten I tied, I'd sit on the bank the rest of the day and throw rocks into the water!"

I know you're very busy. You are a third grade teacher and, of course, you tie flies and fish. But you also earned a guiding license.

"Yes, I took the guide's test for the State of New York. I have all the qualifications, but I don't take people

Rocked Out
Hook: Skalka G, sizes 14 to 8.
Bead: Black tungsten bead to match the size of the hook.
Thread: Olive 8/0 (70 denier).
Abdomen: Nature's Spirit insect green dubbing.
Rib: Size 6X monofilament.
Thorax: Black hare's-ear dubbing.
Back: Jan Siman Magic Shrimp Foil, olive.

Straight Up
Hook: Tiemco TMC100 SPBL, sizes 20 to 16.
Bead: Copper tungsten bead to match the size of the hook.
Thread: Olive 8/0 (70 denier).
Tails: Wood-duck flank fibers.
Abdomen: Tying thread.
Rib: Small copper wire.
Thorax: SLF Spiky Squirrel Dubbing, natural gray.
Wing case: Medium peacock Mylar.

fishing in New York. I have the license, so I can say I'm an officially registered New York guide, but I really don't guide there. When I fish in New York, it's for my own relaxation."

How long have you been guiding?
"I've been guiding for eight years. I started working for a place in Connecticut called Housatonic River Outfitters. A good friend got me the job. At first I wasn't sure if guiding was really for me—I had a couple of bad initial trips. But then I took out a client who was a really nice fellow, and it was very satisfying. All of a sudden I was excited about guiding."

How many days a year do you guide?
"I guide fifty to seventy days out of the year. I do a lot of late-afternoon trips—say from four to eight o'clock. I get a lot of guys who want instruction on the nymph-fishing techniques. A lot of them come straight out of Manhattan. I pick them up at the train station, and we go fishing on this beautiful local stream that has trout. They can bring their waders or whatever they can stuff into their briefcases when they go to work, but I can also supply everything—waders, rod, reels, or whatever they need."

You're developing a reputation as a leading proponent of European nymph-fishing techniques. How did you discover the flies and methods?
"It was about five years ago. My friend said we should try these techniques. We understood nymph fishing using strike indicators, and we had all the other trout-fishing techniques down, and we thought we should give these European methods a try. Being a fly fisherman—like so many fly fishermen—I thought that my methods were the best, but then I studied the European methods and tried them. I tied the flies and rigged the leader the way they do, and I caught a lot more fish. I really clobbered them. And I caught fish in

places that I would have walked by in the past. It was quite eye opening.

"For instance, some fish were obviously taking the flies as they were descending down the water column, but in fly fishing we always talk about insects emerging—we don't think that fish will strike when our flies are descending to the streambed, but they do. With the European methods, you're in constant contact with your flies, and you can detect strikes when they are still dropping. I call these 'reaction strikes.' A trout might not really want to take your fly, but it splashes when it hits the water, it gets into the fish's field of vision, and the nymph might have a bright hot spot—all of this triggers a reaction from the fish, and you catch it."

There's no denying that it's fun casting to rising trout, but what about the rest of the time? Can you really catch more fish using nymph and larvae imitations?

"Ten years ago I thought you had to have at least some real insect emergence going on in order to catch a lot of trout. Sure, you can always catch at least a few fish because there are always some opportunistic feeders, but I thought you'd be really limited with respect to total numbers. But with these new methods, I've discovered there are things you can do to increase your catch rate even when nothing is hatching and there is no obvious feeding activity taking place.

"For example, you know those pockets near the edge of the stream where the water is barely moving? A lot of times fish that aren't feeding hold in those lies to get out of the stronger current. If you cast an indicator rig in there with split shot and a weighted fly, it'll just drop to the bottom, and the fish won't notice it. With the European method, however, I can slowly drag a fly through that water and pick up some fish. It's really very interesting and a revolutionary way of thinking about fishing trout streams."

365 Nymph
Hook: Tiemco TMC100 SPBL, sizes 20 to 14.
Bead: Silver tungsten bead to match the size of the hook.
Thread: Brown 8/0 (70 denier).
Tail: Dark coq de Leon.
Abdomen: Tying thread.
Rib: Small black wire.
Thorax: Dark brown SLF Spiky Squirrel.
Wing case: Black Thin Skin.

François
Hook: Tiemco TMC100 SPBL, sizes 20 to 14.
Bead: Copper tungsten bead to match the size of the hook.
Thread: Olive 8/0 (70 denier).
Body: Pheasant-tail fibers.
Rib: Small copper wire.
Hot spot: Datum Glo-Brite #5.

WMD
Hook: Tiemco TMC2499, sizes 18 to 12.
Bead: Copper bead to match the size of the hook.
Thread: Dark brown 8/0 (70 denier).
Tail: Wood-duck flank fibers.
Abdomen: Tying thread.
Rib: Narrow copper wire.
Thorax: Dark brown SLF Spiky Squirrel.
Hot spot: Datum Glo-Brite #7.

Over the past few years, a lot of tyers have been adding hot spots to their nymph and larvae patterns. Brightly colored thread, dubbing, or floss—anything you can use to wrap a narrow band around the fly—increases the visibility of these flies. Do you believe this increases the effectiveness of artificial flies?

"I like red, orange, and yellow hot spots. When you think about red, orange, and yellow, those are the first colors to dissolve in the water as they drop deeper into the water column. But when we fish for trout, we're fishing water that is at most four to five feet deep. Red is visible up to about three feet, so it works really well for shallow-water situations. Orange is a good all-around color—it can be dull orange or fire orange; they both work. I've also had good success with flies containing bright fluorescent yellow, especially in deeper water. If a run is five to six feet deep, a fluorescent-yellow hot spot on the fly is very effective."

Almost all of your patterns have hot spots, don't they?

"Oh God, yes. But don't misunderstand: A fly will catch fish even if it doesn't have a hot spot. I absolutely believe, however, that a fly will catch *more* fish if it has a hot spot. Just adding a hot spot to a pattern doesn't *make* the fly, but it will definitely enhance it.

"You can improve a lot of older patterns by adding hot spots. Add a collar of fluorescent-yellow thread to a standard Pheasant-Tail Nymph, and it will probably catch more fish. It's still a Pheasant-Tail, but the hot spot is an important enhancement."

What do you use to make hot spots?

"I often use size 8/0 tying thread to wrap a hot spot on a fly. Fire orange is a really good color, but so are shell pink, fluorescent pink, fluorescent yellow, and cerise.

You can also use fluorescent-orange tungsten beads. White beads are also very good for adding hot spots. And, of course, you can also use dubbing to make hot spots; one or two wraps of Ice Dub in the appropriate color makes a perfect hot spot. The Pineapple Express is a good example of a fly with a hot spot made out of Ice Dub."

I'm hearing a lot of good things about the Pineapple Express. Is that one of your favorite flies?

"Yes, it is. We've hammered a lot of fish with that pattern over the past few years. My fishing partner couldn't believe I put that in *Fly Tyer* magazine; that pattern and the Triple Threat are really good patterns."

You mention a product called Datum Glo-Brite for making the hot spots in a lot of the recipes for your flies. What is that material?

"Datum Glo-Brite is a floss from the United Kingdom. I've been told that there are fluorescent colors, and then there are dyes that are actually made using fluorescent material. I do know that when you place a spool of regular fluorescent fly-tying thread or floss next to a spool of Datum Glo-Brite, you can see a big difference; the Glo-Brite almost lights up. It's one of those things that if I didn't see it, I wouldn't believe it. But it's really hard to find Glo-Brite in the United States, so you can substitute with fluorescent tying thread, floss, or dubbing."

It seems like you use a lot of smaller nymphs.

"It depends upon the fishery, and it depends upon how I'm fishing. If I'm fishing multiple nymphs, I use a larger fly for the anchor and one or two smaller flies as droppers."

Pineapple Express
Hook: Tiemco TMC100 SPBL, sizes 20 to 14.
Bead: Copper tungsten bead to match the size of the hook.
Thread: Olive 8/0 (70 denier).
Tail: Wood-duck fibers.
Abdomen: Pheasant-tail fibers.
Rib: Small copper wire.
Thorax: Orange Ice Dub.
Hot spot: Datum Glo-Brite #5.

Triple Threat
Hook: Tiemco TMC100 SPBL, sizes 18 to 14.
Thread: Brown 8/0 (70 denier).
Bead: Gold or copper tungsten bead to match the size of the hook.
Tails: Wood-duck fibers.
Abdomen: Striped peacock herl and Fly DK Quill Body #3 (UV).
Rib: Small copper wire.
Thorax: Jan Siman dubbing, peacock bronze.
Hot spot: Datum Glo-Brite #5.

Polish Woven Nymph

Hook: Skalka G, sizes 12 to 8.

Bead: Black tungsten bead to match the size of the hook.

Thread: Size 6/0 (140 denier), color to match the top of fly, usually brown or olive.

Abdomen: Contrasting colors of four-strand embroidery floss.

Rib: Brassie copper wire.

Thorax: Brown Spiky Squirrel Dubbing.

Iced Cased Caddis

Hook: Tiemco TMC100 SPBL, sizes 18 to 12.

Bead: Black tungsten bead to match the size of the hook.

Thread: Olive 8/0 (70 denier).

Abdomen: Peacock Ice Dub.

Rib: Small copper wire.

Thorax: Insect green Super Fine Dubbing.

Your Polish Woven Nymph is on the larger side. Is that an anchor fly?

"Yes, it is. That is something big to get down quickly."

The Iced Cased Caddis you sent is also larger than most of the other patterns. Is that another anchor fly?

"That Iced Cased Caddis is dynamite anywhere you find Grannom cased caddisflies. But you can use that in a variety of sizes. Right before the Grannom are ready to hatch, you can use that in size 12, and then it is my anchor fly."

It seems like many patterns used as anchor flies are extremely large, but yours are still on the small side, aren't they?

"The key is to make something small that is packed with as much weight as possible. Pack in the bead and wire until you almost can't add any more materials to the hook. This creates the best anchor fly. The Polish Woven Nymph works so well because the body just covers the lead wire; it's a very heavy pattern for fishing fast water."

You like using a dry fly as a strike indicator when fishing a nymph. How do you select a dry fly?

"It's really important that when picking a floating pattern for a dry-and-dropper rig, always select a dry fly that can catch trout. It's not just a strike indicator; you want to use a fly that also has a good chance at catching fish. It's surprising, but a lot of guys don't think about the dry fly catching fish; they're more concerned with using it as an indicator. But it has a hook in it, too, so you should use only dry flies that have a good chance of catching fish on your waters. Leduc's Spiky Squirrel is one of my favorite patterns when fishing a dry fly with droppers. I've used that fly to catch trout even on the Letort and Falling Spring, which are noted for their difficult fish.

"I use Spiky Squirrel Dubbing to tie the body on that fly. That material, combined with the cul de canard wing, creates a fly that just won't sink. And it's very buggy looking on the water. A French guy showed it to me."

Do you tie it in different colors to match the real insects?

"No, I tie it in just that one color, but I do vary the size. The color doesn't seem to matter; when the fish are slashing at caddisflies on the surface, they don't seem to be interested in color."

Leduc's Spiky Squirrel
Hook: Tiemco TMC100, sizes 20 to 12.
Thread: Tan 8/0 (70 denier).
Body: Natural squirrel with guard hairs.
Wing: Natural cul de canard.
Head: Small amount of squirrel dubbing.

Rabbit's Foot BWO
Hook: Gamakatsu S-10, sizes 20 to 14.
Thread: Olive 8/0 (70 denier).
Tails: Light dun Microfibbets.
Body: Olive turkey biot.
Wing: Light dun snowshoe rabbit.
Thorax: Blue-winged olive Super Fine
   Dubbing.

Last Resort
Hook: Knapek streamer hook, sizes 8 to 1.
Thread: Olive 6/0 (140 denier).
Bead: 4.0-millimeter tungsten bead.
Tail: Fluorescent orange marabou.
Body: Olive Estaz Metallique.
Wing: Olive Zonker strip.
Back: Brown Whiting Farms Mini Bird Fur.

Hare and Copper
Hook: Tiemco TMC2499, size 18 or 16.
Thread: Tan 8/0 (70 denier).
Bead: Tungsten, your choice of color and
    size.
Tail: Pheasant-tail fibers.
Body: Natural hare's-ear dubbing.
Rib: Small copper wire.
Hot spot: Datum Glo-Brite #7.

You sent one streamer pattern called the Last Resort. What's the story behind this fly?
"I use that streamer under just about any conditions. When the water is high, however, I'll often fish two streamers at the same time. I might vary the colors—yellow, brown, or dark olive. If you look at the fly, you'll see that it has a hot spot at the end of the body. It's an orange marabou tail. I think I get more hook-ups with this fly because the hot spot is close to the hook point.

    "I cast the streamers upstream, almost as if I'm fishing nymphs. I retrieve them to my position, and when they get to within about fifteen feet, I give them a little jiggle.

    "When conditions are tough and you're not catching many fish, try double streamers. One time, in a competition in Pennsylvania, fishing double streamers saved my rear end. I switched to double streamers and caught eight fish."

In addition to new flies, we're also seeing new extra-long nymph-fishing rods. If an angler wanted to add a specialized nymph rod to his arsenal, which should he choose?
"A ten-foot-long, four-weight is my number-one rod," Aaron said. "I will use a ten-foot two-weight or an eleven-foot three-weight for special situations, but my normal rod for day-to-day use is a ten-foot-long for a four-weight line."

When would you use those other, more specialized rods?
"I might use the ten-foot-long, two-weight rod if I wanted to use an extra-light tippet. This way I can react quickly to set the hook, but I won't snap the tippet. If I'm in a larger river, I might step up to an eleven-foot-long rod to be able to keep more line off the water and get a better drift. The Housatonic in Connecticut and the West Branch of the Delaware

are really wide rivers. Sometimes you need that extra reach to get to the fish."

Hi-Viz Klinkhammer
Hook: Varivas 2200 BL, sizes 16 to 12.
Thread: Dark brown 8/0 (70 denier).
Body: Light brown Super Fine Dubbing.
Thorax: Black synthetic peacock.
Hackle: Grizzly.
Wing post: Fluorescent orange and
chartreuse polypropylene.

You're gaining quite a reputation for teaching these new fishing methods. How do your clients respond?
"At first some of them don't believe it's fly fishing. In the United States it's been labeled as just lobbing flies. They don't realize that you must have a good casting technique to present the flies properly. The biggest obstacle is getting people to understand that you do a lot of casting; once they realize this, they really get into it. It's a really versatile method of fishing; there are times when you'll cast up to thirty feet to reach trout, and there are times when you will catch the fish right at your feet."

When the topic of European nymph fishing comes up, a lot of American anglers respond that it's nothing more than high-sticking. I know you've heard that. How do you respond?
"Watch a guy fishing a strike indicator with the usual high-sticking method. There's usually a huge belly of line going from the rod tip to the water. This belly has enough weight to counterbalance the weight of the flies and split shot and can actually pull the flies off the bottom. The Europeans, however, often keep the rod at a fairly low angle. They use the long rod to reach the fish and keep the line off the water, whereas the guy using the high-stick method just casts the flies and leaves a lot of line on the water. Adjust the rod angle to meet the conditions and water you're fishing. And at the end of the drift, always give the line a little hook-set motion. I do believe I catch fish that I don't detect."

Do you ever fish wet flies in combination with nymphs?
"Sometimes I'll add another tag and tie on a wet fly to catch fish that are feeding throughout the water

column. This can be very effective when the trout are feeding on emergers closer to the surface."

How was your summer? Were you busy fishing and guiding?
"This past year I guided every day in July except for the seven days I went to Colorado. I also guided almost every day in August. A lot of these guys are going out with me to learn about these new nymph-fishing methods, and they love being able to catch more trout."

———————————

Chapter 9

Craig Mathews
and Blue Ribbon Flies

Craig Mathews of West Yellowstone, Montana, is one of our sport's leading fly designers. He consistently creates new fresh- and saltwater patterns that appear in the fly boxes of knowledgeable anglers around the world. And his shop, Blue Ribbon Flies, is a favorite stop for fly fishers visiting his area's famed rivers.

Craig isn't originally from Montana; he moved there more than thirty years ago. Since that time, he has become a leading figure in the fly-fishing industry and is a recognized conservationist. He firmly believes that while it is great to catch fish, we are all responsible for protecting the natural resources we enjoy.

Craig started by telling me how he came to live in Montana and get into the professional fly-tying business.

"I moved from Grand Rapids, Michigan, about thirty-three years ago. I came as the police chief in 1978. I got involved in this business in 1980. I was tying flies back then for Bud Lilly, and I traded flies for gear.

"I'll tell you the truth about how I go into the professional fly-tying business. My sister was born with a birth defect, and she grew to teach handicapped kids in Michigan. I taught her how to tie flies, and she went on to teach her students. She eventually came back to me and said, 'Look at this!' I was pleased that it was taking off. Well, I told her that she and I would get into the wholesale fly-tying business and hire handicapped children to tie the flies. Initially, when we started, Orvis and L. L. Bean were customers. We had nine handicapped fly tyers. I think it was a win-win for everyone involved."

Iris Caddis
Hook: Tiemco TMC 100SPBL, sizes 20
   to 14.
Thread: Brown 8/0 (70 denier).
Shuck: Amber Zelon.
Abdomen: Zelon blended with hare's-ear
   dubbing.
Wing: White Zelon.
Thorax: Zelon blended with hare's-ear
   dubbing.

So you actually moved to Montana to become a policeman.
"Yes, I was the chief of police at that time. My wife was the dispatcher, and she also got involved in the business. I retired from the police department in 1982; that's when I got into the fly-fishing business full-time."

Your fly shop has become legendary, and you offer a lot of guided trips.
"Yes, in addition to the shop, we have fourteen guides who work for us six to eight months a year. We keep them pretty busy."

You sent a really large collection of great flies. We need to spend some time talking about them. Let's start with the Iris Caddis.
"The Iris Caddis was named for the dubbing material we once used for the trailing shuck. It was an ingredient called Iris Dub. I think it came from Germany, but that was a long time ago. Today we use Zelon for the shuck."

What's the body?
"That's a Zelon dubbing blend. We blend Zelon with a couple of natural furs, primarily rabbit or beaver. The wing and shuck are straight Zelon."

This fly must lie flush on the surface. Is it more of an emerger imitation?
"Yes, it is. It's probably the best caddis emerger we've ever fished."

It's such a simple-looking fly.
"Yes, it is simple to tie, and it floats like a cork. You can tie it with Antron, and a lot of people will argue this point, but Antron doesn't float as well as Zelon, at least not in my opinion."

It looks like an adaptable pattern.

"Oh, you bet. We tie it to imitate every caddis species from size 8 down to the microcaddis, say size 22.

"That fly works especially well during *Hydropsyche* emergences. That's our big caddisfly hatch out here. The hatch lasts about six weeks from late June until maybe the first week of August on rivers like the Yellowstone, Madison, and Henrys Fork. On rivers that have a thermal influence, like the Firehole, there are two emergences: the spring and then again in the fall."

I've fished the Firehole River. It's an incredibly unique place. Do you get customers who want to fish there?

"Oh boy, yes. I just love that river."

Some of your patterns, such as the Sunken Stone and Improved Sunken Stone, look very unique. What are the stories behind these flies?

"We started coming up with the Sunken Stone when we were fishing for steelhead back in the early 1980s. One of our local tyers kind of improved on it and brought it out for trout fishing in the late 1980s.

"The foam-bodied version is even newer. We introduced the Improved Sunken Stone about two years ago."

So you're still improving your flies.

"Yes, we're always looking for ways to improve them."

Like the Iris Caddis, the Sunken Stone must lie low on the water.

"Yes, it does. And you can skitter that one and pull it under to imitate a drowned or struggling adult stonefly; it'll pop back up in front of fish and drive them nuts. It's also a good waking fly for steelhead."

Sunken Stone
Hook: 6X-long hook, size 6.
Thread: Orange 6/0 (140 denier).
Tail: Black Zelon.
Body: Orange hare's-ear dubbing.
Wing: Deer hair.

Improved Sunken Stone
Hook: 6X-long hook, size 6 or 4.
Thread: Orange 6/0 (140 denier).
Body: Orange foam.
Wing: Deer or elk hair.
Head: Orange dubbing.

Drake Foam Emerger
Hook: Regular dry-fly hook, sizes 12 to 6.
Thread: Gray 8/0 (70 denier).
Tail: Tan Zelon.
Body: Tan Zelon blended with hare's-ear
    dubbing.
Rib: Brown 3/0 (210 denier) tying thread.
Wing: Gray foam.
Hackle: Tan grizzly.

The Drake Foam Emerger is another pattern that you've designed to lie low on the water.
"Yes, it does. Very often, when the big drakes emerge, they have a very low profile when they're trying to escape their nymph shucks. When this is going on, they're setting flush on the surface, and the bigger fish key in on them; the smaller fish will hit the fully emerged duns, but the larger trout want the low-profile emergers."

The body on this fly looks like pure rabbit dubbing.
"No, that's another Zelon blended dubbing. That one has just a pinch of Zelon. You can use straight rabbit dubbing, but I do prefer just a pinch of Zelon."

The PMD Foam Emerger is a cousin to the Drake Foam Emerger, but that body looks like it has more Zelon.
"That is actually just Super Fine Dubbing."

PMD Foam Emerger
Hook: Regular dry-fly hook, size 16.
Thread: Gray 8/0 (70 denier).
Tail: Tan Zelon.
Body: Yellow dubbing.
Rib: Yellow 6/0 (140 denier) tying thread.
Wing: Gray foam.
Hackle: Dun.

PMD Dun
Hook: Regular dry-fly hook, size 18 or 16.
Thread: Yellow 8/0 (70 denier).
Shuck: Amber Zelon.
Body: Light olive dubbing.
Wing: Amber Zelon and elk hair.

Let's talk about the X-Caddis, one of your most famous trout patterns.

"My wife, Jackie, came up with the X-Caddis. We came up with the Sparkle Dun back in 1983, and we were having a tough time matching a caddis emergence on the Henrys Fork, and one day Jackie said, 'Why don't you do with caddis patterns what you did with the Sparkle Dun—give it a trailing shuck.' So, I added a trailing Zelon shuck, a Zelon dubbed body, and a simple deer-hair wing to create the original X-Caddis. Since then, we improved on that fly. The X2 has a little more sparkle, it has a slightly lower profile, and we added an underwing of Zelon."

You really like Zelon, don't you?

"Yes, I do. Unfortunately Dupont stopped making it, but John Betts and we bought the last six hundred-pound skid of it. We have a lot of Zelon left."

PMD Foam Spinner
Hook: Regular dry-fly hook, size 16.
Thread: Gray 8/0 (70 denier).
Tail: Dun hackle fibers.
Body: Light olive dubbing.
Wing: Dun hackle.
Back: Gray foam.

X2 Caddis
Hook: Regular dry-fly hook, size 14 or 12.
Thread: Brown 8/0 (70 denier).
Shuck: Amber Zelon.
Body: Green hare's-mask dubbing.
Underwing: White Widow's Web or Zelon.
Wing: Elk hair.
Head: Hare's-ear dubbing or a substitute.

Zelon Midge
Hook: Curved-shank emerger hook, sizes
    22 to 18.
Thread: Olive 8/0 (70 denier).
Tail, abdomen, and wing: White Zelon.
Thorax: Dark Zelon.

Giant Nature Stonefly Nymph
Hook: Curved-shank nymph hook, sizes 8
    to 2.
Thread: Black 6/0 (140 denier).
Tail and antennae: Olive biots.
Abdomen: Black Zelon dubbing and
    orange Egg Yarn.
Rib: 3/0 (210 denier) black thread.
Thorax: Black Zelon dubbing.
Legs: Pheasant-body feather.
Wing case: Black latex or a substitute.

You tie at least one pattern using nothing but Zelon.
"The Zelon Midge is a tremendous fly. The trailing shuck is Zelon, and to make the abdomen, I just wrap of a thread rib over the shuck fibers. The splayed wing is Zelon, and I figure-eight wrap dark Zelon around the base of the wings to create the thorax. That's another simple but very effective fly that I fish almost every day on the Madison River during the winter."

Do you fish a lot during the winter?
"We probably have our best dry-fly fishing during the winter, and no one is here. The midges hatch throughout the winter, and the fish are kind of naïve, and they rise freely. I tell people not to book a trip over the winter just to fish, but if you're coming to ski or tour, be sure to pack a fly rod. If you're here for three days, you'll have some really fine fishing on at least one of those days. The water is very low, and you don't even need waders. You're fishing right along the edges of the rivers, in three and four inches of water—it's a kick."

One of the most beautiful flies I've received for this project is your Giant Nature Stonefly Nymph.
"Thank you."

What's the wing case?
"That's simply latex. The abdomen—all the dubbed body parts, actually—is a Zelon dubbing blend, and the belly of the abdomen is something like Egg Yarn pulled forward. It's really simple to tie, and it is totally indestructible salmonfly nymph imitation. It catches both trout and steelhead."

Can you tie smaller versions of this fly?
"Oh, you bet. I use it to tie imitations of different species of salmonflies. It's kind of time-consuming to

make, but since it's so indestructible, it is well worth the effort.

"Nick Lyons was with me about the time I perfected that pattern, and he went nuts with how many trout we caught with it."

I see that when I write the recipes describing your flies, if something looks like dubbing, I can't go wrong if I specify Zelon. Do you have any tips for tying with Zelon?
"No, you won't go wrong by listing Zelon as an ingredient in most of these patterns. Just remember that pure Zelon is hard to use as dubbing; you have to blend a natural fur with it. That's one of the key reasons we add a little rabbit or beaver as a binder."

Of all your very contemporary-looking flies, you then hit me up with the Mighty Midge. That's a very traditional-looking wet fly.
"That's a great little fly. I got that pattern from my close personal friend Yvon Chouinard. He and I fish together a lot, and one day he showed me that fly. It has that little starling hackle, and it just lays waste to the fish on the Madison. It's a deadly fly."

Do you think it imitates anything?
"We tie it in red, light olive, and brown. Those imitate the three primary colors of midges we find in that area. The abdomen is just thread, the thorax is peacock, and the hackle is starling. Simple, huh? And deadly."

The Egg-Laying Caddis is somewhat different from your other patterns; you tie this fishy-looking fly using a cul de canard feather as the wing.
"Rene Harrop said in the Angler's Club of New York journal that we introduced CDC in the United States. It was back in 1980, and CDC was new to American tyers. One of our biggest customers for the stuff was

Mighty Midge
Hook: Curved-shank emerger hook, sizes 20 to 16.
Thread: Black 8/0 (70 denier).
Abdomen: Red thread or floss.
Rib: Gold wire.
Thorax: Peacock herl.
Hackle: Starling.

Egg-Laying Caddis
Hook: Regular dry-fly hook, sizes 18 to 14.
Thread: Gray 8/0 (70 denier).
Tail: Chartreuse or bright green Zelon.
Body: Cul de canard.
Wing: Cul de canard.
Head: Cul de canard used as dubbing.

Mel Krieger. We no longer use a lot of cul de canard, but it works on the Egg-Laying Caddis. And the body is also CDC woven onto thread; it actually comes prespooled. It also floats like a cork; it's good for about a dozen fish before you have to baby it and dry it out. But that's another pattern that you can tie to imitate a variety of caddisflies."

Do you design all of the patterns you sell through Blue Ribbon Flies?

"I think that originality in fly tying is only undetected plagiarism. So much of the credit for all of our flies goes to our entire team. I still use forty fly tyers around the country who develop new patterns. We all feed off one another to create new flies. It's fun, and it keeps me enthused; I still fish 150 days a year!"

In addition to being an angler and business owner, you're a committed conservationist. Tell me about these activities.

"Several years ago we came up with our One Percent idea when Yellowstone Park came to the local gateway communities and said they didn't have funding to provide everything visitors expected. Way back when I was police chief, we lobbied the state legislature to create a resort tax to fund police, fire, and water services. When park officials came to us looking for support, it just occurred to me that we could tax ourselves 1 percent and send the money to the park. As you can imagine, however, you can't just send money to a national park, but the Yellowstone Park Foundation had just come on line, so we gave the money to them to fund projects in the park.

"Look, I make a really good living off Yellowstone National Park, and I just felt that I should give something back. At the same time, Yvon Chouinard and his company, Patagonia, were doing pretty much the same thing, so in 2001 we held a meeting in Los Angeles

Zelon Ant
Hook: Regular dry-fly hook, sizes 18 to 14.
Thread: Black 8/0 (70 denier).
Body: Black dubbing.
Back: Black foam.
Wing: White Zelon.
Legs: Black round rubber or a substitute.

and founded One Percent for the Planet. We now have almost 1,700 business members worldwide, and we've raised more than $60 million. It's a real commitment.

"A member business must certify that they are indeed contributing 1 percent of their gross sales to conservation; the beauty is that each member sends their check to their favorite cause. You feel really proud that you help protect a resource that is dear to your heart. The first check is the hardest one to write, but after you see the impact you can make, you can't wait to write the second check. It's a tremendously successful and worthwhile program."

———————————

Chaos Hopper
Hook: Regular dry-fly hook, size 8.
Thread: Brown 6/0 (140 denier).
Body: Tan foam.
Wing: Gray Zelon.
Legs: Yellow round rubber.
Indicator: Yellow foam.

Rusty Foam Spinner
Hook: Regular dry-fly hook, size 16.
Thread: Gray 8/0 (70 denier).
Tail: Dun hackle fibers.
Body: Brown dubbing.
Wing: Dun hackle.
Back: Gray foam.

Chapter 10

Mike Mercer:
"I Still Love to Tie and Fish"

COURTESY OF MIKE MERCER

Poxyback Green Drake Nymph
Hook: Tiemco TMC2302, size 12 or 10.
Thread: Olive 8/0 (70 denier).
Tail: Thread natural ring-neck pheasant-tail fibers.
Abdomen: Buggy Nymph Dubbing, Z-Wing.
Rib: Small copper wire.
Carapace: Golden brown mottled turkey tail.
Gills: Olive ring-neck aftershaft feathers.
Wing case: Buggy Nymph Dubbing, olive.
Thorax: Buggy Nymph Dubbing, olive.
Legs: Golden brown mottled hen-back feather.
Wing case coating: Five-minute epoxy.
Head: Buggy Nymph Dubbing, olive.

I've admired Mike Mercer's terrific patterns for a very long time. They show ingenuity and a real mastery of pattern design. Just by examining his flies, you can tell that Mike is a real angler.

I tied Mike's Poxyback nymph imitations for many years and was especially partial to his Poxyback Green Drake and Poxyback Golden Stone; these have been some of my go-to patterns for years.

Mike lives in California and works at the well-known The Fly Shop of Redding. In addition to being one of our sport's most recognized fly designers, he has a job at The Fly Shop that we would all envy.

"How long have you been with The Fly Shop?"
"Oh boy, I've been here for thirty-three years. I came to work here about six years after they opened the doors."

The Fly Shop is one of the most-respected fly shops in the country, isn't it?
"Yes, it's become one of those iconic shops. We've been very fortunate."

Is The Fly Shop still under the same ownership?
"Yes, it is. There was a partnership for the first several years, but then Mike Michalak bought out his partner, and he's owned it ever since."

Mike Mercer: "I Still Love to Tie and Fish"

I remember that The Fly Shop received the Retailer of the Year Award at the annual Fly Fishing Retailer Show a few years ago.

"Yes, we did. In fact, we've won quite a few awards. But I don't know, maybe it's just one of those survival things: like, 'Who are we going to give the award to now?'"

Quite a few fly shops have gone out of business over the past few years.

"Sadly, that's true, but we're still thriving. I think a small part of our success is due to the attrition in the number of fly shops, but I hate that. Mom-and-pop shops are the heart of fly fishing. We're like a large mom-and-pop store, but it's really sad to see all the little guys going away."

The small shops play a large role in introducing people to the sport of fly fishing.

"They're absolutely a huge part of it. I consider those shops good, friendly competition. They also generate a lot of business for us."

There's a big learning curve to fly fishing. Fly shops play a large educational role, don't they?

"Yes, they do. Learning to fly fish requires a real commitment. And it's fun to watch that beginning angler when he catches his first fish on a fly, and the lights go on in his eyes. It could be an eighty-year-old man or a six-year-old kid, but they get so excited. I remember when I caught my first fish on a fly; I was full of shock and awe. I'd been fishing with worms for years, and I felt total disbelief that these fish would actually eat a synthetic fly. I was in total shock when this little smallmouth bass came over and took my fly. At that point I bought into the whole thing; my whole life changed. And to see this in other people is so cool."

Psycho Prince Nymph
Hook: Tiemco TMC3769, sizes 18 to 12.
Thread: Camel 8/0 (70 denier).
Bead: Gold.
Tail: Dark brown turkey biots.
Rib: Small copper wire.
Carapace: Dark mottled golden brown
    turkey tail.
Abdomen: Orange Ice Dub.
Wing tuft: Electric banana Angel Hair.
Wing: Amber turkey biots.
Collar: Arizona Synthetic Peacock
    Dubbing.

Mercer's Poxyback Crayfish
Hook: Tiemco TMC200R, size 8.
Thread: Orange 6/0 (140 denier) or 8/0 (70 denier).
Antennae: Sili Legs, pumpkin/black speckled.
Claws: Clumps of muddy orange marabou.
Legs: Muddy orange hen-back feather.
Eyes: Melted plastic eyes.
Carapace: A slip of turkey tail, coated with five-minute epoxy.
Dumbbell eyes: 5/32 inch.
Body: Select Buggy Nymph Dubbing, lava brown.

You have a really unique job at The Fly Shop, don't you?
"I've actually had all the jobs over the years. Now I'm part of a team of six people that sells international travel trips. I sell trips to fish all over the world, but my specialty is Alaska and Chile. All of us here have our specialties. It's a great way to make a living. Anglers call and e-mail and say they want to take a trip someplace, but there are so many lodges and options that they don't know what to do. It's fun to walk them through the steps and help them plan their dream trip. It's so satisfying when they return and tell you what a great time they had."

Do you have to travel and check out the lodges you recommend?
"You bet I do; all of them. It's fun, but it's also a very important part of the job."

You're one of the best fly designers in the country, and your patterns appear in fly boxes across the United States and around the world. How long have you been designing new patterns?
"I've been seriously designing my own flies since I was in my early twenties—that's almost thirty years. I tied a lot when I was a kid—I started when I was twelve years old—but I just imitated what other people were making. I started guiding when I was eighteen, and I guess I was about twenty when I said, 'These flies just aren't cutting it.' That's when I started thinking about making my own patterns.

"Most flies work on freestone streams, but on places like Hat Creek, Fall River, and the big spring creeks, the regular flies just weren't working. It was like the trout were tired of them; you watch fish come up to them and then turn away. I remember when the Flashback Pheasant-Tail Nymph hit, and the fish were all over them. But in the course of just one or two years that fly wouldn't work as well. I started asking

86

a lot of questions: What are the fish really eating, and what really triggers them to strike? I started seining the water where I was fishing and collecting insects, and I paid a lot more attention to how the trout were reacting.

"I just lived for fishing back then. I was just a kid, and if I wasn't guiding, I was fishing on my own— literally every single day for three or four years. Living like this you can't help but learn a lot. I eventually began thinking that there had to be a better way to catch those fish, and I wanted to see if I could tie flies that more closely matched what the trout were eating.

"This was also the same time when a lot of the writings of Swisher and Richards were coming out, and I was also a big fan of Ernie Schwiebert—I loved his exacting style, and his thought processes really resonated with me. I didn't want to tie just a clump of Pheasant-Tail Nymphs—that sucks—I wanted to be a little more imitative. It was a cool time of life; there was about five years where I just lived to fish, and I've never come as close to learning so much."

Where were you guiding?

"Hat Creek, Fall River, McCloud River, Upper Sacramento River, and the Pit River.

"The Lower Sacramento, with all of its big rainbows, is getting all the press today, but back then it wasn't that good; there was a bunch of mine effluent and dioxins leaching into the river, and while there were big fish back then, there weren't very many of them. And there were only two species of caddisflies— nothing else. We learned that the caddisflies were the only insects that could survive in the river. Now, since the river has been cleaned up, it's gone from having fair fishing to having really good fishing with the additional new insects: more species of caddisflies, PMDs, blue-winged olives, October caddis, salmonflies, golden stones, a few green drakes, and a few Hex. With

Poxyback Callibaetis Nymph
Hook: Tiemco TMC200R, sizes 18 to 14.
Thread: Chartreuse or light green 6/0 (140 denier).
Tail: Three natural gray ostrich herl tips.
Rib: Pearl Flashabou.
Abdomen: Tan Damsel Buggy Nymph or olive/tan Antron dubbing.
Gills: Natural gray marabou clumps.
Thorax: Same as the abdomen.
Legs: Wood-duck flank fibers.
Wing case: Two slips of dark mottled turkey tail feather, one on top of the other and coated with five-minute epoxy.
Head: Same as the thorax.

Profile Spinner, Hexagenia
Hook: Tiemco TMC2499SPBL, size 8.
Thread: Tan 8/0 (70 denier).
Tail: Barred ginger hackle stems.
Extended abdomen: Yellow Larva
    Lace Dry Fly Foam colored with a
    waterproof marking pen.
Rib: Tying thread.
Hackle: Ginger.
Down Wing: Dun Zelon.
Wing post: Orange and yellow yarn.
Thorax: Antique gold Hare-Line dubbing.

Mercer's PMD Trigger Nymph
Hook: Tiemco TMC3761, sizes 18 to 14.
Thread: Brown 6/0 (140 denier) or 8/0
    (70 denier).
Bead: Small gold metal bead.
Tail: Three ring-neck pheasant-tail fibers.
Abdomen: Brown turkey biot.
Thorax: Select Buggy Nymph Dubbing, brown.
Legs: Speckled partridge fibers.
Wing bud: Pale yellow Ice Dub.

clean water and a device on the dam that regulates the temperature of the water entering the river, the Lower Sacramento has completely turned around and become a fantastic fishery."

What are the key triggers in a good nymph imitation?
"While it's impossible to say what a fish really sees, I'm convinced they see things like dark camouflaged backs and light-colored bellies on nymphs. So often when they're swimming toward the surface, or stoneflies are tumbling through the water, the fish see these differences in color. I think it is important to design these contrasting colors into your nymph imitations.

"The wing cases of some nymphs, such as mayflies, fill with gases and become distended and blotchy looking before the wings burst out. This is the stage when the nymphs are susceptible to the trout because they're swimming to the surface. One of the most pronounced improvements I made on my nymphs was adding that little strip of Flashabou down the middle of the wing case under the epoxy on the back. Man, that made a huge difference."

So, you were making Poxyback nymphs before you added the flash?
"Yes, the plain Poxybacks came first."

How long have you been tying Poxyback Nymphs?
"Probably almost twenty-five years. And I keep coming up with new ones."

What was the first Poxyback Nymph?

"It was the Golden Stone Poxyback, but it's not the one with the biot abdomen that has become so popular; the original had a body of picked-out dubbing. We still stock it here at the shop. The first one that got any real publicity, however, was the Poxyback PMD Nymph. It worked phenomenally well, even better than the Golden Stone. The Golden Stone caught fish, but it just looked so cool and had fly-shop bin appeal; the Poxyback PMD Nymph, however, worked a lot better, and it's still one of my top sellers."

Poxyback Biot Golden Stone
Hook: Tiemco TMC2302, sizes 18 to 6.
Bead: Gold, size to match the hook.
Thread: Tan 8/0 (70 denier).
Tail and antennae: Sulphur orange turkey biots, mottled with a brown waterproof pen.
Underbody: Round lead-free wire strips down both sides of the hook shank.
Abdomen: Sulphur orange turkey biot, mottled with a brown waterproof pen.
Wing case: Golden brown mottled turkey tail coated with five-minute epoxy.
Thorax: Buggy Nymph Dubbing, golden stone.
Legs: Golden brown mottled hen-back feather.
Head: Buggy Nymph Dubbing, golden stone, colored on top with a brown waterproof pen.

Poxyback PMD Nymph
Hook: Tiemco TMC2302 or TMC5262, sizes 18 to 14.
Thread: Camel 8/0 (70 denier).
Tail: Three yellow ring-neck pheasant-tail fibers.
Rib: Pearl Flashabou.
Carapace: Dark mottled turkey tail.
Abdomen: Buggy Nymph Dubbing, PMD.
Thorax: Buggy Nymph Dubbing, PMD.
Gills: Cream/gray marabou clumps.
Wing case: Dark mottled turkey tail coated with five-minute epoxy.
Legs: Yellow ring-neck pheasant-tail fibers.
Head: Buggy Nymph Dubbing, PMD.

When did you start adding the Flashabou wing stripe?

"The Micro Mayflies with the Flashabou wing stripe were the first flies that got any publicity. They've been out for a lot of years, and they're still my best-selling nymphs. I attribute a lot of their success to the flash."

What's it like to design a new fly?

"Let's use a new nymph as an example. Sometimes you get it right on the first try; you tie the fly, take it fishing, and it works really well. Usually, however, it comes in stages. I start whittling it down, trying to match the

Gold Bead Poxyback PMD Nymph
Hook: Tiemco TMC2302 or TMC5262, sizes 18 to 14.
Thread: Camel 8/0 (70 denier).
Bead: Brass bead, gold color.
Tail: Three yellow ring-neck pheasant-tail fibers.
Rib: Pearl Flashabou.
Carapace: Dark mottled turkey tail.
Abdomen: Buggy Nymph Dubbing, PMD.
Thorax: Buggy Nymph Dubbing, PMD.
Gills: Cream/gray marabou clumps.
Wing case: Dark mottled turkey tail coated with five-minute epoxy.
Legs: Yellow ring-neck pheasant-tail fibers.
Head: Buggy Nymph Dubbing, PMD.

Copper Bead Poxyback Baetis
Hook: Tiemco TMC 200, size 18.
Bead: Brass bead, copper color.
Thread: Chartreuse 8/0 (70 denier).
Tail: Three pheasant-tail fibers dyed yellow.
Abdomen: Super Fine Dry Fly Dubbing, blue-winged olive.
Abdomen carapace: A slip of lemon wood-duck fibers.
Rib: Same as the tying thread.
Gills: Sparse clumps of gray/olive marabou.
Wing case: A slender slip of mottled turkey tail coated with five-minute epoxy.
Thorax: Same as the abdomen.
Legs: Sparse clumps of lemon wood duck.
Head: Same as the abdomen.

triggers that will turn on the fish, and finally—at least to my eyes—I get it to the final cut, and it's done. It's just obvious to me that it's done. But next I go fish the fly, and maybe even then I make more adjustments."

How did you hit on the idea of the Flashabou back stripe?

"Flashback styles of nymphs were already around, but they seemed a little too gaudy, and I didn't care for them that much. I wanted just a little bit of flash on my flies, and it was a total accident that it worked so well. But if you look at the wing cases of real emergers, you don't see all that brightness; there's just a little thin strip. That's what I had in my mind, and 'boom,' it really worked. And it didn't matter what nymph I put it on: It dramatically improved any fly. In the long run I learned just how important it is to imitate that initial moment when the wing case opens and those gases start shining through there. I don't think the fish really want that big blast of color—not that Flashbacks don't catch fish, because they work well—but there's something about this in a technical trout-fishing situation that really improves the performance of the fly."

What's so interesting is that even a novice or intermediate-level tyer could apply these features to their own nymphs. It's not hard to add a strip of flash and drop of epoxy to the wing case of even Hare's-Ear and Pheasant-Tail Nymphs.

"You're absolutely right. I try to tell people that, 'Look, I've stolen techniques from here and there and added my own to come up with new flies. Yes, take these ideas and put them on your own flies.' I really like that about fly tying."

You also add gills to many of your flies.

"I'm a real fan of gills and legs. It goes back to that idea of adding and subtracting things to see what works best. In the case of the PMD Poxyback, it works way better with gills. I tie some nymphs without gills, and they work great, especially flies that have extremely

Ruby Micro Mayfly Nymph
Hook: Tiemco TMC3769, sizes 20 to 14.
Bead: Copper, size to match the hook.
Thread: Camel 8/0 (70 denier).
Tail: Three natural ring-necked pheasant-tail fibers.
Abdomen: Red Flashabou.
Rib: Small silver wire.
Wing case stripe: Pearl Flashabou.
Wing case: Golden brown mottled turkey tail.
Thorax: Buggy Nymph Dubbing, lava brown.
Legs: Natural ring-necked pheasant-tail fibers.
Wing case coating: Five-minute epoxy.
Head: Buggy Nymph Dubbing, lava brown.

thin bodies, maybe tied using only thread; a lot of times gills don't seem to matter. But on more traditional nymphs, I think the gills make a big difference and are an improvement.

"I've experimented with a lot of materials to add gills to flies: sometimes filoplume, sometimes ostrich herl, and sometimes marabou."

With respect to your dry flies, you really like parachutes, don't you?

"That's really good; I didn't know anybody picked up on that. Yes, I'm a huge fan of parachutes."

Profile Spinner, Pale Morning Dun
Hook: Tiemco TMC100, size 18 or 16.
Thread: Camel 8/0 (70 denier).
Tail: Blue dun spade feather fibers.
Abdomen: Rusty turkey biot.
Wing post: Orange and yellow
    polypropylene yarn.
Down Wing: Dun Zelon.
Thorax: Rusty brown Super Fine Dry Fly
    Dubbing.
Hackle: Blue dun dry-fly saddle hackle.

**Profile Spinner,
Foam Body Green Drake**
Hook: Tiemco TMC2499SP, size 12 or 10.
Thread: Olive 8/0 (70 denier).
Tail: Olive grizzly-neck hackle stems.
Extended abdomen: Yellow Larva
    Lace Dry Fly Foam, colored with
    waterproof pens.
Rib: Tying thread.
Wing post: Orange and yellow yarn or
    white calf tail.
Down Wing: Dun Zelon.
Thorax: Buggy Nymph Dubbing, Micro
    Mayfly.
Hackle: Olive grizzly-saddle hackle.

But you're doing something different with your parachute patterns: There are little wisps of fibers coming out of the sides. What is that material, and why is it there?

"That's just Zelon. It represents spinner wings. Those flies work fine without it, but in more challenging situations, those patterns really outperform. And I've never been a big fan of long, split Microfibbet tails. Some guys like them, and they catch trout with their flies, but I've had problems with fish bumping them away. I like straight little hackle-fiber tails. Sometimes I'll split the tails, but a lot of times I don't. I don't know if all of this is true—sometimes you get an idea in your mind, and you can't shake it—but I've done very well with smaller, less-pronounced tails.

Profile Spinner, BWO
Hook: Tiemco TMC100, sizes 22 to 18.
Thread: Olive 8/0 (70 denier).
Tail: Blue dun spade fibers.
Abdomen: Olive turkey biot.
Wing post: Orange macramé yarn.
Down Wing: Dun Zelon.
Thorax: Super Fine Dry Fly Dubbing, blue-winged olive.
Parachute hackle: Blue dun dry-fly saddle hackle.

Profile Spinner, Brown Drake
Hook: Tiemco TMC2499SP, size 12.
Thread: Brown 8/0 (70 denier).
Tail: Brown grizzly stripped hackle stems.
Extended abdomen: Larva Lace Dry Fly Foam, yellow, folded over a needle and colored with waterproof marking pens.
Rib: Same as the tying thread.
Wing post: Orange and yellow macramé yarn.
Down Wing: Dun Zelon.
Thorax: Select Buggy Nymph Dubbing, amber caddis.
Parachute hackle: Dark dun saddle dry-fly hackle.

Missing Link Caddis
Hook: Tiemco TMC102Y, sizes 18 to 12.
Thread: Camel 8/0 (70 denier).
Abdomen: Tying thread coated with
   Softex.
Rib: Pearl Flashabou.
Thorax/wing splitter: Peacock Ice Dub.
Wing: Elk-body hair.
Hackle: Dark dun dry-fly hackle.

"By the way, my Missing Link is another example of how I design a fly: I work on it, and I just know when it's done. And that fly has been enormously successful."

I've never heard of that pattern. Is it new?

"Yes, it's fairly new; I've been tying it for only a couple of years. I'm so pumped about that fly I can't think straight. I actually tied it to imitate a dying caddis, but it works for everything. I'll use it in size 18 when the fish are eating the little size 24 *Pseudocloeons*, and they take that with no problem—better than a tiny parachute. It's crazy. I've never had a fly that will do this.

"I also use it as an attractor. I used an Adams for a large part of my life, but now I go straight to the Missing Link. And it doesn't matter what the fish are on—caddis, small stones, mayflies, even terrestrials—there's just something about it that gives them confidence.

"We were on a small stream in Montana last year that contains cutthroats. We've fished it a lot. We always walk in and fish grasshoppers. I don't know what happened—maybe somebody got in there ahead of us—but our 'hopper patterns didn't work; the fish would come up, check out the fly, and go back down. The real grasshoppers were there, but the fish weren't interested in our artificials. So, we started fishing some different things, and I tried the Missing Link. Sure enough, the first fish came up and took it. It was total dumb luck on my part, but there's just something magical about the Missing Link that *the trout like*."

What sizes do you tie it in?

"I tie it on wide-gap hooks, but they would correspond to normal sizes 20 to 16. I also tie them in green-drake sizes. They all work.

"Look, I've had great days with all my flies, and I've had bad days with all my flies. But with the Missing Link, it's the one fly that never fails."

Can someone who doesn't tie flies buy the Missing Link?
"Yes, they can. Umpqua Feather Merchants picked it up, but they've had it for only about a year.

"You know, sometimes I feel like I've been cheating with all of my nymphs. I mean, sometimes the fish will eat a cigarette butt. Nymphs are nymphs. You can always catch fish with nymphs, but dry flies are a different scenario. A lot of the dries I've tied over the years have worked, but nothing has consistently

Flush Floater Salmonfly
Hook: Tiemco TMC2302, size 6 or 4.
Thread: Camel 8/0 (70 denier).
Tail: Round black rubber.
Abdomen: Orange Larva Lace Dry Fly
    Foam; color the last segment with
    a dark gray Prismacolor waterproof
    marking pen to imitate the egg sac.
Thorax: Select Buggy Nymph Dubbing,
    dark stone.
Rear collar: Orange dubbing to match the
    foam body.
Forward collar: Same as the thorax.
First underwing: Pearl Krystal Flash.
Second underwing: Black moose mane.
Third underwing: Elk-body hair.
First overwing: Orange macramé yarn.
Second overwing: Yellow macramé yarn.
Legs: Round black rubber.
Head: Same foam as the abdomen,
    colored on top with a dark gray
    Prismacolor waterproof marking pen.
Antennae: Round black rubber.

Flush Floater Golden Stone
Hook: Tiemco TMC2302, size 10 or 8.
Thread: Camel 8/0 (70 denier).
Tail: Sili Legs, pumpkin/black flake.
Abdomen: Larva Lace Dry Fly Foam,
    yellow colored with a light tan
    Prismacolor waterproof marking pen.
Thorax: Select Buggy Nymph Dubbing,
    golden stone.
Collar: Same as the thorax.
First underwing: Pearl Krystal Flash.
Second underwing: Black moose mane.
Third underwing: Elk-body hair.
First overwing: Orange macramé yarn.
Second overwing: Yellow macramé yarn.
Legs: Sili Legs, pumpkin/black flake.
Head: Same foam as the abdomen,
    colored on top with a light tan
    Prismacolor waterproof marking pen.
Antennae: Sili Legs, pumpkin/black flake.

outproduced the way the Missing Link does. This one is crazy, and it'll be fun to see what happens with it. Look, I know I sound like I have a giant ego, but this fly is just that good. And look, it's not about fly sales: I've given you the fly and recipe, so anybody can tie it on their own."

Umpqua Feather Merchants has carried your patterns for many years. How many flies do you have with them?
"That's a tough question to answer. Should I include all the color variations or just count unique patterns? If you're talking about simply single, unique designs—leaving out the variations—it's more than forty flies.

"I've been having a lot of fun with my tying lately. For a long time I'd send Umpqua four or five flies every year, and they'd pick up one or two for their catalog. But this past year I went kind of crazy and created all these new designs, and they're picking up several of them. I've been tying and developing flies for a lot of years, and I'm as enthusiastic as ever. I still love to tie and fish."

———————

Chapter 11

Kevin McKay
and the New Age of Fly Fishing

Gathering information and learning how to tie flies and to fish have become easier due to the Internet. Fishing reports, fly patterns, river maps—they're all just a few mouse clicks away. (You don't know what a "mouse click" is? Then where have you been living?)

It must seem odd reading about the virtues of the Internet in a printed book. As an editor of the world's largest magazine dedicated to tying flies, I hear the question all the time: "Do you think the Internet will put you out of business?" At first I wondered about this, and so did every other publisher and editor but not anymore.

Publishers are discovering that you have to deliver your content on all platforms: print and digital. Rely on one format—print *or* digital—and you might be screwed; use both mediums to deliver information and reach readers, and you'll stay in business and might even grow.

It's partially a question of quality: Large photos of beautiful fishing scenes and flies do not translate well to a computer screen, they're not terribly interesting on a digital tablet, and they suck on a smartphone. I use all of these devices, so I know what I'm talking about. These images simply look better on the printed page.

It's also a question of expectations. I stopped losing sleep over readers who want only pattern recipes: They can all go to the Internet. There are scads of websites that are little more than lists of flies and patterns, and they are good sources of raw information.

The same can be said for cooking recipes: If you simply want to know how to bake a cake or cook barbecue, go online. The Internet is perfect for creating websites that contain cooking recipes, yet cookbooks remain one of the most popular categories in publishing. Why? Because there are still enough readers for whom quality matters. They have higher expectations. They enjoy owning, reading, and even fondling beautiful books and magazines; no one enjoys fondling a laptop.

And yet the Internet offers unparalleled potential to help people learn to fish, cook, and do hundreds of other things.

Something else I hear is that young people are not getting into fly fishing. Well, the Internet is the best way to reach the next generation of fly fishers.

Even though I make the bulk of my living in the world of print, I spend a lot of time online. I appreciate the efforts of the folks who are designing high-quality websites, and I recognize their contributions to helping people, especially young people, learn to tie flies and fish.

I asked a friend and Maine registered guide, Kevin McKay, to participate in this project for two reasons. First, I needed someone to represent fly fishing in Maine. My home state contains thousands of miles of rivers, streams, lakes, and ponds full of trout and landlocked salmon, and it is a popular destination for fly fishers. Second, I wanted someone to represent the impact that "new media" are having on fly fishing. A website such as Kevin's (the address is www.maine flyfish.com) is an excellent forum for anglers to share information and learn from one another. It's not a commercial website (almost all fly shops have those): It's an information-based site. I'm sure there are one or more similar websites dedicated to fishing where you live.

But before we discussed his website or flies, I wanted to learn more about Kevin's guiding.

How long have you been guiding?

"I've been guiding for ten or eleven years. It's getting busier each season. You know how it is: It starts slowly and picks up as time goes on."

Is the business going well?

"Yes, it is. I'm always trying to push that hundred-trip mark, but guiding is just a part of what I do. I have a family, so I've been very busy: I have a real full-time job, I guide full-time, and I'm a full-time dad."

And then you're working on your website.

"And then I'm doing the website. I'm always adding new content. Recently I've been making fly-tying videos. This has been fun. The videos are geared more toward beginning tyers. My kids and their friends have been getting on the website to see how to tie basic patterns."

How long have you been maintaining your site?

"I think the Web was going on even before I started guiding. The first website was called the Maine Fly Fishing Journal. When I first got into fly fishing, I felt that I'd go into a fly shop, and they'd look at me like I had three heads if I didn't know exactly what I wanted or I didn't already know how to fish. The information wasn't there, and it just seemed like a lot of people didn't want to share what they knew."

I think that's one of the limiting factors in growing the sport of fly fishing: Fly shops should be the first point of contact for new anglers to get good, solid information, but some of them can be quite intimidating. Some shops are very good at welcoming new anglers; others are not.

"I agree. It seemed like an elitist club. But then I met some guys at work who were into fly fishing, and they showed me what I needed. We went to the L. L. Bean store, and they helped me buy my first outfit.

McKay Special
Hook: 6X-long streamer hook, size 6 or 4.
Thread: Black 6/0 (140 denier).
Tail: Red quill.
Body: Yellow Uni-Stretch.
Rib: Silver tinsel.
Wing: White marabou.
Throat: Red marabou.

"But I have to tell you, I was still looking for good information, and it was just hard to find. So, I started Maine Fly Fishing Journal."

That sounds like a pretty big step. What did you put on your website?

"It started pretty simple. I'd take a trip—say to the East Outlet of the Kennebec or wherever—and I'd post a fishing report. I'd talk about the fishing, the insects I was finding in the river, the hatches, and anything else that occurred to me. I'd talk about the flies I tried and list those that worked and those that did not work, and I'd post a photo. I wanted other people to do the same so we could share information."

How did you start guiding?

"That's another one of those things that sort of happened by accident. My brother-in-law, who has friends who work on Wall Street, said that he and his buddies wanted to go fishing with me. I said that would be fine, and he replied that they would want to pay me. 'What do you mean, pay me?' I asked. He said that they'd pay me. Wow, that was great. That's what started the ball rolling for me to get a guide's license."

Things were really starting to cook for you—fishing, guiding, and maintaining the website. Are things still evolving?

"A friend recently helped me revamp my website. One of the things he suggested was that the name of the original site was too long to generate traffic. So, I started searching for a good name that would have 'Maine' in it. I discovered that 'maineflyfish.com' was available, so I immediately registered it. It seemed like a pretty obvious name that would help generate more traffic."

Brown X-Caddis
Hook: Regular dry-fly hook, sizes 16 to 12.
Thread: Brown 8/0 (70 denier).
Tail: Yellow Zelon.
Wing: Deer hair.

Okay, you had the website name. What did you do next to develop the site?

"A friend in southern Maine named Richard Babine had put together a book on basic fly fishing. He scanned the whole thing and gave it to us for the website, so that content is available. I'm doing videos, and I write book and DVD reviews—we post anything related to fly fishing in Maine and a lot of other places.

"But the website is a real team effort. The members of the forum are key to developing the site; they really pull it together. They participate and make it what it is. We even have members who take new anglers fishing; for instance, a couple of guys take new people striper fishing. They've been doing this for a couple of years; I think it's an annual thing. They call it 'Newbie Day.' That's really great and illustrates the community of the site, and I'm very thankful for it."

A website like this truly is a team effort, isn't it?

"It absolutely is a team effort. For example, the fishing reports are a huge draw. Everyone wants to know where to fish, not just the guys from Maine, but especially visitors to Maine; a lot of people find us because they want to know where to go when they get here. I need the users of the site to post fishing reports: Where did they go, what was hatching, what flies did they use?

"To help generate this sort of content, I started giving away fly rods. If people put up fishing reports, they get a chance to win a rod. It's a great way to get reports and to thank people for participating. It takes some time—there's no fancy technology here: I just write down all the names of the people who post fishing reports, and my son picks a name out of the hat.

"Look, I don't want someone to give up their secret fishing spot, but if you visit some place like the Mousum River, which is a stocked river, tell us what happened. That's a great tool to help someone get into fly fishing. We have a core group of guys who offer this type of information. Everyone helps each other."

You do some other things to promote your website and fly fishing in Maine. For instance, you host a fly-fishing movie night at a local theater or restaurant.

"Yes, I do. We've been doing movie night for a few years. I reached out to a company called Gray Ghost Productions to see if we could show their films. It's worked very well. Last year we did it as a fundraiser for restoration of the Penobscot River. These events are always popular."

Another thing that's very well received is the January event you call the Freeze Up.

"No one in Maine is doing anything like the Freeze Up. That's another thing that happened by accident. We were fishing one day in December, and someone said he always fished on the first of January. I suggested that we meet on the river and have a cookout. I think five of us showed up the first time, but last year we counted eighty people. We fish, eat, and have a good time. It's a great chance to get out and see friends in the middle of winter.

"The State of Maine has also been helpful with the Freeze Up. They give us a permit to stock rainbows in the river for us to catch. They stock fish there anyway, so it's not a problem."

Where do you have the Freeze Up?

"We held it on the Presumscot River the first couple of years, but that river can freeze over. Now we go to the Mousum River because it tends not to freeze. Fly fishing in Maine—in January—isn't always easy.

"But you know, even the Freeze Up is a team effort. Everyone brings food. One guy brings salmon from Alaska, and another member brings cheesecake that his wife makes. It's a really good time."

Let's talk about your guide services. Where do you guide?
"I do a variety of fishing. I have an eighteen-foot jetboat, a drift boat, canoes stashed on a remote pond, and I even have float tubes and a small aluminum boat. I know that some guides specialize on certain rivers—or for certain species of fish—but I can tailor a trip to what a client wants. For trout and salmon, I do float trips on the West Branch of the Penobscot, the East Outlet of the Kennebec, the Moose, the Roach—a variety of rivers. If a client wants, we can fish three rivers in the same day."

So a client can see a variety of water.
"Oh, definitely. We can cover a lot of water. Each trip is different, and it's up to the client."

Let's talk about your fishing and flies based on the season. Where might you fish in the spring, and what flies would you use?
"I've started the season fishing in the Rangeleys; that's where I developed that green caddis larvae. Those rivers are full of green larvae, but you'll find them on many other rivers. I've used that fly to catch big brook trout in the rivers over there, but it works in many other waters.

"Another spring I was guiding some folks from Tennessee in the Moosehead Lake area; we were doing one of those three-river trips. We were on the Moose River, and I suggested they use sinking lines, heavy

West Branch Caddis
Hook: Regular dry-fly hook, sizes 16 to 12.
Thread: Brown 8/0 (70 denier).
Body: Brown dubbing.
Wing: Wood-duck crest feather.
Hackle: Brown.

Caddis Larva
Hook: Tiemco TMC2487, size 14 or 12.
Bead: Black.
Thread: Black 6/0 (140 denier).
Abdomen: Chartreuse Vinyl Rib.
Thorax: Peacock herl.

The Chicken
Hook: Mustad 94720, size 4.
Thread: White 6/0 (140 denier).
Tail: White marabou.
Body: White Crystal Chenille.
Throat: Red rabbit fur.
Collar: White marabou.

tippets, and my fly called The Chicken. I told them to just cast out and let the fly swing through the water. I suggested that pattern because the smelt might be running, and the larger trout might be chasing the baitfish. On the first cast, one of the guys broke off on a really good fish.

"Later in the day we went to the East Outlet of the Kennebec and changed to fishing a yellow stonefly nymph. They caught some nice salmon.

"When I nymph fish, I almost always start by using a black or yellow stonefly imitation. A new nymph angler needs to learn to flip a few rocks before he selects his flies. Examine several rocks, and count the nymphs and caddis larvae you find. Start by selecting an imitation of the most common insect you find. But every river in Maine contains big black and yellow stoneflies, and imitations of these insects are some of the first flies I use. Over the years a big yellow stonefly has been my number-one pattern."

Secret Stone Nymph
Hook: Mustad R74, size 6 or 4.
Bead: Black bead.
Thread: Brown 6/0 (140 denier).
Tail: Olive biot.
Body: Yellow Antron yarn.
Legs: Coq de Leon.
Wing case: Brown Scud Back.
Antennae: Olive biots.

Green Copper John
Hook: Regular wet-fly hook, sizes 16 to 12.
Thread: Black 6/0 (140 denier).
Bead: Gold.
Tail: Black biots.
Abdomen: Green Ultra Wire.
Thorax: Peacock herl.
Wing case: Opal Mirage tinsel.
Legs: Pheasant-tail fibers.

Is the Secret Stone Nymph one of your flies?

"Yes, that's one of my patterns. But look, I don't tie tons of flies; I'm more of a practical fly tyer. I tie because I need some flies for fishing. If I need yellow stoneflies tomorrow because I'm guiding, and I have only two in my fly box, then I'll tie some more tonight."

Where do you use your Hex mayfly?

"I have a pond where I take a few clients. My biggest brook trout from that pond weighed five and a half pounds. I've caught a lot of large trout in that pond and almost all on Hex imitations. It's a long hike in, so it gets very little pressure. You can still catch some really nice trout in Maine. But the Hex hatch brings out the big fish."

Tell me about The Chicken.

"The first day I used that fly, I caught thirty-two or thirty-four fish at the Roach River. I have friends who

Hex Dun
Hook: Regular dry-fly hook, size 8.
Thread: Yellow 8/0 (70 denier).
Tail and abdomen: Yellow deer hair.
Wing: White calf tail.
Hackle: Yellow grizzly.

Griffith's Gnat
Hook: Regular dry-fly hook, sizes 22 to 18.
Thread: Black 8/0 (70 denier).
Body: Peacock herl.
Hackle: Grizzly.

Bead-Head Woolly Bugger
Hook: Mustad 79580, size 6 or 4.
Head: Gold cone.
Thread: Olive 6/0 (140 denier).
Tail: Olive marabou.
Body: Olive chenille.
Hackle: Grizzly.

also love it. All that marabou really turns on the trout and salmon."

It's gratifying to see a young guy like Kevin McKay get into fly fishing. He loves the sport and is willing to share what he learns with others. And he does it in a very modest, unassuming way. With younger, tech-savvy anglers like Kevin around, the future of fly fishing and tying is assured.

———————

Chapter 12

Harry Murray
of the Beautiful Blue Ridge

The Shenandoah Valley in western Virginia is one of the most beautiful and historic places in the United States. Lush, green mountains and hundreds of miles of naturally flowing trout streams offer a wealth of opportunities for visiting fly fishers.

No one knows more than Harry Murray about fishing the Shenandoah Valley and the Blue Ridge Mountains for both native brook trout and smallmouth bass. He designs flies, has published several books and dozens of magazine articles, owns a fly shop, and teaches fly-fishing classes. It sounds like his plate is full, but for Harry, fly fishing is his passion; in his real life, he is a pharmacist.

I really enjoyed talking with Harry about fly fishing for native mountain brook trout. It reminded me of the years I lived in eastern Tennessee and fished the trout streams in the Great Smoky Mountains and Cherokee National Forest, another underappreciated angling resource.

COURTESY OF HARRY MURRAY

You live in one of the most beautiful parts of the country; nothing surpasses the Shenandoah Valley. Are you from that area?

"Yes, I am: six generations. The home where I was born and raised is right across the street from where the fly shop is today."

How long have you had the fly shop?

"Well, I have a fly shop and drugstore together. I got out of college in 1962 and opened both businesses almost simultaneously."

That's one of the oldest fly shops, operated by the original owner, I've known of.

"It's a good thing I have the pharmacy to help pay the bills."

At least you're an honest fly fisherman.

"I try to be."

You have excellent fishing for both smallmouth bass and trout. This book is more about trout flies and fishing. What's the geographic range of the trout fishing in your area?

"We fish the Blue Ridge Mountains, which run from Front Royal, Virginia, all the way down to the North Carolina line. The Blue Ridge, of course, is part of the Appalachian chain. You have good fishing all the way through the mountains of Tennessee and northern Georgia."

I think a lot of people underestimate the quality of the fishing in the Appalachians.

"This fishing we have is the real thing. These are all wild brook trout, and I'm going fishing tomorrow. Our hatches start just about this time of the year. Our quill Gordons will be coming off within the next week or so. And then we work our way into the other hatches: the blue quills and then the March browns and all the way into the sulphurs.

"You see, once the water temperature gets over forty degrees, these brook trout are willing to feed on top. I've already been catching a few fish on nymphs, but they haven't been willing to look up because the water has been down in the mid-thirties. But as it warms up and gets closer to forty, they'll start feeding on the surface, and we'll be getting our quill Gordon hatch."

What is the first major hatch?

"The quill Gordon."

And what's the second hatch?

"The dark blue quill."

When will they start emerging?

"They'll start the latter part of March."

This is only the first of March. All of that is happening this early in the season?

"Yes, it is. And by the middle of April we'll be into the March browns, and then the gray fox follow those a couple of weeks later and then the light cahills. Our sulphurs get going around the middle of May, and they run into June and sometimes even July. And we also get really good hatches of little yellow stoneflies; they start in late April and run into July, and once in a while we'll have little yellow stoneflies into August."

It's interesting that you mention the sulphur mayflies because that insect is usually associated with the slower waters such as the Pennsylvania limestone streams.

"We have them, but some years the hatch is heavier than others. The sulphur is a heavy hatch when it's on, but you might go two or three days and not hit it, and then on the fourth day they're everywhere. I've never figured that one out.

"One time my son and I were camping on a stream in the Blue Ridge. He said he was going to go fishing while I put up the tent. After a few minutes, he came running back to camp to get me—I thought a bear was after him. 'You've got to see this,' he said, 'get your fly rod and come up.' There was one pool that was about twenty feet long and about ten feet wide. There were about eleven brook trout feeding on both the duns and spinners. We had just fantastic fishing to the sulphurs.

"The great Art Flick helped me identify all of these insects. Art was a very close, personal friend. When I got out of college, there really wasn't any good work on the hatches of this area. There were

Murray's Sulphur Dry Fly
Hook: Mustad 94840, size 16 or 14.
Thread: Cream 6/0 (140 denier).
Tail: Light ginger hackle fibers.
Body: Sulphur orange dubbing.
Wing: Mallard-flank fibers.
Hackle: Light ginger.

some textbooks, but that was about it. So, I started collecting the insects in little pill bottles and alcohol solutions and sent them to Art. He helped me identify the hatches, and I put that information in hatch charts in two of my books.

"Now, don't confuse the timing of these hatches with, say, the hatches as they occur in the Catskills; our hatches are about two or three weeks ahead. And some years we might have a good green drake hatch, and other years we do not. But the quill Gordons, blue quills, March browns, and sulphurs are very dependable. In fact, we have very good hatches of quill Gordons."

Do you rely on the Catskill-inspired fly patterns?
"Not really. That's why I developed the Mr. Rapidan. Theodore Gordon was one of our best fly designers, but the body on the Quill Gordon fly that you and I know is a far cry from matching the real insect, so I was trying to develop a pattern that would better match the mayfly. The body on the Mr. Rapidan more closely matches the color of the real quill Gordon."

So, the other Mr. Rapidan patterns followed that fly?
"Yes, they did; one thing followed another."

And you have free-rising fish in these small mountain streams?
"Oh, absolutely."

Would you say that most of the mayfly imitations you've designed are more heavily hackled than the Catskill style of flies?
"I think so. When I look back at the Darby patterns and the old Rube Cross patterns, my flies have a lot more hackle because I'm fishing really rolling water."

Mr. Rapidan Delta-Wing Caddis
Hook: Mustad 94840, size 16 or 14.
Thread: Tan 6/0 (140 denier).
Body: Quill Gordon Fly Rite Dubbing.
Hackle: Brown and grizzly.
Wing: Yellow calf tail and light elk hair.

How large are the rivers where you are fishing? From my experience, these are headwater streams.

"We're fishing primarily headwaters because that's where you'll find the best populations of wild trout. These streams are ten to fifteen feet wide, and the pools are ten to fifteen feet long.

"The fish don't run big. A twelve-inch brook trout is a big fish, but you don't gauge the quality of the fishing based on the size of the fish. They can be tough, and on some days you'll catch a lot of trout on the surface, but sometimes you'll come into a pool and see a fish feeding, run every fly you have by him and he thumbs his nose at your patterns. It's not all a giveaway."

As you know, I lived in Knoxville and fished the Smoky Mountains, which offer a very similar type of fly fishing. People who have never done this type of fishing need to realize that while most of the fish aren't large, it's a wonderful opportunity to scale down your tackle and use a shorter and much lighter rod.

"Yes, it is; I mostly use a two- or three-weight rod."

Do some guys fish with nymphs?

"You bet they do. I teach in my classes that there are two prime times to use nymphs: during high water and then when the water is cold and the fish aren't rising. If we have just two or three inches of rain and streams rise, we're forced to go to nymphs. If we have cold water, say in the mid-thirties, we're again forced to go to nymphs. After that we're hitting the hatches and using dry flies, and by the early part of the summer we switch over to beetles, crickets, and ants."

Mr. Rapidan Bead-Head Nymph
Hook: Mustad 3906B, sizes 16 to 10.
Thread: Tan 6/0 (140 denier).
Tail: Pheasant-tail fibers.
Body: Hare's-ear dubbing.
Rib: Fine copper wire.
Wing: Mallard flank.
Legs: Mottled Indian hen fibers.

Black Miracle Stonefly Nymph
Hook: Mustad 3906 B, sizes 16 to 12.
Thread: Black 6/0 (140 denier).
Tail: Black biots.
Abdomen: Black dubbing.
Rib: Blue wire.
Thorax: Black dubbing.

Murray's Housefly
Hook: Mustad 94840, size 16 or 14.
Thread: Black 6/0 (140 denier).
Body: Peacock herl.
Wing: Grizzly hen.
Back and head: Black deer hair.

Murray's Little Black Stonefly
Hook: Mustad 94840, sizes 20 to 14.
Thread: Black 6/0 (140 denier).
Body: Black dubbing.
Hackle: Black.
Wing: Black goose biots with clipped tips.

You did send a couple of terrestrial imitations. I think your Housefly is particularly interesting.
"I tied that one to fish the Pennsylvania spring creeks right up the road. Those creeks were beat to death with every other kind of pattern, and I just wanted to show the fish something a little different. I think Chauncey Lively used to talk about the light pattern a fly created, and with those wings, it does create a different light pattern."

It's a beautiful little fly.
"Last year—it was probably early June—we just had houseflies all over the place. They'd get on your arms and kind of drive you crazy. They were also getting into the streams, and the fish were feeding on them. Last year we took a lot of fish on that pattern."

When does your fishing season end?
"The fish will feed, and the water temperature stays above forty degrees, until early December, but our only little stumbling block is that we do have spawning brook trout in mid-October, and, depending upon the section of the stream, they'll continue spawning until the middle of November. We discourage bothering them when they're spawning. But as far as the water temperature goes, we can catch them on the surface until the first of December."

Do you get early black stoneflies in the spring?
"Oh yes, right now. I'm seeing little black stoneflies on the snow drifts throughout the Blue Ridge Mountains.

And in real quiet, stopped-up pools—something with a log jam in it—you'll find brook trout feeding on these stoneflies just like you'd see brown trout rising in a spring creek.

"That little dark stonefly I sent to you has been very effective when the little black stoneflies are on the water."

What flies do you use later in the year?
"Ants and other terrestrials are very effective."

Do you ever use things like the Royal Wulff and other attractor patterns?
"Sure, they work great. The Royal Wulff is a fine fly."

Tell me the story about the Inchworm.
"We have a terrific number of those insects. It actually represents several things. We have one insect down here the local boys call an 'oak worm,' which is a little more tannish than the inchworm; you'll see them hanging down from the trees all the time. We start seeing the real inchworm around the middle of April until the middle of June, but that fly matches a lot of little wormlike things.

"One of my fishing partners was with me one day. He was kind of leaning on a fence, watching me fish downstream, and his line was dangling over the water with an Inchworm. The fly was just bobbing off the water next to the back, and a pretty good-sized brown trout grabbed it. He realized that he was imitating the appearance of a real inchworm, and he used that

Murray's Little Bronze Stonefly
Hook: Mustad 94840, sizes 20 to 14.
Thread: Black 6/0 (140 denier).
Body: Black dubbing.
Hackle: Grizzly.
Wing: Gray goose biots with clipped tips.

Murray's Fly Beetle
Hook: Mustad 94840, size 16 or 14.
Thread: Black 6/0 (140 denier).
Body: Peacock herl.
Back and legs: Black deer hair.
Wing: Light elk hair.

Murray's Inchworm
Hook: Mustad 94840, size 14.
Thread and rib: Green 6/0 (140 denier).
Body: Green deer hair.
Head: Peacock herl.

dapping technique to catch some real nice trout. The Inchworm is a really good fly for us."

Are stoneflies important?
"The little yellow stoneflies are very important. We also get the giant stoneflies, but I think they're just too big for these fish. But the little yellow stoneflies run in sizes 18 and 16, and the fish love them; it's a very dependable hatch."

Tell me a little more about your terrestrial patterns. When, for instance, would you fish your ant pattern?
"With respect to ants, they start showing up along our mountain streams even in early April, and I'll use that sort of fly even then. You see, when Marinaro did his stream studies on the Letort, he was coming up with two thousand pounds of aquatic insects per acre of stream bottom, even though a lot of it was cress bugs.

Yellow Miracle Stonefly Nymph
Hook: Mustad 3906 B, sizes 16 to 12.
Thread: Yellow 6/0 (140 denier).
Tail: Yellow biots.
Abdomen: Yellow dubbing.
Rib: Gold wire.
Thorax: Yellow dubbing.
Wing case: Yellow quill.
Legs: Mottled Indian hen fibers.

Mr. Rapidan Ant
Hook: Mustad 94840, sizes 22 to 18.
Thread: Black 6/0 (140 denier).
Body: Black dubbing.
Wing: Yellow calf tail.
Hackle: Grizzly.

Penn State University said that this wasn't possible, so they did their own research and came up with 2,400 pounds per acre of stream bottom. On the other hand, biologists tell me that a rich mountain freestone stream cranks out only about 150 pounds of insects per acre of stream bottom, so the fish have to feed on whatever food presents itself.

"This is a very important point, and I stress it in my classes. We spend a lot of time learning how to read the water. These fish will get on feeding stations at the head or tail of a pool or some other good positions and stay there all day long. The point is to then present the fly to the fish, and because of the general low amount of available food, the trout have little choice but to strike."

Olive Magic Caddis Pupa
Hook: Tiemco TMC2457, size 14 or 12.
Thread: Olive 6/0 (140 denier).
Body: Olive dubbing.
Rib: Gold wire.
Hackle: Brown mottled Indian hen.
Head: Peacock herl.

Chapter 13

Dennis Potter
and the River House Fly Company

The Upper Midwest is home to some of North America's finest trout fishing, much of which is centered around Michigan's legendary Au Sable River.

Dennis Potter has been fishing the Au Sable for most of his adult life. In fact, he loves the Au Sable so much that he bought a summer home on the river many years ago. He calls his retreat the River House and named his business the River House Fly Company.

For the River House Fly Company, Dennis designs flies, offers classes, and travels to give high-tech fly-tying exhibitions. Dennis is always experimenting with new materials to create fresh patterns, and he has come up with some winning designs.

Tell me more about the River House.

"The River House is our fly-fishing getaway. We've had it for more than twenty years. We're a mile below Gates's Au Sable Lodge, on the main stem of the Au Sable. We're on what is dubbed the 'Holy Water.' It has been fly fishing–only, catch-and-release since the 1980s. It's heavily fished, but it still offers excellent trout fishing. It was my dream—many, many years ago—to have this place, and I made it work."

When does your fishing season begin?

"The river is open all year, and it's catch-and-release only, which is a nice thing. So, if you want to fish nymphs or streamers, you can go fishing even in the winter when there is nothing really hatching; it is lovely—just gorgeous—in the winter. The banks are lined with cedar trees."

COURTESY OF DENNIS POTTER

Dark Tungsten-Bead Soft Hackle
Hook: Heavy-wire nymph hook, sizes 16 to 12.
Thread: Brown 8/0 (70 denier).
Bead: Tungsten.
Abdomen: Turkey tail.
Thorax: Peacock Arizona Synthetic Dubbing.
Hackle: Hungarian partridge.

Even though you're in Michigan, the water doesn't ice over?
"No, it does not. There are a lot of springs in the river, especially from my neck of the river and on downstream, that help keep the temperature up and prevent the water from freezing. You might get some terribly cold weather that you would never consider going fishing, and then you might get a very little amount of shelf ice out from the bank, but for the most part the river itself is too warm to freeze over.

"We're on a hill above the river, and you can hear a big seep rolling across the rocks and flowing into the river. Gallons and gallons of water every hour, and it's always about fifty-two degrees. When I go fishing during the winter, I'll target where those seeps flow into the river with small streamers. I know there'll be a decent-sized trout sitting in that warmer water rather than in the colder water in the middle of the river."

When do the hatches begin on the Au Sable?
"The hatches start with the early black stoneflies. On the right day, these insects can generate some good dry-fly activity. But for the really good dry-fly action to start, especially for the big brown trout, we need the water to rise to about fifty-two degrees.

"After the early black stoneflies, we get the early olive mayflies in April."

In many parts of the country, the hendricksons are considered the first hatch of the season. Do you get hendricksons?
"We get fabulous hendrickson hatches, but you usually get some olives first. And with the hendricksons, you get a bunch of other bugs mixed in: a small mahogany and then light hendricksons, brown drakes, and then the Hex hatch."

*Michigan is famous for its **Hexagenia** hatch. When does this occur in your area?*
"You have good fishing to the Hex hatch if you're on the right water. This happens around the very end

Crystal Stone
Hook: Scud hook, size 10 or 8.
Thread: Size 8/0 (70 denier).
Tails: Goose biots.
Abdomen: Turkey biot.
Wing case: Crystal Hair.
Thorax and legs: Pearl Cactus Chenille.
Note: Dennis Potter selects materials in
    black, olive, or white.

Rivergod Emerger, Slate Wing Olive
Hook: Tiemco TMC101, size 18.
Thread: Olive 8/0 (70 denier).
Tails: Wood-duck fibers.
Shuck: Dark brown, McFlylon or EP Fibers.
Abdomen: Tying thread.
Wing: Medium dun Crinkled Zelon.
Thorax: Olive Super Fine Dry Fly Dubbing.

I. C. Spinner
Hook: Dry-fly hook, sizes 24 to 12.
Thread: Rusty brown 8/0 (70 denier).
Tail: Dun Microfibbets.
Abdomen: Tying thread.
Wing: Light gray EP Fibers or Float Vis.
Indicator: Fluorescent yellow EP Fibers or Float Vis.
Thorax: Rusty brown Super Fine Dry Fly Dubbing.

of June and first of July. And then we have fabulous fishing to Tricos. We have terrific Trico hatches."

We've talked a couple of times, and you always get excited when you talk about the Tricos.
"That's the hatch I wait for all year. If I could fish to only one hatch, it would be the Tricos. On the North Branch of Au Sable, we'll often have fishable numbers of Tricos by the Fourth of July, and I've hit Tricos on the main stem the third weekend of September. And no one is looking for them. I'm convinced that unless you have a really big chill in late September that there are probably Tricos in some sections of the main stem into October. So, between the North Branch, South Branch, and main stem of the Au Sable, we have more than two months of fishing to Tricos, and I just love them. It's the tiny black curse; they drive me crazy, but I just love them."

Do a lot of anglers plan to fish the Trico hatch?
"For a lot of the people who don't have the time or desire to fish all of the hatches, they start with the hendricksons around the end of April. They'll fish through the hendricksons, and then they'll do some sulphur stuff and maybe some brown drake and then they'll hit the Hex, and then they're done. By the time the Hex hatches are over, half to three-quarters of the fly fishermen are gone. When I fish Tricos, there's all kinds of water where you might see a few people, but you do have a lot more elbow room. But the Tricos are a super hatch, but it's not chased like the other hatches."

Do you see an influx of people who want to fish the Hex hatch?
"Oh, I don't know; I don't think so."

I ask because it gets so much publicity.

"I know, but I guess I've done my Hex time—years and years ago. And I caught some big fish; that's when you'll catch your big browns. Once these fish reach fifteen or sixteen inches, they stop feeding during the day. They hide during the day and then come out at night to feed.

"It's a little-known fact, but fish in a river can migrate great distances to feed throughout a twenty-four-hour cycle. I'm talking about miles of travels. Many years ago a telemetry study was done on a couple of twenty-inch brown trout in the Au Sable. One of them stayed in the local area, and once these researchers figured out their equipment, one of these fish was already swimming up out of the main stem and into the East Branch. It spent every night foraging in the East Branch, and every morning around five o'clock it would drift back downstream into the main stem and lay up under the same logjam. It made this ten-mile round trip every day.

"You could be here for the Hex hatch. The trout start rising, and you catch a good fish. There's a good chance that this fish just moved into that part of the river from somewhere else. It's endlessly fascinating.

"I love the western rivers—the Missouri and the rest—where you have big brown trout rising throughout the day, but that's a real exception here. Every once in a while on a hendrickson hatch or an early evening spinner fall, you might get some big monster to come out and slash at those little bugs, but that's definitely the exception."

Of all the flies you sent, only one is a streamer: All the rest are insect imitations. Does anyone use crayfish patterns and the like to target the larger fish?

"Oh, sure. I just don't tie that stuff. There are a lot of people who fish only large streamers. I say they have 'big-fish syndrome.' They do a lot of that way

Fly Bugger
Hook: Streamer hook, size 6.
Thread: Olive 6/0 (140 denier).
Eyes: Dumbbell.
Tail: Damsel green marabou.
Hackle: Olive.
Body: White Crystal Chenille.
Markers: Color the fly using permanent markers.

Opal and Elk Caddis
Hook: Dry-fly hook, sizes 18 to 12.
Thread: 50 denier GSP.
Body: Opal tinsel.
Rib: Fine gold wire.
Hackle: Dun or grizzly.
Wing: Dark elk hair.

downriver. They fish big streamers with full-sinking lines all day long, obviously with the hope of catching— or even just seeing—a really huge fish. I just don't care about that anymore. I've caught my big fish over the years. I think that's another reason I don't get excited over the Hex hatch as much anymore; I'm such a visual person, and I want to see what's going on. Give me smaller brook or brown trout all day long, and I'm perfectly happy."

You love to experiment with new materials. Opal tinsel is one of your favorite materials, even on dry flies.
"I carry no dubbed caddisflies—none. All my X-Caddis, all my Elk-Hair Caddis—all of my caddisflies have bodies tied using opal tinsel. I beat this into people: Tie a few of your favorite caddis or mayfly patterns with opal tinsel bodies. I don't know why, but it is as close to a magical material as I have ever used."

How did you hit on the idea?
"I used to fish the One-Fly contest in Jackson Hole back in the late 1980s and early 1990s. I knew from previous experience that the cutthroat trout love that prismatic pearl tinsel. I started experimenting with a huge tinsel Trude and some other flies and had good success; they solved some problems better than dubbed flies. And then opal tinsel came along, and I naturally made the switch. This stuff is just outrageous. I don't know what the fish think it is, and I don't give a damn: The fish just eat it."

Do these flies work as well throughout the day, or are they low-light flies?
"They work well throughout the day, but the material also almost glows in the dark. Put a chunk of it in your hand and walk into a dark room; I don't know the exact terminology to describe what's happening—it reflects any ambient light or whatever; it glows green."

What you describe reminds me of all the nymph fishermen who are adding hot spots to their patterns. They swear that small, bright pieces of color improve their flies. You're describing much the same thing.

"I remember when a buddy and I were fishing to a pod of rising fish on the Missouri River. My buddy used a regular X-Caddis, and I used an Opal X-Caddis, and I hooked ten fish before he had a strike. And not only did rising fish move to take my fly, but fish that were feeding only subsurface rose to take the fly. David, I know people look at me like I'm full of shit and just telling another fish story, but anyone who seriously tries it reports excellent results."

What other new materials are you using?

"I've become a big fan of EP Fibers, especially for the wings on my parachute patterns. I tie only two dry flies with hair wings: the Opal and Elk Caddis and the Opal X-Caddis. All the other flies have synthetic wings: the down-wing stoneflies, the caddisflies, and the parachutes. EP Fibers are great for this."

Your Brown Drake is a beautiful pattern.

"The wing on that fly is either EP Fibers or something I'm playing with called McFlylon; that's also a great product for tying the wings on flies. These products weigh nothing, they come in a lot of colors, you can trim them to shape, and they never hold water. They're the perfect material for making the wings on dry flies.

"Any natural material—hair, feathers, or whatever—eventually absorbs moisture. There's nothing you can really do to prevent this. You can put some floatant on it, and it'll help a little bit, but once it absorbs water, you have to retire that fly. This doesn't happen with the synthetic fibers. And I never put floatant on a parachute wing. Why bother? The wing isn't supposed to be in the water, and the floatant just adds weight and will help knock the fly over.

Opal Wulff
Hook: Dry-fly hook, sizes 18 to 12.
Thread: Brown 6/0 (140 denier) or 8/0 (70 denier).
Tail: Moose-body hair.
Body: Opal tinsel.
Wing: Light gray McFlylon or EP Fibers.
Hackle: Brown.

Potter's Brown Drake
Hook: Tiemco TMC100, size 12 or 10.
Thread: Brown 6/0 (140 denier).
Tails: Pheasant-tail fibers.
Abdomen: Yellow or natural deer hair.
Wing: Light gray McFlylon or EP Fibers.
Hackle: Brown.

Fat-Head Beetle
Hook: Dry-fly hook, sizes 16 to 10.
Thread: Black 8/0 (70 denier).
Underbody: Peacock.
Body: Black foam.
Wing: Slate EP Fibers.
Legs: Black round rubber legs.
Indicator: Fluorescent pink or yellow
    Egg Yarn.

"On a parachute—and I'd love to know how many thousands of parachutes I've tied over the years—if the wing is too tall, it can also cause the pattern to be top-heavy. Ideally, the diameter of the wrapped hackle should be about one and one-half times the height of the wing. It's not so much the amount of hackle as it is the quality and the length of the fibers. If a parachute pattern consistently falls over on the water, the wing is probably too tall for the diameter of the hackle. It's a simple proposition, but a lot of tyers miss this point."

Are terrestrials important for fishing the Au Sable?

"Absolutely. We have our first ant swarm in June. These are about size 16 cinnamon ants. If the ants end up on the water, and the trout start feeding on them, you can go out weeks later and use an ant pattern to catch fish. There's something about the shape of an ant that once they start feeding on them, they just like that shape."

Potter's Moth
Hook: Dry-fly hook, size 12 or 10.
Thread: White, yellow, or olive 50 denier
    GSP.
Body: Tan dubbing.
Rib: Opal tinsel.
Underwing: Gray polypropylene yarn.
Wing: Dark elk hair.

Rubber Leg Lightning Bug
Hook: Scud hook, sizes 18 to 12.
Thread: Olive 8/0 (70 denier).
Bead: Tungsten.
Tails: Round rubber legs.
Abdomen: Opal tinsel.
Wing case: Opal tinsel.
Thorax: Peacock.
Legs: Round rubber legs.

Your Magma Ant is an interesting pattern.
"The year before last I wanted to create a big, gaudy, general-purpose searching type of ant pattern. I wanted it to have the right shape, but I added opal tinsel and threw everything at it. That's how I came up with the Magma Ant. I've fished it around here and out West and have had great success with it."

I know that when you're not tying or fishing, you are on the road visiting clubs and appearing at shows. A lot of guys are using cameras and monitors or projectors with their presentations, but you're an expert at this and have taken it to a whole new level. How long have you been doing this?
"I've been offering the fly-tying video theater since the early 1990s. In the beginning, of course, it required a lot of really heavy equipment; it was a nightmare. Today, carrying a thirty-two-inch LCD monitor is nothing, and the whole procedure is so much easier."

Do you bring all the equipment?
"I bring the entire show: It's ten pounds of you-know-what in a five-pound bag. Everything goes into my little Subaru, and off I go: the Ott lights for tying, the camera gear, the monitor, even my own comfortable chair. If the crowd is too large, then the club can provide a bigger monitor or digital projector, but I do bring a pretty big monitor. I really prefer the monitor because the image is so clear and sharp; if I go into digital autofocus with the camera, I can make size 8/0 thread look like rope. It's very easy to see what I'm tying and follow along. The audience at a club or show has to see what you're tying, or it's just not worth it."

Where do you offer your services?
"I'm all over the Upper Midwest, certainly in Michigan, and I go to Wisconsin, Indiana, Ohio, and Ontario. Frankly, I go just about anywhere I can drive. I don't mind the drive, and to do it right and give the people

Crimson Magma Ant
Hook: Dry-fly hook, size 12.
Thread: Red 8/0 (70 denier).
Body: Bright red dubbing.
Gaster (connector): Opal tinsel.
Hackle: Brown.
Legs: Round rubber legs.
Wing: Light gray McFlylon or EP Fibers.

what they expect, I have to bring my equipment. It works out very well."

How many events do you do in a year?
"Between shows, club events, and fly-shop demos, I easily have twenty or more bookings over the fall and winter. I suspect I'll be busier next year—it just keeps growing—but I want to do only so much. It's a high-class problem, but I don't want to be gone every weekend."

I don't want to mislead anyone: The River House is not a business, and no one should go to the Au Sable with the idea that they'll visit your fly shop or anything like that, right?
"No, it's nothing like that. I teach some fly-tying classes at my home, but I don't have a shop. When it comes to my business, wherever I am that day, that's the address of the River House Fly Company."

———————

Chapter 14

Al Ritt
and Rocky Mountain National Park

Of all the great places to fish in North America, I read very little about Rocky Mountain National Park and its trout.

Let's remedy that now.

Al Ritt is a talented fly designer and guide living in Colorado; his original patterns are sold by Montana Fly Company. His stomping ground is Rocky Mountain National Park and some of the surrounding waters. Al is also associated with Peak Engineering, the manufacturer of premium fly-tying vises and other tools. When he's not fishing or designing better fly-tying tools, Al is often on the road attending fly-fishing shows, leading classes, and offering seminars. And in this world of mass-produced imported flies, Al still accepts orders for custom flies.

I caught Al between trips, and he told me about fishing the beautiful Rocky Mountains.

"I do some guiding, mostly in the Rocky Mountain National Park," Al explained. "I guide on a little bit of private water around the Red Feather Lakes, and I also guide on a ranch that has a section of the Big Thompson River and some trophy trout ponds."

Rocky Mountain National Park sounds interesting. What's the fishing season?

"The park never closes to fishing, but the water does ice up. We can usually start fishing sometime in March, and you can fish into November. There's a lot of elevation change, and obviously the higher water ices up earlier."

Does the running water also ice up?

"Yes, both the still and moving waters ice over. The waters up there are very small, so even the streams ice up in the winter."

Are you fishing to stocked or native fish?

"The park hasn't been stocked in many years. Although not all of the fish are native to the region, today it's all natural reproduction. And there are just a ton of fish up there."

What species of fish live in the park?

"We have Colorado River cutthroat and greenback cutthroat—those are both indigenous species. The introduced fish are rainbow, brook, brown, and Yellowstone cutthroat trout. There's quite a bit of variety, and there are a lot of fish."

So, it's possible to catch a variety of fish on a trip?

"Yes, you can. If you're taking a guided trip, or you're researching a trip and call a local fly shop, tell your guide or the shop owner what you want to catch, and they'll point you in the right direction. Not all waters contain every species of trout, so you might have to be selective about where you fish in order to target certain species. But many of the waters are very close together, so you can easily move around and catch several different species in the same day."

Is there good access?

"Oh, sure—it's a national park."

How large are the trout in the Rocky Mountain National Park?

"You can expect to catch a range of sizes. A typical fish measures eight to fourteen inches, but there are some much, much larger fish. Some brown trout measure twenty inches long. That's not something you'd want to count on every day, but they do exist."

ARF Midge Pupa
Hook: Dohiku 644.
Thread: Red 8/0 (70 denier).
Antennae: White Organza.
Bead: Gun metal glass.
Underbody: Tying thread.
Rib: Silver wire.
Overbody: Clear Micro Tubing.
Wing: White Organza.
Thorax: Sybai Fine Flash, peacock.

What types of flies do you prefer to fish: dry flies, nymphs, or streamers?

"I really prefer using dry flies, but all of these fishing methods are very effective. Because the streams are so small, however, you don't find the trout holding in really deep water a lot. And it's a fairly short growing season, so they're very opportunistic, which makes it nice for fishing attractor dry flies and terrestrials. These fish aren't pushovers, but I'd say that they're more spooky than picky when it comes to choosing a meal."

It's a national park, so I'm sure it gets a lot of visitors. Are the trout heavily pressured by anglers?

"Yes, there are a lot of people up there, but most of them are hiking and sightseeing. There are a fair number of fishermen in those areas where you can see water from the road, but like in most places—especially destinations where you get a lot of visiting anglers—if you can't see the water from your car, you stand a good chance of having it to yourself."

That's true: Most people don't want to walk very far to start fishing.

"I think part of it is a confidence problem. You're in an unfamiliar area, and it's a big park with a lot of wild space. It can be sort of overwhelming for a lot of people."

Let's start talking about your flies. You sent a number of soft-hackle patterns. Why?

"I really like soft hackles."

Even for fishing the park?

"Oh, yes, they work really well up there."

What are your preferred colors?

"The Hare's-Ear or Pheasant-Tail tones work well—you know, copper and brown. But blue is another very productive color. I have no explanation why a soft hackle with a blue body works so well, but it does.

ARF Tung-Syn Pheasant-Tail Soft Hackle
Hook: Dohiku 302SP.
Thread: Tan 8/0 (70 denier).
Bead: Tungsten copper.
Tail: Krystal Flash, root beer over pearl.
Abdomen: Glitter D Rib, root beer.
Wing case: Mirage Tinsel.
Thorax: Sybai Fine Flash, peacock.

ARF Gen-X Soft Hackle (Copper)
Hook: Dohiku 302.
Thread: Yellow 8/0 (70 denier).
Tail: Opal Mirage Flash.
Abdomen: Copper brown Ultra Wire.
Thorax: Peacock Ice Dub.
Hackle: Brahma hen dyed brown.

The Master's Fly Box

ARF Gen-X Soft Hackle (Hot Orange)
Hook: Dohiku 302.
Thread: Hot orange 8/0 (70 denier).
Tail: Opal Mirage Flash.
Abdomen: Tying thread.
Thorax: UV Ice Dub, cinnamon.
Hackle: Hen grizzly dyed orange.

"I don't know if I sent all the colors, but I tie the Gen-X series in tan, copper, orange, brown, olive, chartreuse, and blue. If there are no hatching insects, I'll use an olive, tan, or blue Gen-X."

The Devil's Doorman is an interesting, heavy pattern. Tell me about this fly.

"It's an attractor nymph that I can fish deep; the red tails and bead spot make it a good target for the fish. All the weight comes from the tungsten bead. I use the beads sold by the Flymen Fishing Company; I think these are the heaviest beads on the market."

How did you develop the Devil's Doorman?

"I really liked the beads, and frankly I just liked the color combination. The dubbing for the body is bloody-black Tri-Lobal Dubbing; I use that a lot. That dubbing has a

ARF Gen-X Soft Hackle (Chartreuse)
Hook: Dohiku 302.
Thread: Chartreuse 8/0 (70 denier).
Tail: Opal Mirage Flash.
Abdomen: Chartreuse Ultra Wire.
Thorax: UV Ice Dub, olive.
Hackle: Brahma hen dyed olive.

ARF Devil's Doorman
Hook: Daiichi 1150.
Thread: Red 6/0 (140 denier).
Bead: Flymen Fishing Company Nymph-
    Head tungsten bead, bloodworm red.
Tails: Red goose biots.
Abdomen: Bloody black leech Tri-Lobal STS.
Rib: Red Ultra Wire.
Shellback: Red pearl Mirage Tinsel.
Legs: Black pheasant-tail fibers.
Thorax: Bloody black leech Tri-Lobal STS.

nice sheen with some red undertones. All the materials come together to make a good attractor pattern."

The Humpulator is a big dry fly. Do you use these large attractor flies in the park?

"I use that pattern in smaller sizes in the park. I designed that fly to fish as an indicator with droppers, especially when fishing during float trips when you don't have a lot of time to dry off your floating fly. None of the materials in the Humpulator absorb water, so you can keep fishing and not miss good lies because you're tending to your fly. I also use that pattern for fishing lakes; I still use it as an indicator with droppers."

The Harey Yellow Stone is a nice stonefly imitation.

"Yes, it is, but I also use that basic design to tie caddis imitations. The key to that fly is the snowshoe-hare

ARF Trailing Bubble Harey Caddis (Tan)
Hook: Daiichi 1110.
Thread: Tan 8/0 (70 denier).
Tail: Opal Mirage Flash.
Abdomen: Tan Super Fine Dubbing.
Underwing: Opal Mirage Flash.
Wing: Tan snowshoe-hare foot fur.
Thorax: Tan Super Fine Dubbing.
Hackle: Barred light ginger.

ARF Trailing Bubble Harey Yellow Stone
Hook: Daiichi 1110.
Thread: Yellow 8/0 (70 denier).
Tail: Opal Mirage Flash.
Egg sac: Red foam.
Abdomen: Yellow Super Fine Dubbing.
Rib: Yellow grizzly hackle.
Underwing: Opal Mirage Flash.
Wing: Off-white or bleached cream
    snowshoe-hare foot fur.
Spot: Red foam.
Thorax: Yellow Super Fine Dubbing.
Hackle: Barred Light Ginger.

ARF Humpulator
Hook: Daiichi 1280.
Thread: Yellow 8/0 (70 denier).
Tail: Tan calf-tail hair.
Back: Tan foam.
Abdomen: Yellow polypropylene yarn.
Rib: Brown hackle.
Underwing: Opal Mirage Flash.
Wing: Tan calf-tail hair.
Post: Fluorescent orange Hi-Vis yarn.
Thorax: Golden brown Ice Dub.
Hackle: Golden brown grizzly.

ARF Trailing Bubble Harey Caddis (Peacock)
Hook: Daiichi 1110.
Thread: Black 8/0 (70 denier).
Tail: Opal Mirage Flash.
Abdomen: Peacock herl.
Underwing: Opal Mirage Flash.
Wing: Tan snowshoe-hare foot fur.
Thorax: Olive Super Fine Dubbing.
Hackle: Grizzly dyed olive.

ARF Midge Adult
Hook: Dohiku 301.
Thread: Black 8/0 (70 denier).
Abdomen: Black stripped quill.
Wing: White Organza.
Thorax: Sybai or another peacock-colored dubbing.
Shellback and post: Gator Hair, fluorescent pink.
Hackle: Yellow grizzly.

wing; it doesn't absorb water and floats longer than a hollow hair such as deer hair."

You like tying the tails on many of your flies using Krystal Flash. You sent several patterns with this style of tail.
"I add the Krystal Flash to imitate any trailing gas bubbles of the emerging insects. It's also a good attractor. I've been doing it for about seven or eight years, and I think it's improved a lot of my flies. But if it seems like the wrong choice when fishing, it's easy to pluck the Krystal Flash tails from the fly."

The ARF Midge Pupa is one of the smallest flies you sent. You made it using some really interesting materials. I'm not familiar with what you used to tie the thorax; it's called Sybai.
"That's a dubbing from Europe, but you can substitute with many other brands of dubbing. Sybai has great color, and it's very fine. Just select your favorite brand of dubbing."

Where would you use this fly?
"I use it a lot for fishing still waters, but I also use it in tailwaters and spring creeks where you have a lot of midge activity."

At the other end of the spectrum, at least in terms of size, is your Matuka-style streamer tied with the rabbit-strip wing. Where do you use this fly?
"Lakes and streams. It works anyplace you need to imitate something larger. I tie it in six different colors. Use that fly when you need to imitate a leech, a baitfish, or even a crayfish."

You tied this pattern using the Flymen Fishing Company's Fish Skulls. How do you like them?

"I love using Fish Skulls. A Fish Skull makes a fantastic transition from the thread head to the body of the fly; they make the whole pattern come together. It's harder using a cone because there's always that junction between the body and the back of the cone. And you add the Fish Skull to the hook after you've tied the fly; it's the last thing you do. Fish Skulls are also a very convenient way to add weight to your patterns."

I suppose you could switch to using Fish Skulls on many of the patterns you were already tying.

"Absolutely. I converted many of my conehead patterns to Fish Skulls. Fish Skulls are far easier to use, and they make better-looking flies."

What sizes do you tie this streamer?

"I tie it mainly for a little bit smaller waters, so mostly in sizes 6 and 8. But you could certainly make it in larger sizes for steelhead and salmon."

How do you fish it? Do you strip it through the water?

"I let the water temperature be my first guide. In colder water, I fish it slower; in warmer water, I fish it faster. If I see fish following the fly, but they're not striking, I speed up the retrieve so they have less time to make up their minds; I try to get them to react a little more aggressively."

ARF Skulled Electric Zonker
Hook: Daiichi 1720.
Thread: Olive 6/0 (140 denier).
Tail: Black-barred olive marabou and olive and pearl Krystal Flash.
Body: Dark olive Tri-Lobal STS.
Wing: Olive squirrel Zonker strip.
Rib: Chartreuse Ultra Wire.
Head: Golden chartreuse Flymen Fishing Company Fish Skull.

Your crawfish patterns are particularly nice. Do you use these in both still and moving water?

"Yes, they work well in both."

How long did it take you to develop this fly?

"That was one of the longer ones; it took a while to develop that fly. I wanted a pattern that I could stick right on the bottom and be weedless without having to actually add a weed guard. The obvious start was to flip the hook over. I started by weighting the entire body and using just a bundle of rubber legs for the claws. Fairly early on I removed all of the weight except that which was at the hook eye and added the foam claws on the end of the rubber legs. This elevated the angle of the fly into the realistic fighting-crawfish position."

Ritt's Fighting Crawfish (Orange)
Hook: Daiichi 1730.
Thread: Orange 6/0 (140 denier).
Weight: Plain lead dumbbell eyes.
Antennae: Orange UV Krystal Flash.
Eyes: Black round rubber.
Claws and arms: Orange Foam claws
    mounted on orange barred rubber legs.
Carapace: Mottled orange Thin Skin.
Underbody: Orange yarn.
Body: Burnt Orange Crawdub SLF Dubbing.
Legs: Orange grizzly-saddle hackle.
Rib: Hot Orange Ultra Wire.

Ritt's Fighting Crawfish (Dirty Tan)
Hook: Daiichi 1730.
Thread: Tan 6/0 (140 denier).
Weight: Plain lead dumbbell eyes.
Antennae: Tan UV Krystal Flash.
Eyes: Black round rubber.
Claws and arms: Brown foam claws
    mounted on tan barred rubber legs.
Carapace: Mottled bustard Thin Skin.
Underbody: Tan yarn.
Body: Tan Crawdub SLF Dubbing.
Legs: Golden yellow grizzly-saddle hackle.
Rib: Ginger Ultra Wire.

How would you fish this fly? What type of line do you use?

"On still waters, I fish fairly shallow, even if the lake is deep. I find that if they're actively feeding, the trout are usually in the shallower water. If I'm using a ten-foot-long leader, I can fish almost ten feet deep with a floating line. The advantage of the floating line is that I can easily make the next cast."

Your damselflies are another set of stillwater flies. The SlimFlash Damsel is a very simple pattern that even a novice tyer can master.

"Yes, by the time you make five or six of them, most people will find that they're not very complicated. And they really do catch trout."

This fly has no weight, does it?

"I do carry some damselfly nymph imitations that have metal bead-chain eyes, but the one you have has plastic bead chain. Damselfly nymphs are in the water throughout the year, but early in the season, before the damsels start emerging, I fish deeper using the weighted version. But when they migrate, they move close to the surface of the water. As the insects start emerging, and I know they're higher in the water column, I switch to a nymph that has the lighter plastic eyes."

When do damselflies emerge in your area?

"More toward the middle of the day—late morning until early afternoon. But the damselflies—at least the nymphs—are always present, and the trout are aware of them."

You also sent a damsel dry fly. I think this is one of the most overlooked types of flies, even among stillwater anglers.

"Well, they're a little tough to fish. One of the most difficult things is that damselfly imitations set so low in the water, and the Hi-Viz spot on that fly makes it easier to see on the surface. And the sparse Organza

ARF SlimFlash Damsel
Thread: Light olive 8/0 (70 denier).
Hook: Daiichi 1710, size 10.
Tail: Light olive marabou.
Abdomen: Light olive marabou.
Rib: Opal Mirage Flash.
Thorax: Light olive marabou.
Eyes: Black plastic bead chain.
Wing case: Opal Mirage Tinsel and olive
　　Antron yarn.

ARF Hi-Vis Damsel
Thread: Olive 8/0 (70 denier).
Hook: Daiichi 1130.
Abdomen: Braided damsel body.
Wing: Clear White Organza.
Post: Hi-Vis chartreuse.
Wing case: 2-millimeter-thick olive closed-
　　cell foam.
Thorax: Golden olive Super Fine Dubbing.

wings don't twist the leader when casting. I make the wings a little shorter than what you'd find on the real insect. The shorter wings don't tangle on the hook point and reduce twisting in the air. I think you can get away with this on a damselfly imitation because the wings are clear on the real insect; I want the fly to just give the impression of wings on the water."

Are damselflies important to where you fish?

"I think they're far more important than people realize. We have some tremendous damselfly hatches, but a lot of anglers aren't aware of them because the insects crawl onto the land to emerge. But you'll find a lot of fish cruising in the shallows and feeding opportunistically whenever a damselfly lands on the water."

Chapter 15

Fishing the Canadian Prairies with Philip Rowley

I'd like to introduce you to another Canadian fly fisherman who is having a major impact on our sport.

Philip Rowley lives in Alberta, the home of the Bow River, but he travels across North America in search of good fly fishing for his television show, *The New Fly Fisher*. His show airs in the United States as well as in Canada. My wife, who has only a passing interest in fly fishing (although she's really damned good at it), enjoys the show, and she quickly recognized Phil when I introduced him to her.

Phil is making a nice living as a professional fly fisherman. In addition to his television show, he works with Superfly International, a major supplier of fine fly-tying materials. Phil is also a busy author and lecturer; you'll see him at fly-fishing clubs and shows across the continent.

I've never visited Alberta, so I asked Philip to describe where he lives.

"I live in Sherwood Park, which is a small municipality that's just a stone's throw east of Edmonton, Alberta," he said.

Is there fishing in your area?

"Yes, there is. When most people think of Alberta, they think of the Bow River and the streams, and always I joke: 'Just keep thinking that.' We have a lot of great fishing up here that most people don't even know about.

"I had an opportunity to chase my dream when I was given an offer to work for Superfly International, which is a Canadian fly-tying materials supplier. And I was eventually given an opportunity to pursue a television show called *The New Fly Fisher*."

COURTESY OF PHILIP ROWLEY

Herl May-Flashback
Hook: Mustad S82, sizes 16 to 12.
Tail: Mottled turkey-flat fibers.
Rib: Fine wire.
Shellback: Mottled turkey quill.
Body: Ostrich herl.
Wing case: Mottled turkey quill topped with pearl or Mirage Mylar.
Thorax: Ostrich herl.
Legs: Mottled turkey-flat fibers.
Note: Select materials to match the local *Callibaetis* nymphs. Favorite colors include tan, olive, olive dun, and light olive.

Clear Water Pupa
Hook: Mustad C49S, sizes 16 to 12.
Thread: Size 8/0 (70 denier), color to match the natural insect.
Rib: Fine wire.
Body: Midge Braid.
Wing case: Pearl Mylar.
Wing buds: UNI Mylar, peacock/orange (orange side out).
Thorax: Tying thread.
Gills: Stillwater Solutions Midge Gill.

Tell me about Superfly. They offer a line of signature tying materials developed by Brian Chan and yourself, right?
"That started around 2003. Superfly approached Brian and me to see if we would be interested in designing a line of materials for tying stillwater flies. It started with the materials and has expanded into flies and other equipment that we're slowly bringing on line. The materials were the catalyst. It's kind of funny how it all worked out. Brian and I came to visit the folks at Superfly, and I was sort of wondering if I could live here. I didn't realize that this is exactly what would happen."

What was it like designing your own line of materials?
"We met over the course of a weekend, and we talked about the kinds of materials we'd like to include in the product line. It was kind of unique because as fly tyers, we're typically bound by what we can buy in the fly shop. Here, however, we were saying what materials and colors we wanted. We came up with some core colors, and then we spread those across the materials we like to use when we tie. It has since evolved, and we've added more materials and additional unique colors. It's called Stillwater Solutions, and it has been pretty successful. You'll find the materials all across Canada and into the United States. Even Cabela's carries it."

Do you think the interest in stillwater fishing is increasing?
"I'd like to think so. I still love fishing streams and rivers, but I think people are interested in learning about fishing lakes. They're a little intimidated by lakes at first, but they get really interested when they see that there are fewer anglers. And then they discover just how large the trout get. I tease some of my river and stream buddies that we use different scales to measure our fish: they measure them in inches, and stillwater anglers measure them in pounds."

A lot of the fly shops in places like Montana and Colorado tell me that more anglers are discovering stillwater fishing because the best rivers are so crowded.

"Yes, they're crowded, and lakes and ponds aren't subject to runoff the way rivers are. And still waters aren't subject to environmental conditions such as flooding. In 2007 the Bow River had a really vicious flood, and anglers didn't know what to do. Events like these give people a chance to try fishing local lakes and ponds, and they discover they like it. If you like big fish, still waters are great. And if you like matching the hatch, lakes and ponds offer a cornucopia of invertebrates that you can learn to imitate. It's very challenging—and rewarding."

What are the challenges that put people off from fishing still waters?

"When they get to the shore of a lake, you see no visible features such as runs, eddies, or pools. It's just flat water. You have to unravel where to go and what to do. And then you have to learn how to imitate all the different sources of food. There's no current to animate your fly, so a lot of times you have to do it with your hands. You have to learn how to move the fly through the water, how long you let it sink, and so forth. I find that most new stillwater anglers don't retrieve their flies slow enough, and they don't let their flies sink deep enough. It's just a new fishing environment, and they have to learn to adapt to it. In our seminars, we do on-the-water instruction where they can get out on the lake and practice what we teach them. They then come in for the afternoon, and we debrief and give them some ideas on how to improve their fishing."

Are people receptive to this type of fishing and instruction?

"I've been taking people to the southwest portion of Manitoba. That section of the province has some fantastic stillwater fishing, and it gets very little

Red Back Pheasant
Hook: Mustad C49S, sizes 16 to 8.
Thread: Black 8/0 (70 denier).
Rib: Fine gold wire.
Body: Claret pheasant-tail fibers.
Shellback: Red holographic Mylar.
Thorax: Peacock herl.
Head: Small gold bead.
Gills: Stillwater Solutions Midge Gill.

pressure. On some lakes the trout average five pounds. And then there's a great diversity of fish species: big rainbow trout, big brown trout, and a unique brook-brown trout hybrid called a tiger trout. Tiger trout are very colorful and superaggressive; you can take them on top by stripping a Chernobyl Ant across the surface. These fish are very aggressive and cooperative. These trips sell out within weeks of advertising them."

What's the fishing season in that area?

"Like most stillwater fishing seasons, it begins around May first and runs to the end of October—either by regulations or by weather."

What hatches do they have?

"All the same hatches we have throughout the West. There are chironomids, damselflies, caddisflies, mayflies, and dragonflies. In addition to the insects, there are also leeches, forage fish, and scuds. If you like matching the hatch—if you like solving that puzzle—still waters have a healthy assortment of foods that will keep you busy tying and fishing for a long time."

What type of watercraft do you use for fishing ponds and lakes: a boat, canoe, or float tube?

"I do some guiding, so I like using a flat-bottomed, fourteen-foot-long pram or jon boat. I like keeping my clients together because it's just easier. The boat is very stable, has pedestal seats, and is very comfortable. We double anchor, although some of the European lock-style techniques are getting more popular, and I use them a lot."

What kind of techniques are you talking about?

"The boat's drift is controlled by a drogue, which is essentially a big underwater parachute that drags behind you to slow your drift while you cast and fish. You're moving very slowly, but you are always casting to new water and presenting your fly to new fish. In North America, on the other hand, we tend to anchor up on likely looking structure and then fish."

I've never seen anyone use a drogue.
"You can't really buy them over here. You can buy a conical drogue, or a sea anchor, but the best is called a European paradrogue; they're rectangular in shape and offer a greater surface area. The paradrogue is also easier to control."

Tell me about The New Fly Fisher. *What's that all about?*
"*The New Fly Fisher* is a television show designed to teach people how to fly fish. We shoot all over North America: fresh water, salt water, everything. It's not just the usual fishing show; we try to be more educational. In addition to showing some nice water and fish, we talk about what equipment to bring, what flies to bring, how to read the water and a rise, casting techniques, and everything else that will help you be successful."

Let's talk about some of the flies you sent. I absolutely love your Grizzly Dragon. I know this is one fly I'll tie and fish this season.
"Oh, you like dragonfly nymphs."

In my mind, a dragonfly nymph is one of the most difficult flies to design. I'm always experimenting with new patterns, and this one looks like a real winner.
"Yes, dragonfly imitations are a little difficult to both design and fish. When I wrote my first book, *Fly Patterns for Still Waters*, I used aquariums to study and photograph the different food sources. Real dragonfly nymphs don't play well with other insects; they're superaggressive. As fly tyers and anglers, we generally target two types of nymphs: the slender, hourglass-shaped darners and the squat, more spiderlike dragonfly nymphs. Dragonfly nymphs are ambush

Grizzly Dragon
Hook: Mustad R74, size 8 or 6.
Underbody: Preformed foam body.
Body: Grizzly marabou.
Wing case: Olive Midge Flex.
Legs: Light olive, olive, or dark olive Midge Stretch Floss.
Eyes: Black foam.
Head: Dark olive-green Soft Blend dubbing.

Draggin
Hook: Mustad R74, size 4.
Thread: Olive 6/0 (140 denier).
Underbody: Black foam.
Body: Dark olive-green Sparkle Blend
    Dubbing and peacock Crystal Chenille
    spun together in a dubbing loop.
Wing case: Dark brown raffia.
Thorax: Olive deer hair.
Legs: Yellow/black Sili Legs.
Eyes: Black foam.
Head: Dark olive-green Sparkle Blend
    dubbing.

feeders; they bury themselves in the weeds and debris and wait for food to come to them.

"I had a dragonfly nymph that was one inch long in July, and by October he was two and a quarter inches long. It had eaten everything in the tank except three leeches, and it had a go at one of them. They'll eat each other, and they'll rip caddisflies out of their cases. At times the aquarium looked like a scene out of the movie *Gladiator*: There were bits and pieces everywhere."

What do you use to make the underbody of the Grizzly Dragon?

"That's foam. My philosophy for designing dragonfly nymphs is based on an English pattern called the Boobie. It has a buoyant construction, so it has a foam underbody and foam eyes. I present the fly using a fast-sinking line and a short leader. The line essentially lies on the bottom, and the fly remains relatively weedless by skipping and dancing just about the weed tops. Real dragonflies like to inhabit weedbeds, sunken debris, and rocks, which aren't fly-friendly areas. As a result, a lot of anglers pass up these places; if you toss in a weighted fly, you're likely to snag and lose it. I reverse this and use a buoyant fly and a fast-sinking line."

How do you tie the fly?

"I tie on the underbody; we actually sell preformed underbodies, but you can also cut out your own. I then make a dubbing loop and use Marc Petitjean's Majic Tool to insert the marabou in the loop; I suppose if you're careful, you can insert the marabou feathers using your fingers. I then close the loop and wrap the body."

Do you trim the marabou body to shape?

"You can do that, but once the fly gets wet, all the fibers come together and form the shape of a dragonfly nymph."

What is the wing case?

"You can use turkey feather, but on that fly I'm using another Stillwater Solutions product called Midge Flex."

I suppose you could use raffia or a variety of materials to fashion the wing case.

"Frankly, if you're imitating one of the crawling nymphs, you don't even need it; the real nymphs don't have them. I think we add a lot of these features more for the fishermen than the fish. Besides, if the fish can see that amount of detail, then please explain why they don't see the hook or leader."

How do you fish this fly?

"Okay, a dragonfly nymph is capable of jetting through the water by absorbing water into its abdomen and then shooting the water out of its rectal gill chamber. For the most part, however, a dragonfly nymph crawls; it hunts its prey like a cat, and then it makes a final pounce. For the most part, use a steady hand twist—with maybe an occasional quick strip—and then let it rest. Vary the retrieve to make it look like it's moving randomly."

Pearly Damsel
Hook: Mustad R70, sizes 14 to 10.
Thread: Size 8/0 (70 denier), color to match the body.
Tail: Marabou.
Rib: Fine copper wire.
Shellback: Pearl Mylar.
Body: Marabou.
Wing case: Midge Flex.
Thorax: Marabou.
Legs: Marabou.
Eyes: Black or olive monofilament.
Head: Marabou.
Note: Select marabou to match the local damselfly nymphs.

Grizzly Damsel
Hook: Mustad C53S, sizes 12 to 8.
Thread: Size 8/0 (70 denier).
Tail: Grizzly marabou.
Rib: Fine gold or copper wire.
Shellback: Pearl Mylar.
Body: Grizzly marabou.
Wing case: Midge Flex.
Thorax: Grizzly marabou or partridge
    aftershaft feathers.
Legs: Partridge.
Bead: Gold or copper.
Note: Select materials to match the
    damselflies in your local waters.
    Favorite colors include olive, light
    olive, *Callibaetis,* olive dun, and tan.

I suppose the Grizzly Damsel is part of the same family of flies.
"Yes, it is, but that fly is made using the same material throughout. The tail is a tuft of grizzly marabou, the body is dubbed grizzly marabou fibers, the thorax is the aftershaft feather placed in a dubbing loop, and then there is a partridge hackle in front of that. One of the challenges of designing a damselfly nymph imitation is creating a pattern that has a lot of movement. With those materials, that fly is constantly moving. I tie that in sizes 10 and 12, and I make it in olive, light olive, and tan."

How do you select the color of fly when you fish?
"A lot of people ask me how to select the right color of fly when fishing. I tell them to match the color of the weeds in the lake, and you'll be in the ballpark. All these insects are well camouflaged, and they generally match the color of their surroundings."

I'm looking at the Grizzly Sedge Pupa. This is another realistic-looking pattern.
"The Grizzly Sedge Pupa uses just the aftershaft feathers for the thorax. A lot of people get the misconception that once a caddis larva turns into a pupa, that there's this missile effect, and it quickly travels to the surface of the lake, but that's not correct.

"Through my aquarium studies, I've seen pupae take three or four days before they rise to the surface. They remain along the bottom, prestaging, and it seems to take them a while to get enough buoyancy to rise; this is when they are very vulnerable to the trout."

How, then, do you fish the Grizzly Sedge Pupa?
"Fish the Grizzly Sedge Pupa very slowly near the bottom. I tie this pattern with those soft materials so it has a lot of inherent movement; I can fish it very slowly, and it still looks alive."

You tied this on a size 8 hook, which strikes me as large.
"Some of our caddis species get as large as size 6. The traveling sedges are like the salmonfly hatch of the lakes; they're big bugs that really attract the fish. Fishing dry flies is really exciting."

The Waste Troll Minnow has an interesting name. What's the story behind this fly?
"The Waste Troll Minnow is part of my waste-troll series of flies. Simply, it looks like the stuff from your waste troll that you throw away, and yet when that fly gets wet, it morphs into the shape of a minnow. The grizzly marabou is so slender that it flows right into a teardrop minnow shape. I use that fly a lot in the prairie lakes. In British Columbia you don't have a lot of forage fish, but in the prairies we have a strong forage-fish base,

Grizzly Sedge Pupa (Traveling Sedge)
Hook: Mustad C53S, sizes 12 to 8.
Thread: Size 8/0 (70 denier), color to
    match the body.
Body: Dark olive-green Sparkle Blend
    Dubbing and olive Crystal Chenille,
    spun together in a dubbing loop.
Wing case: Olive Midge Flex, 1/8 inch wide,
    olive.
Thorax: Olive grizzly marabou.
Wing pads: Olive mottled turkey quill.
Swimmerets: Olive Super Stretch floss.
Beard: Pearl UV Crystal Flash.
Head: Peacock herl.

Waste Troll Minnow
Hook: Mustad 34007, size 8 or 6.
Thread: Olive 6/0 (140 denier).
Tail: Grizzly marabou.
Body: Grizzly marabou and UV Polar Chenille.
Topping: Olive marabou.
Gills: Red marabou.
Cheeks: Olive partridge.
Eyes: 3-D.

and the trout learn very early about the value of having a little sushi in their diets. You need to have at least a handful on minnow patterns in your box if you plan to fish the prairie lakes and ponds."

Stillwater Dun
Hook: Mustad C49S, sizes 16 to 12.
Tail and extended body: Partridge.
Body: Soft Blend dubbing.
Wing: Gray polypropylene yarn.
Hackle: Dun grizzly.
Note: This fly can be tied in olive, *Callibaetis,* and dark summer duck to match both stillwater and moving-water mayfly duns.

Chromie
Hook: Mustad C49S, sizes 16 to 8.
Thread: Black 8/0 (70 denier).
Butt: Red holographic Mylar.
Rib: Red holographic Mylar.
Body: Silver Flashabou or SuperFlash.
Thorax: Peacock herl.
Head: Black bead.
Gills: Stillwater Solutions Midge Gill.

Most of the flies you sent are subsurface patterns. Do you mostly fish under the surface of the water?
"Yes, I do. Lakes don't have all the dry-fly fishing you'll find on rivers and streams. Within each region you'll find a lake that has a reputation for good dry-fly fishing, but most of the time you're fishing with nymphs, pupae, and other subsurface patterns.

"I think part of it has to do with the depth of the water. You might be fishing eight, ten, or even twenty feet of water, and that's just a long way for a fish to go for a meal. This is why, even during a hatch, you might do better fishing deeper with subsurface flies."

The Stillwater Dun is the one dry fly you sent.
"That specific fly is meant to be a *Callibaetis* imitation, but you can tie it in any configuration you wish. And I tie it in two styles; sometimes I tie it thorax style, and other times I make it as a parachute fly. And, of course, you can use it to fish moving water."

I can't let you get away without talking about fishing chironomids. A lot of anglers seem intimidated by these flies. Can you offer any tips?
"I think you're right; a lot of people are intimidated by those insects and the flies. But I find chironomids everywhere I go, and they are certainly important to the trout. I do schools every year at Fortress Lake; that's a big trophy brook trout fishery in the Canadian Rockies. Big leech and minnow patterns all work, but for about two weeks around Father's Day, the fish go absolutely bonkers over chironomids. We use stomach pumps to sample what the fish are eating,

Fly Craft Fullback-Flashback
Hook: Mustad S82, sizes 12 to 8.
Thread: Black or olive 8/0 (70 denier).
Tail: Olive or burnt orange partridge.
Rib: Fine copper wire.
Shellback: Olive dun pheasant-tail fibers.
Body: Dark olive green, dark summer duck, or black Soft Blend or Sparkle Blend dubbing.
Wing case: Olive pheasant-tail fibers and pearl or Mirage Mylar.
Thorax: Dark olive green, dark summer duck, or black Soft Blend or Sparkle Blend dubbing.
Legs: Olive or burnt orange partridge.

and this is especially important with chironomids because the size and color can change throughout the day. I remember pumping what had to be more than two hundred chironomids out of one fish; all black chironomid pupae, and they were all wiggling. If you want to succeed at fly fishing still waters, you can't underestimate the importance of chironomids."

Balanced Leech
Hook: Mustad 32833BL jig hook, size 10 or 8.
Thread: Black 8/0 (70 denier).
Tail: Black marabou blended with a few strands of pearl or pearl UV SuperFlash or Flashabou.
Rib: Fine red wire.
Body: Black Soft Blend Dubbing.
Bead: Gold tungsten, mounted on a straight pin and secured to the hook shank.

CDC Scud
Hook: Mustad R70 or R50, sizes 14 to 10.
Thread: Olive 8/0 (70 denier).
Rib: Fine gold or copper wire.
Body: Soft Blend dubbing and CDC, colors to match natural scuds.
Shellback: Midge Flex, color to match the body.

Chapter 16

Scott Sanchez:
A Wyoming Favorite

Scott Sanchez has been a contributing writer to *Fly Tyer* magazine for many years. He is also the regular fly-tying columnist for *American Angler* magazine. In addition to churning out great articles describing the newest fly-tying materials and techniques, he has written several highly regarded books describing how to tie both freshwater and saltwater flies.

Scott lives in Wyoming and has ample blue-ribbon water on which to test his patterns. He remains one of my favorite tyers, and I'm always eager to talk with him about fly tying and fishing.

"I was born and raised in Salt Lake City," Scott said, "but I've moved in and out of Wyoming for a lot years. Today I work at Jack Dennis's Fly Shop."

You used to guide, right?

"I used to do some guiding when it was a lot easier to do permitwise. Now, where I live, the federal government owns 97 percent of the land. It's a real pain in the butt with the amount of permits you have to get, and you have to have livery insurance and things like that, which make it so hard for guides. I only bring this up because I think this is something people should know who hire our local guides; they really have to do a lot in order to take anglers fishing. Anyway, I thought that if I was going to go through all that to make money going fishing, I might as well just fish with my friends."

What rivers are you fishing?

"I spend a fair amount of time on the Snake and the Green down by Pinedale and the Salt River, but it seems like I'm doing more small-stream fishing."

How large are those streams?

"Some of these are definitely creek-size. They're freestone streams. Pretty much everything we have here is freestone."

How large are the fish in these streams?

"Anywhere from six to fourteen inches long. Anything larger is a real bonus. But they probably average eight to ten inches."

I bet you have a lot of these waters all to yourself.

"Yes, I do. That's the wonderful thing about them."

So, you're really into small streams.

"Oh, I like floating larger rivers, but it's fun to fish small streams. That's how I grew up fishing around Salt Lake City."

Are the small streams you fish tributaries of the larger local rivers?

"Yes, they are. And there's a lot of access to them because they flow through federal land. We have tons of national forests around here."

You sent a nice collection of flies. Are these all your own patterns?

"I pretty much came up with those patterns. You get a lot of ideas from other tyers, but I think of those as my flies."

What fly would you recommend for fishing your small streams?

"A variation of that Convertible Damselfly—tied in tan—is a great attractor pattern on those streams. Tie it in tan or brown—it's a great small-stream fly. It could be a mayfly, a stonefly—or a cheeseburger. It can represent a lot of different things, and the fish really like it."

Convertible Damselfly
Hook: Dai-Riki 270, sizes 14 to 8.
Thread: Blue 6/0 (140 denier).
Tail: Blue buck tail.
Abdomen: Blue dubbing on rear half of hook shank.
Rear wing: Gray calf tail.
Front wing: The butt ends of the rear wing.
Thorax: Blue dubbing.
Hackle: Two grizzly hackles.

Swamp Monster
Hook: Dai-Riki 270, sizes 12 to 6.
Thread: Chartreuse 3/0 (210 denier).
Eyes: Black painted bead chain.
Tail: Olive rabbit hair.
Body: Olive rabbit-fur dubbing.
Rib: Tying thread.
Wing case: Rabbit hair.
Legs: Chartreuse rubber legs.
Head: Olive rabbit-fur dubbing.

When I saw your Convertible Damselfly and Swamp Monster, which also looks like a damselfly nymph imitation, I thought you were using these for fishing still waters. Do you fish trout ponds and lakes?

"Yes, I do some backcountry lakes where you have to hike in. For us, spring runoff in the rivers can last a pretty long time—sometimes it can last until the middle of July. This is a good time to fish the ponds and lakes. I'll spend time on a lake fishing with shooting heads for lake trout. A lot of time you can catch lake trout in five feet of water, so this is definitely a boat deal; you anchor your boat on both ends and sit over a shoal. I've had twenty- and thirty-fish days doing this."

What fly would you recommend for this type of fishing?

"That little Swamp Monster damselfly is good for that. It works as a great generic imitation—it might be a damsel, or it might be a dragonfly. It's just wiggly—the most important thing is that it has motion."

Double-Sided Beetle
Hook: Dai-Riki 320, size 12 or 10.
Thread: Black 6.0 (140 denier).
Underbody: Black dubbing.
Back: Black foam.
Wing post: Pink polypropylene.
Hackle: Yellow grizzly hackle.

You also sent a collection of ants and beetles. Tell me about those flies.

"I fish beetles and ants almost all the time. I love fishing those patterns. I fish them on small streams, spring creeks, and on the Snake River—almost everywhere. It seems like the trout are always eager to eat ants and beetles. Those are some of my real go-to flies."

Do you use your ants and beetles throughout the season, or do you save them for later in the summer?

"I use them throughout the season, but they really come into their own later in the year. Our grasshopper fishing doesn't start until mid-July or later. You'll find them in dry places away from the stream earlier in the season, but the ones closer to the stream come out later than most people would think. The ants and beetles seem to come out once the snow melts."

Suspended Beetle
Hook: Dai-Riki 320, sizes 16 to 12.
Thread: Black 8/0 (70 denier).
Shellback: Black Swiss Straw.
Underbody: Peacock Mylar dubbing.
Rib: Fine green wire.
Indicator: Black foam and orange Hi-Vis or
    polypropylene fibers.
Legs: Fine black rubber.
Hackle: Black.

Suspended Ant
Hook: Dai-Riki 320 hook, sizes 20 to 12.
Thread: Black 8/0 (70 denier).
Abdomen: Black Body Stretch or Scud
    Back.
Midbody: Tying thread.
Indicator: 2-millimeter-thick black foam
    and orange Hi-Vis or polypropylene
    yarn.
Hackle: Brown grizzly.

Black Rubber-Legged Biot Bug
Hook: Dai-Riki 285, size 12 or 10.
Bead: Black brass or tungsten bead head.
Thread: Black 8/0 (70 denier).
Underbody: .030-inch lead wire.
Rib: Copper wire.
Abdomen: Black dubbing.
Tail/sides: Black turkey or goose biots.
Thorax: Black dubbing.
Wing case: Black Spandex.

Olive Rubber-Legged Biot Bug
Hook: Dai-Riki 285, size 12 or 10.
Bead: Black brass or tungsten bead.
Thread: Olive 8/0 (70 denier).
Underbody: .030-inch lead wire.
Rib: Olive wire.
Abdomen: Olive dubbing.
Tail/sides: Olive turkey or goose biots.
Thorax: Olive dubbing.
Wing case: Olive spandex.

I see that you also like flies tied with biot bodies.

"Yes, I sent you a couple of those flies. Those patterns are sort of variations of my original Biot Bug. Those are in the size 10 range to imitate midsize stoneflies: yellow sallies and smaller golden stoneflies. We have a ton of stoneflies in that size range during the late spring and early summer. The thing about those flies is that they have tungsten beads and wire underbodies, so you can get them down without a lot of effort. They work really well with a big foam dry fly as an indicator."

So, you use variations of the same general pattern to imitate a wide variety of insects.

"Sure, why not? Most bugs have the same generic profile within their species."

Tell me about the Ultra Zug.

"That's another good generic nymph imitation. You can change the color and size to match just about anything. It's also a pretty good deep caddis emerger; it has that ragged collar and the profile of a deep pupa."

It's pretty nondescript-looking. Do you fish it dead drift, or do you give it some action?

"I primarily fish it with a dead drift and then swing it at the end. If you don't get a strike on the drift, the fish see it rise like an emerger at the end of the drift, and then they often hit it."

The name of the Everything Emerger pretty much says it all: I suspect you can tie versions to match almost any type of aquatic insect.

"That pattern came about on a parking lot on the Henrys Fork. The original concept was to combine a couple of flies: Craig Mathews's X-Caddis, which is still one of the best caddis emergers out there, and the Hair-Wing Dun, which has that same basic profile. You can do a lot of things with the Everything Emerger.

   "Once, when we were on the South Fork, and there were PMDs in one spot and yellow sallies in another spot. The insects were both roughly the same size and color. You could pull up the hair wing to imitate the mayfly, or you could mash down the wing with your thumb to create a stonefly profile. You could match both insects without changing flies. That's when I started calling it the Everything Emerger: It could be a mayfly, it could be a stonefly, it could be a caddisfly or even a midge. The cripples of all these insects look pretty much the same; they all have screwed-up legs and wings."

Do you consider it an imitation of an emerger or a cripple?

"You can use it to match either form. I mean, both forms of insects are on the water at the same time, so the trout are taking it for either an emerger or a cripple—or both."

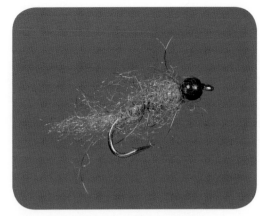

Ultra Zug Free-Living Caddis
Thread: Black 8/0 (70 denier).
Bead: Black metal bead.
Body: Lime dubbing.
Rib: A strand of pearl Krystal Flash.
Collar: A tuft of Peacockle dubbing spun behind the hook eye. Trim the fibers to length.

Everything Emerger
Hook: Dai Riki 320, sizes 20 to 12.
Thread: Rust brown 8/0 (70 denier).
Shuck: Brown Antron or Zelon.
Body: Tan dubbing.
Rib: Doubled rust brown tying thread.
Wing: Dark elk or deer hair.
Legs: The butt ends of the wing.

How long does it take you to design a fly?

"You're always adapting patterns and materials to create a fly to solve a problem; maybe it's the fish you couldn't catch, or you're trying to simplify a fly. It doesn't take a long time to come up with a new fly—sort of like a rough sketch—but you will tweak the pattern for years."

Have you seen any interesting new materials lately?

"Polar Dub looks interesting. It has some nice sheen but no flash. I've been using that for tying trailing shucks and wings on my flies. It looks buggy.

"I'm also finding some interesting applications for Gorilla Glue. That's what I used to tie that Gorilla Glue Ant I sent to you. It expands three or four times its size as it dries."

Did you add the color?

"Yes, because it needs water as an activator. You can add a drop of acrylic paint, and it works great. And you can also paint it. Black paint works especially well, but to get tan you have to add brown paint. You can experiment with it to get the exact colors you want.

"You can do all kinds of wild shit with Gorilla Glue. You can make ants and beetles. I actually wrote an article for *American Angler* magazine in which I filled a monofilament frame with glue, kind of like tying a Mother of Epoxy fly. You just barely fill the frame, and the glue bubbles up and fills the area. I've also used it to make grasshopper bodies and heads. You just have to be quick because it has a pretty short working time.

"You apply this stuff on your fly, and watch it grow. It's almost addictive to use. I was teaching a class, and it was just one thing I wanted to show the students, but people were still making bodies an hour and a half later!"

Gorilla Glue Ant
Hook: Dai-Riki 320, sizes 8 to 16.
Thread: Black 8/0 (70 denier).
Body: Fast-set Gorilla Glue (white) tinted
    with brown acrylic paint.
Legs: Black rubber legs.
Indicator: Orange polypropylene EP
    Fibers.

Does the glue float?

"Yes, because when it expands, it forms air bubbles. You'll put a small drop on the hook—you'll barely see it at all—and it'll expand to something like four times its size. That's why it's so perfect for making the bodies on ants and beetles.

"By the way, felt soles might be on their way out, but if you have felt-sole wading boots, Gorilla Glue is ideal for repairing the soles. You can never fully dry the soles before you want to glue them back on, and water is the catalyst for the glue, so it's perfect for this application. I repaired some felt soles three years ago with that stuff, and they're still holding. I've also repaired the dry compartments on my drift boat—there's really no such thing as a totally dry compartment—using Gorilla Glue. They're tough to caulk because there's always a bit of moisture, so I hit it with the Gorilla Glue, it bubbles up, and you're done."

The Lipstick Minnow is an interesting-looking fly; it's different from everything else you sent.

"The Lipstick Minnow came from a trip I was taking to Hawaii fifteen or twenty years ago. At that time there was no information about fly fishing in Hawaii, and it's pretty tough to do anyway. They have a lot of small, clear minnows, and the light-tackle spin fishermen where using something called Glitter Strips, which were basically strips of silicone that had glitter in them. I thought epoxy flies might work, but they take a lot of time to make, and I knew I'd lose a lot of flies in the coral. My solution was to wrap an underbody using metallic thread, add some strands of Krystal Flash, and slip a piece of clear plastic tubing onto the hook shank as the body. I glued the eyes in place using Goop. It's really easy to make, and you can create a lot of flies quickly. Although I tied it for fishing the salt, it's also a great fry imitation for trout."

Lipstick Minnow

Hook: Mustad 34011, size 4.

Thread: Silver, pearl, or multicolor metallic Mylar sewing thread or metallic rod wrapping thread. If not available, use gray 3/0 (210 denier) tying thread.

Tail: Gray marabou or fur.

Underbody: Metallic thread.

Sides: Two strands of silver holographic flash and four strands of pearl Krystal Flash.

Body: 3/16-inch-diameter clear vinyl aquarium tubing.

Head: Goop or a similar adhesive.

Eyes: 3-millimeter molded eyes.

Everfloat Caddis Emerger
Hook: Dai Riki 320, sizes 16 to 12.
Thread: Black 6/0 (140 denier).
Tail: Olive Polar Dub.
Wing: Natural cream rabbit-foot fur.
Body: Olive Polar Dub.
Back: 1-millimeter-thick olive foam.
Head: Black Polar Dub.
Rib: Pearl Krystal Flash.
Collar: Olive Polar Dub.

What's the story behind the Everfloat Caddis Emerger?
"That's another caddis emerger I created. That fly came about while fishing the Mother's Day hatch on the Yellowstone River; when that hatch is on, there's no better trout fishing. As you find in a lot of places, fish love to eat pupa. I joke around that we fish dry flies during a caddis hatch because we want to, not because the fish are really keying in on them. A lot of times the fish are really taking the easy food, which are the pupae, and I wanted to come up with a floating emerger that would allow me to fish a sunken pupa below it. That Razor Foam back and bunny-foot wing make it buoyant; it'll actually float with a bead-head pupa imitation."

Most of your flies seem more impressionistic than realistic.
"I don't think the fish are really that smart. Some flies are such precise imitations that you can interpret them as only one type of forage. You sometimes wonder if the fish reject these flies because something might be out of place, or they're really feeding on something else. On the other hand, you wonder if they might accept a more generic imitation. We don't always know what the fish are thinking, even though we pretend that we do."

What type of flies do you prefer fishing: dry flies or subsurface patterns?
"I spend a lot more time fishing dry flies because I live in cutthroat country. You have spring and fall seasons when the water is really cold—or getting cold—and nymphs work better; you'll catch a larger percentage of white fish, but these are good times of the year to fish nymphs. But I don't fish nymphs all that much in the middle of summer, other than maybe a rubber-legged stonefly, and I don't know if you'd call it a nymph or an emerger."

How late in the year do you fish?

"Sometimes we have gorgeous Novembers, and I'll fish until then, especially for brown trout, but as it cools down, the cutthroats seem to hunker down. I think it's a survival mechanism. You look at rivers like the Snake—it's a pretty harsh place—and the area can have wide temperature swings throughout the year. The fish seem to move to find the best places to survive. But you can fish the flies I sent from spring through the fall, and you'll have good luck catching fish—say April until November."

———————

Chapter 17

Lisa Savard
and New Hampshire's Upper Connecticut River

Savard with her son

I first wrote about Lisa Savard more than ten years ago for a feature article in *American Angler* magazine. I spent a couple of days at her place, Lobstick Lodge, on the upper Connecticut River in northern New Hampshire.

Far northern New Hampshire, above the town of Pittsburgh, is a beautiful place. It's sparsely populated and heavily forested. It is also home to some of the finest fly fishing in New England.

Lisa has prospered since we first met. She has added on to the lodge, hired more guides, and expanded her fly shop. She is a real success, and it's been a lot of fun watching her business grow.

I thought it was important to include a chapter about the fine trout fishing in New Hampshire, and contacting Lisa was an obvious choice. It has been a couple of years since I was last at Lobstick, and I first wanted to hear how her business has changed.

"We have forty-three cabins now," Lisa said. "We're an Orvis-endorsed outfitter, and we have a larger fly shop right here at the main office. We have guides that will take you wade fishing or in a drift boat on the Connecticut River."

When we met, you were still guiding. How long have you been a guide?
"I was spending a lot of time guiding back then. I've been guiding about fifteen years."

When we fished together, we waded, but you also guide using a drift boat.

"Yes, I do. I especially like doing double drift-boat trips. These days I like someone to help launch the boat, but rowing is no problem. I love drifting the Connecticut River."

It's all wade fishing near the lodge. I suspect that's what most anglers are coming to do, right?

"That's what most anglers are familiar with because that's what gets all the press."

Describe the wade-fishing areas.

"The main area is called the 'trophy stretch.' It's pocket water at the top where it comes out of First Connecticut Lake. As it drops in elevation, the river forms more pools before it enters Lake Francis. This section contains brook, brown, and rainbow trout as well as landlocked salmon. It's very easy to wade, and the flow is generally between one hundred fifty and three hundred cubic feet per second.

"Between First Connecticut Lake and Second Connecticut, it is all fly fishing only. This area runs sixty to one hundred cubic feet per second, so it's also very easy to wade and enjoyable. And then there's a stretch between Third Lake and Second Lake, which is smaller, and the access isn't quite as good, but it contains native brook trout. And then there's another great section to wade below Murphy Dam, which is the last lake in the chain; there you'll have flows from three hundred to five hundred cubic feet per second. This last section contains some very good brown trout, and it is very wadable.

"Check out a map, and you'll see a lot of opportunities to fish the upper Connecticut River. There's a lot of water to fish."

You're pretty specific about the water flows. Are the flows fairly constant?

"Yes, they are. These lakes are managed for flood control and recreation, not power generation; power generation occurs about two hours downriver. So, the flows are generally fairly constant, which is great for wading anglers. We often go five or six weeks with no change in water volume. And what's really interesting is that if we have a big water event—a big rain or whatever—the flows are always clear from the dams to the first tributaries below the dams, so we always having good fishing."

How far away is the portion of the river that you fish from drift boats?

"The start of our drifts is in Stewartstown, which is seventeen miles south of the lodge."

That's not far to go.

"No, it's not. And there's another place we launch which is twenty-six miles from the lodge."

Someone can visit you and see quite a variety of water, couldn't they?

"Yes, they can. Plus, we have seven fly fishing–only ponds nearby, and we have many more ponds than that. And there are also several smaller tributaries to the Connecticut River that can fish quite well."

What type of fish is in the ponds?

"Pretty much brook trout."

Since we're on the topic—and I love stillwater fishing—let's talk about the ponds and then return to the river. What hatches do you have in the ponds?

"Basically blue-winged olives. Some ponds have a green-drake hatch but not all of them. But we're a real caddis area—caddis, caddis, caddis. In early spring, though, the ponds have good midge hatches, and a Griffith's Gnat works very well. And that Olive CDC Caddis I sent to you works well as an imitation of either a caddisfly or mayfly because it doesn't have a prominent hackle, but it does have the right profile; we often use an olive-bodied CDC Caddis on the ponds in the spring. We live and die by that fly almost everywhere.

"That CDC Caddis looks like a lot of things. The cool thing about that fly is that you can give it a little skitter and pull it just under the surface, and the cul de canard will make it pop back up so it'll look like an emerger. Do that right in front of a trout, and sometimes it'll whack the fly right there. That's a very good pattern and an excellent fishing technique."

Olive CDC Caddis
Hook: Regular dry-fly hook.
Body: Olive dubbing.
Thread: Olive 8/0 (70 denier).
Wing: Olive cul de canard.

In terms of the river, what size of fish do people catch?
"We have a lot of ten- to twelve-inch fish; the typical New England trout."

Do you get larger salmon in the rivers in the autumn?
"Yes, we do; they can go eighteen inches."

Do you get larger brook trout in the autumn?
"We get larger brook trout throughout the season courtesy of the big green truck—I don't know how you want to word that. But the state stocks lots of big brook trout throughout the year. We have a great stocking program."

Bead-Head Pheasant-Tail Nymph
Hook: Regular wet-fly hook, sizes 16 to 12.
Thread: Brown 6/0 (140 denier).
Bead: Gold bead.
Tail: Pheasant-tail fiber tips.
Abdomen: Pheasant-tail fibers.
Rib: Copper wire.
Thorax: Peacock herl.
Wing case: Pheasant-tail fibers.

What are some of your favorite nymph patterns?
"That Bead-Head Pheasant-Tail and Prince Nymph are two of our favorite flies; we use them a ton."

Do you use single flies or droppers?
"When I guide, I almost always use droppers. I place something heavy at the top, like a stonefly or a larger Pheasant-Tail Nymph. I use the fly that I think will be 'the one' on the bottom."

Prince Nymph
Hook: 2X-long wet-fly hook, sizes 18 to 14.
Thread: Black 6/0 (140 denier).
Tail: Brown biots.
Body: Peacock herl.
Rib: Round gold tinsel or wire.
Wing: White biots.
Hackle: Brown.

Do you use the Pheasant-Tail throughout the season?
"Absolutely."

What are the primary hatches on the Connecticut River?
"Caddis, caddis, caddis, caddis—throughout the entire season. In July we get the little yellow sally stoneflies, and in August we get these big honking stoneflies. We use a Stimulator to match these. These stoneflies are so large that they could eat chickadees."

I didn't realize you had big stoneflies.
"They're awesome. You can use a Stimulator through out the day, but right as it's getting dark, splat your fly right on the water. Do this when you almost can't see to fish anymore. This technique almost always brings a strike."

Gray Caddisfly
Hook: Regular dry-fly hook.
Body: Gray dubbing.
Thread: Gray 8/0 (70 denier).
Wing: Gray cul de canard.

Stimulator
Hook: Curved-shank nymph hook, sizes 14 to 12.
Thread: Orange 8/0 (70 denier).
Tail: Deer-hair tips.
Body: Dirty orange polypropylene yarn.
Body hackle: Brown.
Wing: Deer hair.
Hackle: Grizzly.

And you do this in August?

"Yes, in August. Remember, we're on a tailwater, so we have good fishing throughout the season. The dams on First Connecticut Lake and Lake Francis are bottom-release dams. The water from the dam on Lake Francis comes out sixty feet below the surface of the lake, and it's especially cold; even in the middle of summer, when the air temperature is in the eighties and even nineties, the water temperature in this section of the river is around fifty-two degrees. That's what keeps the water so cold where we drift, even in the summer."

Do you think people realize that upper New Hampshire is such a good destination for summer fishing?

"They do if they attend one of my seminars at the winter fly-fishing shows. I really emphasize this."

You sent an Adams Irresistible. When do you use this fly?

"We use the Irresistible a lot when we float the river. When you get downriver, you're apt to see more mayfly action. We have blue-winged olives and cahills in the Pittsburgh area, but as you move downriver, you'll find more mayflies. It's tough describing all of the hatches in the river because of the variety of water.

"For instance, around Pittsburgh and near the lodge, you have broken pocket water and plunge pools, but as you move farther below Pittsburgh, the river becomes more pastoral, and you'll have sulphurs, Tricos, and even ant hatches. You'll even use grasshoppers. You won't use any of those flies, however, on the upper stretches, even though these two major sections of the rivers are only twenty miles apart.

"Also, as you move downriver, the flow slows up and your casting must be more accurate; you and your line and the boat will all drift into groups of rising trout. When you're above Pittsburgh, however, your fishing will be more active: You'll cast over here into some pocket water, and then you'll cast over there into more

Irresistible
Hook: 2X-long dry-fly hook, sizes 16 to 12.
Thread: Black 3/0 (210 denier).
Tail: Moose or some other black hair.
Body: Deer hair, spun and clipped to
     shape.
Wing: Grizzly hackle tips.
Hackle: Brown and grizzly.

Tan X-Caddis
Hook: Regular dry-fly hook, sizes 18 to 14.
Thread: Tan 8/0 (70 denier).
Tail: Zelon.
Body: Tan dubbing.
Wing: Deer hair.

Hatching Pupa
Hook: Regular wet-fly hook, sizes 18 to 14.
Thread: Brown 8/0 (70 denier).
Tail: Wood-duck flank fibers.
Abdomen: Stripped peacock herl.
Rib: Red Ultra wire.
Thorax: Peacock herl.
Hackle: Partridge.

Red Copper John
Hook: Regular wet-fly hook, sizes 18 to 14.
Bead: Gold bead.
Thread: Black 6/0 (140 denier).
Tails: Brown biots.
Abdomen: Red Ultra Wire.
Thorax: Peacock herl.
Legs: Hen-hackle fibers.
Wing case: Turkey or a slip clipped from a
    freezer bag and coated with epoxy.

pocket water. In this quick water, the fish decide right away whether or not they're going to strike your fly, but just twenty miles away downriver, the fish will say, 'Hum, I think that fly was tied in Sri Lanka.'"

You sent a lovely traditional wet fly. I'm not familiar with this specific pattern. What is it?
"That's a Hatching Pupa. We use that all over the place, even when we travel out west. I use that in the river as the second fly I think the fish will take. When I drift, I might use an Adams Irresistible, and two feet to eighteen inches after that I'll tie on the Hatching Pupa and let it ride in the surface film as an emerger. Ellis Hatch tied that fly. He was a fish and game commissioner for New Hampshire, and he rules when it comes to fly tying around here. That's his pattern."

This red Copper John is very small. Do you use a lot of small flies?
"When it comes to the Pheasant-Tail and Bead-Head Prince, they'll be sizes 14 and 12. The red Copper John, however, is smaller."

What do you think it imitates?
"I don't know; maybe something red in the river. All I know is that it catches fish."

It's a little-known fact, but John Barr, who designed the original Copper John, says that his favorite color is red. He says that it catches more fish than any other color, including the original copper-colored fly.
"It really does work well, and it works better more toward fall."

What's this big fly with the dumbbell eyes? It's similar to a Woolly Bugger.

"That's the Woolly Bomber. That was once an Orvis pattern, but they dropped it. It's an awesome fly, so we get Ellis to tie them for us. I have caught the largest brook trout here using that fly. When I hear of a big fish in a pool, I'll pop one of those bad boys on and often pull it out of the pool. When lake trout come out of the dam, I'll catch them using that fly."

Oh, so you also get lake trout in the river.

"Once in a while. They're stupid, but they're big. Big is good."

You also enjoy classic streamers, such as the Black Ghost and Magog Smelt.

"The Black Ghost is a searching pattern, and the Magog Smelt is a good representation of a real smelt. When you pick up a smelt and look at it in the light, there's

Woolly Bomber
Hook: 4X-long streamer hook, sizes 10 to 4.
Thread: Black 6/0 (140 denier).
Tail: Black marabou and pearl Krystal
   Flash.
Body: Black chenille.
Hackle: Grizzly-saddle hackle.
Eyes: Lead dumbbell.
Head: Black chenille.

Black Ghost
Hook: 4X-long streamer hook, sizes 10 to 4.
Thread: Black 6/0 (140 denier).
Tail: Yellow hackle fibers.
Body: Black floss.
Rib: Silver tinsel.
Throat: Yellow hackle fibers.
Wing: White marabou and pearl Krystal
   Flash.

Magog Smelt
Hook: 4X-long streamer hook, sizes 12 to 6.
Thread: Black 6/0 (140 denier).
Tail: Teal-flank fibers.
Body: Silver tinsel.
Throat: Red hackle fibers.
Wing: White, yellow, and lavender buck tail.
Topping: Peacock herl.
Shoulders: Teal-flank feathers.

just a tinge of purple. I want my smelt imitations to have just a hint of purple."

Putt's Favorite
Hook: 4X-long streamer hook, sizes 12 to 6.
Thread: Red 6/0 (140 denier).
Body: Silver tinsel.
Head and wing: Gray marabou. Coat the head with cement or epoxy.
Eyes: Paint.

Do you get a good smelt run into the river?
"In May, as a general rule, it begins Mother's Day weekend and lasts for the following two weeks."

Do the smelt ever get blown through the dams?
"Yes, they do, but they're dead, and the big brown trout pluck them off the surface."

And the final fly is a Thunder Creek streamer.
"That's actually a Putt's favorite. Some people call it a Thunder Creek, but over here we call it a Putt's Favorite. There was a fellow named Putt who used to come here, and that was one of his patterns. We tie it in olive and gray. The gray version usually works best because it imitates most of the baitfish, and the olive version is a good substitute for an olive Woolly Bugger."

What's your fishing season?
"It begins right around Mother's Day, and it closes October fifteenth. Because the Connecticut is a tailwater fishery, we have consistently good fishing through the season."

Chapter 18

Eric Stroup:
An Innovative Tyer with a Growing Reputation

Eric Stroup is another of the young-gun fly tyers I selected to include in this book. His flies are superb, and he has a growing reputation as a guide and teacher as well as a fly tyer. He's very friendly and is willing to share what he knows with fellow anglers.

When I opened the package of flies he sent for photographs, I was immediately drawn to his Peaking Caddis. Cased caddisfly larvae imitations have become a big part of my fishing; Maine's landlocked salmon and brook trout swallow them like jelly beans, and I always get excited whenever I discover a new pattern. Eric's Peaking Caddis is not only an admirable imitation of a cased caddis but also is obviously simple to tie. It also answered another fly-tying problem I was trying to solve: Most of my cased-caddis patterns are on the large side, and I wanted something smaller for fishing littler streams or shallower water. You can easily make the Peaking Caddis in a range of small and medium sizes.

I called Eric and immediately asked about the Peaking Caddis. I mentioned an Oliver Edwards pattern called the Peeping Caddis and the fact that that fly is tied using spun and clipped deer hair; that's why it is hard to make in smaller sizes. Eric's Peaking Caddis, however, makes great use of pheasant-tail fibers.

"I wrap six to eight pheasant-tail fibers over lead wire to make the body. If you want to get really fancy, you can square it up using toothless pliers. Wrap the fibers over the lead, and then square up the body to really match the Grannom caddis. Next, coat the body with head cement or superglue. Just work carefully so you don't break the fibers, but the glue holds everything together just fine."

Peaking Caddis
Hook: Dohiku 302, sizes 14 to 8.
Thread: Black 6/0 (140 denier).
Tail: Chartreuse Sparkle Yarn melted on
    the end.
Body: Pheasant-tail fibers.
Hackle: Black hen hackle.

Walt's Worm
Hook: Dohiku 302, sizes 16 to 8.
Thread: Black 6/0 (140 denier).
Underbody: Fine lead wire.
Body: Hare's Ear Plus #1 or a substitute
    gray rabbit dubbing.

Is the Peaking Caddis one of your patterns?
"No, I got it out of an English magazine. They actually dubbed the body, and I did that, but the more I thought about it, the more I realized that using pheasant-tail fibers would be a lot easier and would actually look more like our Grannom caddisflies."

Were they squaring up the body in the article you read?
"No, they were just tying it round. I started squaring it to make it a little more realistic."

[Fly-tying note: I took Eric's advice and tied this pattern using dubbing as well as pheasant-tail fibers. The tail fibers make a far more realistic-looking case. And when I wanted to tie a slightly larger fly and needed longer material to make the case, I substituted with fibers clipped from a dark mottled turkey-tail feather. These flies look great!

Walt's Worm is another unusual pattern Eric shared with me. This fly is deceptively simple, and I wondered if it would really catch trout. He assured me that it is indeed a real fish-getter.]

"Believe it or not, that's probably the most effective pattern I sent to you. It's an imitation of a cranefly larva. We have tons of craneflies in our streams, and that fly was developed by Walt Young and Tom Baltz. Walt created that pattern to fish Spring Creek, and it's an absolutely killer bug. We use it twelve months out of the year, and I'm never on the stream without it. It's actually sort of a Czech Nymph; it has a lot of weight in it."

What colors do you tie it in?
"Olives, tans, and other natural colors. And I make the body using Hare's Ear Plus #1 dubbing; that's the best material."

The Purple Soft Hackle is a lovely classic-type wet fly. Is it an attractor pattern, or do you use it to match a specific insect?

"I use the Purple Soft Hackle to match the *Isonychia* mayflies. It's a great pattern for fishing central Pennsylvania, and it also works well on the West Branch of the Delaware River. I use a lot of the old-style patterns because they work so well. Soft hackles work especially well for a new angler who is struggling to get a good drift."

When do you fish with this fly?

"I use it anytime the *Isonychias* are around, which is basically May until October. I fish it deep, I fish it near the surface—I fish it at all water depths. My favorite place to fish it is in the tailouts of currents. Dead-drift it through the current, and then use the old Leisenring lift to raise it in the water. The fish just hammer it."

It's unusual to see a pattern designed to match a specific insect tied in purple.

"When it gets wet, it turns a little darker and closely matches the color of the real *Isonychia*."

Tell me about your dry fly called the Catskill Sulphur Spinner.

"I started fishing the Catskill Spinner seven or eight years ago. I wanted to match the sulphur spinners. The sulphur mayflies are our best hatch—it's usually from mid-May to about the first of June. Over the past ten years, I don't think I've missed a day on the water during that hatch—mostly as a guide, of course. But I still have days when I can't figure out what the trout want to eat. Fishing during the sulphur spinner fall is some of the most complicated fishing we have. I've noticed over the years that there are times when the trout will only eat the moving bugs. By that I mean the spinners land, rest on the water, and move their wings.

Purple Soft Hackle
Hook: Dohiku 302, sizes 12 to 8.
Thread: Wine 6/0 (140 denier).
Tail: Black hen-hackle fibers.
Abdomen: Purple dubbing.
Rib: Fine silver wire.
Thorax: Peacock herl.
Hackle: Black hen hackle.

Catskill Sulphur Spinner
Hook: Dohiku 301, sizes 18 to 14.
Thread: Orange 6/0 (140 denier).
Tail: Medium dun hackle fibers.
Body: Tan or rust Pearsall's Gossamer Silk.
Rib: Fine gold wire.
Wing: Medium dun hen-hackle tips.
Hackle: Medium dun.

Flat-Wing Spent Spinner (Sulphur)
Hook: Dohiku 301, sizes 18 to 14.
Thread: Orange 6/0 (140 denier).
Tail: Medium dun hackle fibers.
Rib: Tan Pearsall's Gossamer Silk.
Thorax: Rust Fine & Dry dubbing.
Wing: Medium dun hen-hackle tips.
Hackle: Medium dun rooster hackle.

CDC Grannom Caddisfly
Hook: Dohiku 301, sizes 18 to 12.
Tread: Black 6/0 (140 denier).
Body: Blended black, brown, and gray
    dry-fly dubbing.
Hackle: Dark gray cul de canard.
Wing: Natural deer hair.

The ones that are moving get eaten. If you can't imitate some movement, you have to wait until the insects are dead and the trout start gulping the spent spinners. I started fishing this pattern, and it seems to help."

It's curious that this is a spinner imitation, but the wings are tied in the upright position. Most spinner imitations are designed with the wings splayed out from the sides.
"There are times when the typical spent-wing pattern doesn't catch fish during the spinner fall. This is when I use the Catskill Spinner."

The Flat-Wing Spent Spinner is a more typical-looking spinner imitation. Is this one of your patterns?
"The Flat-Water Spinner is probably one of my designs, but a lot of guys tie something similar. A lot of anglers come with the typical polywing spinners, and sometimes those don't cut it. Sometimes you need to switch things up. I tie it in sizes and colors to match a variety of spinners. It's just a good overall pattern."

The CDC Grannom Caddisfly is a really fishy-looking fly. Obviously you're fishing this as an emerging pupa, maybe in the surface film, right?
"No, I fish it as a dry fly. I let those CDC fibers lay right off of it. They seem to move in the current. There are a lot of times where you want to move a caddis pattern on the surface, and with this fly, you don't have to do that: It's already moving for you. And what I like about this fly is that after you catch a fish or two on it, it will sit a little lower in the water, and I think those fibers look like legs, a shuck, and some of the other parts of a natural insect. I've had tremendous success with that fly; I don't even fish hackled caddisfly patterns any more unless I'm using something like the Hi-Viz Caddis. But for actual caddis hatches, this is the fly I use."

What sizes and colors do you tie it in?

"I tie it in all the sizes and colors. The one I sent to you is an actual Grannom imitation, but I adapt the pattern to match all the caddisfly hatches."

The Hi-Viz Caddis is also a great-looking fly. It must float well, too.

"Yes, it does. It's caught a lot of trout."

The October Caddis is an interesting pattern. Normally, I thought that this was considered a western hatch. Do you have October caddisflies in Pennsylvania?

"We have it here. It hatches from October into November. It's a big bug—a true size 10. But they hatch after the sun sets, so it really doesn't offer a lot of opportunities to fish dry flies. But once the hatches get going, you can fish this pattern anytime during the day and catch fish."

Hi-Viz Caddisfly
Hook: Dohiku 301, sizes 16 to 10.
Thread: Tan 6/0 (140 denier).
Tail: Brown polypropylene.
Body: Tan Fine & Dry dubbing.
Rib: Fine gold wire.
Hackle: Brown rooster hackle.
Wing: Natural deer hair and gray or white polypropylene.

October Caddis Soft Hackle
Hook: Dohiku 302, sizes 14 to 10.
Thread: Orange 6/0 (140 denier).
Abdomen: Natureblend light yellowish tan.
Rib: Copper wire.
Thorax: Orange SLF Squirrel Blend dubbing.
Hackle: Partridge dyed orange.

Golden Pheasant-Tail Soft Hackle
Hook: Dohiku 302, sizes 18 to 10.
Thread: Orange 6/0 (140 denier).
Tail: Golden pheasant-tail fibers.
Abdomen: Golden pheasant-tail fibers.
Rib: Fine gold wire.
Thorax: Peacock herl.
Hackle: Partridge.

Sulphur Soft Hackle
Hook: Dohiku 302, sizes 18 to 14.
Thread: Yellow 6/0 (140 denier).
Tail: Light dun hen-hackle fibers.
Abdomen: Yellow Natureblend.
Rib: Fine gold wire.
Thorax: Cinnamon Natureblend.
Hackle: Light dun hen hackle.

Sulphur Klinkhammer
Hook: Partridge Klinkhammer 15BN, sizes
20 to 16.
Thread: Pale yellow 6/0 (140 denier).
Abdomen: Yellow Pearsall's Gossamer Silk.
Thorax: Light olive Fine & Dry.
Wing post: Gray polypropylene.
Hackle: Light ginger rooster hackle.

It's a fairly typical-looking wet fly. Do you fish it down-and-across stream?

"Yes, but I also dead-drift all my soft-hackle patterns. I try to figure out how the fish want a fly, and then I'll match the presentation to meet their preference."

Do the spring creeks have the October caddis?

"Yes, they do. The Little Juniata has a small hatch, but it's very prolific on Spruce Creek. Penns and Big Fishing Creek also have them."

Of course, a guide couldn't operate in Pennsylvania without a collection of sulphur imitations. You sent samples of a sulphur nymph, a wet fly—which serves as an emerger—and a parachute dry fly. Your Sulphur Parachute is tied in the Klinkhammer style. And even though it's a mayfly imitation, you prefer tying it without tails.

"I let the body dip down into the surface film, and it works great."

Let's talk about your fishing. Where do you guide?

"I fish and guide on the Little Juniata, Penns Creek, Spring Creek, Big Fishing Creek. And I do a little on Spruce Creek but not much."

What's your normal fishing season?

"We guide twelve months out of the year. We even get a few clients during the winter, but that is when we do most of our fly-tying schools. I have my book, *Common Sense Fly Fishing*, so we've started Common Sense Weekends: Each weekend we work on a different skill."

Listening to Eric talk about his winter activities reminded me of when my family and I lived in Tennessee, and we would travel to Pennsylvania to visit relatives in Philadelphia. On the way home we would drive to the middle of the state, and then take the interstate south. One year we stopped by Big Spring and found several anglers fishing. The bank was covered in thick snow, and fishermen wore waders to maneuver through the soft powder. I related this story to Eric.

"Oh, sure: You can fish all of these rivers throughout the year. I generally steer people away from Penns Creek in the winter—because Penns is tough fishing anyway—and it gets particularly difficult when the water temperature drops. But they all fish fairly well in the wintertime. Spring Creek is probably your best bet for fishing during the winter."

What fly would you recommend for fishing during the winter?

"Small nymphs work well—size 16 and smaller. Dead-drift them along the bottom. We also have a lot of midge hatches. If you get a couple of warm days, say in mid-February, it's not uncommon to catch thirty or forty fish per day. You won't catch big fish—they'll be smaller—but you can catch a lot of them. And you have a smaller window in the day for fishing, typically from about eleven in the morning until three in the afternoon. But that's a lot of action for such a small period of time."

J-Bug Nymph
Hook: Dohiku 302, sizes 18 to 12.
Thread: Olive 6/0 (140 denier).
Tail: Pheasant-tail fibers.
Body: Olive dubbing.
Rib: Copper wire.
Shellback and wing case: Pheasant-tail fibers.
Legs: Mottled brown hen.

Dark Sulphur Nymph
Hook: Dohiku 302, sizes 20 to 12.
Thread: Dark olive 6/0 (140 denier).
Tail: Wood-duck flank fibers.
Body: Brown rabbit dubbing.
Rib: Copper wire.
Wing case: Black pheasant-tail fibers.
Legs: Mottled brown hen.

Horse Hair Midge
Hook: Dohiku 302, sizes 24 to 16.
Thread: Black 6/0 (140 denier).
Body: White moose mane.
Thorax: Dark brown dubbing.
Legs: Black hen-hackle fibers.

Do the trout actually rise to the hatching midges?
"Oh, yes, we're fishing to rising trout. In fact, we still have some olives coming off. [This interview was conducted mid-December.] It's gotten colder, but there are still a few midges hatching, and the fishing hasn't been bad."

Does the water ever freeze over?
"All of these waters we're talking about get cold, but they don't freeze."

What are your favorite summertime patterns?
"Beetles and ants work well during the summer. You might get a dozen days where the water gets too hot, and the fishing slows, and you might want to stay off the streams, but Fishing Creek is always okay. And Spring Creek is usually okay. Penns Creek and the Little Juniata might slow down if you get some really hot days, but you can always fish them in the early morning."

What tips can you give anglers who wish to come and fish the streams in your area?
"The number-one thing is to bring felt-bottomed boots because our streams are treacherous; they're very slippery. I also recommend using a longer rather than a shorter rod to get a little more reach; being able to keep your line off the water, which you can do with a longer rod, can make a tremendous difference in catching fish. A four- or five-weight rod works best; my favorite rod is a ten-foot, four-weight. And I use a ten-foot-long leader that I tie up, but sometimes I'll go up to a fifteen- or eighteen-foot-long leader. I don't necessarily like using those extra-long leaders, but sometimes that's what the fishing demands."

A lot of famous anglers came from Pennsylvania; they designed some of the most important flies and wrote some of the most important books in the history of our sport. Who influenced you as a fly tyer?

"I'm from George Harvey's neck of the woods. George and Joe Humphreys influenced everything fly fishermen do around here. We grew up looking at and tying their patterns. You can't fish around here and not be influenced by their contributions."

———————————

Chapter 19

Mike Valla: Preserving the Catskill Traditions

Fan Wing Coachman
Hook: Dry fly, size 10.
Thread: Brown 8/0 (70 denier).
Tail: Golden pheasant tippets.
Body: Peacock herl and red floss.
Wing: White hen-hackle tips.
Hackle: Brown.

Writing a book is a journey, and it has many surprising twists.

The trip begins in a simple fashion: You try to get into the heads of your readers. What will they want to know? What will they find useful? And can you present this information in an entertaining way?

With those questions in mind, you sketch out the parameters of your book. In this case, I had to determine what types of flies I should include and which tyers I would ask to participate. So far we've met anglers who live and guide in many parts of the United States and Canada. And we've learned about a lot of different types of flies and fishing.

As I prepared my outline, I was always conscious of the history of fly fishing. How much time should I spend talking about traditional patterns? I know tyers still make and fish many of the classic flies, but is that interest so strong that I should cover those patterns in this book?

It is impossible to avoid the Catskill Mountains and that region's rich fishing traditions when discussing North American fly tying. To discuss only new flies is to pander to the belief that something is good only if it is new, and I'm not much of a panderer. This holds true for fly-tying materials, finished patterns, and skill in tying. Nothing has displaced the importance of quality hackle, and classic Catskill dry flies still catch fish around the world. And making a fine Quill Gordon or Light Hendrickson is far more difficult that just lashing a foam body and bunch of rubber legs to a hook.

Mike Valla is a leading practitioner of the art of dressing classic Catskill patterns. His book, *Tying*

Catskill-Style Dry Flies, is quickly becoming the Bible on the subject. I knew that I wanted Mike, and his flies, in my book.

And that's where the trip took an unexpected turn.

I had met Mike at the Catskill Fly Fishing Center and Museum. We occasionally spoke at the major fly-fishing shows. I knew he was talented at the vise, had a good reputation, and was always willing to share what he knew. I felt he would be an ideal candidate for an interview. What I didn't know was that he was intimately familiar with some of the most important fly tyers of the twentieth century.

How long have you been tying flies?

"I started tying flies in 1967 and immediately enjoyed it. In 1969 I took a bus—alone—from Binghamton, New York, to Roscoe to fish the Catskill rivers. I stopped in Walt and Winnie Dettes' shop, and Winnie said, 'Who the hell are you? How old are you?'

"I said, 'I'm fifteen. I came to fish.'

"Well, Winnie gave me some flies and a map. I was on foot: no food, no water—nothing. I just wanted to catch fish. Winnie sent Walt out looking for me close to dark because she knew I had to catch a bus to get home. Walt wandered up and said that they had an extra bedroom and that I could spend the night with them. I told him to call my mother and ask, and she said to put my ass on the bus—she didn't know who he was. About a couple weeks later I returned and stayed with the Dettes."

Wait a minute. You actually lived with the Dettes? I didn't know that!

"I spent the next three or four summers with them. And when it came to going to college, they helped me get into Cornell. And then I spent a lot of my college breaks with them. This went on through the mid-1970s."

[Mike told this amazing story in a matter-of-fact sort of way. I only knew him as a guy who tied nice

Cahill Quill
Hook: Dry fly, size 10.
Thread: Tan 8/0 (70 denier).
Tail: Ginger hackle fibers.
Body: Stripped peacock-eye herl.
Wing: Lemon wood-duck fibers.
Hackle: Ginger.

Quill Gordon
Hook: Dry fly, size 10.
Thread: Tan 8/0 (70 denier).
Tail: Blue dun hackle fibers.
Body: Stripped peacock-eye herl.
Wing: Lemon wood-duck fibers.
Hackle: Blue dun.

flies, and that he could teach us a lot; that's all I was expecting. I had no idea that he actually lived with the legendary Dettes!]

Did the Dettes show you how to tie?

"I was already tying but not very well. Walt sat me down and showed me the Catskill style of tying. Unfortunately, in 1971 we moved to Texas. Walt had loaned me a Hardy reel, and I mailed it back to him. Walt called my mother and said he wanted me to come up for the summer for my graduation present. That was 1972. And then, of course, I went to Cornell and spent my breaks with the Dettes."

What was it like to tie with Walt Dette?

"I remember his exact words. The first thing he showed me was how to set wings on a fly and wrap hackle. I said that I must be doing it wrong because I was wrapping the feather with the shiny side facing the back of the fly; Walt wrapped it with the shiny side facing the hook eye. And do you know what he said? He said, 'That's how you do it, and there's nothing wrong with that; this is just how I do it.' He never said I was wrong, he would just say, 'Here, try this. This works for me.'

"Look, I knew all about Walt Dette when I met him. I almost fell over into the river when he walked up and said, 'Hi, I'm Walt Dette.' But what I remember most was that he was so kind. He never criticized my tying; he was very kind and offered suggestions and would simply say something like, 'This is how I do it; maybe it'll work for you.'

"I remember that he used to drive me up and down the river to fish. He worked for the City of New York and did water sampling of the water flowing to the city. We'd get up at five in the morning and make sandwiches for our lunches. He'd drive me down the Beaverkill someplace—he'd take me as far as I wanted

Atherton No. 2
Hook: Dry fly, size 10.
Thread: Brown 8/0 (70 denier).
Tail: Light dun hackle fibers.
Body: Light fox fur.
Rib: Narrow gold tinsel.
Wing: Lemon wood-duck fibers.
Hackle: Light blue dun.

to go—and he'd drop me off to fish for the day, and then he'd drive to work. He say something like, 'I'll pick you up at Hendrickson Pool this evening,' and he would often give me a couple of bucks to buy a snack.

"I also remember that when I was getting out of college and needed some money, I said I wanted to sell my camera for one hundred dollars. He sent a check and told me to keep the camera. It took a while, but I eventually paid him back. He was just very kind.

"Here's another story that illustrates Walt's generosity. One evening he drove me down to the river to fish, and I was frustrated because I had a bird's nest in my cheap reel, and I was having trouble getting it out. He told me to wait and said he would go back to the house for another reel. He came back with this Hardy Saint George reel and Wes Jordan bamboo rod and told me to use his tackle when I visited. That's just the way he was."

Cross Special
Hook: Dry fly, size 10.
Thread: Brown 8/0 (70 denier).
Tail: Blue dun.
Body: Light fox fur.
Wing: Lemon wood-duck fibers.
Hackle: Blue dun.

You must have learned a tremendous amount about tying from the Dettes. Can you share some of it with us? For instance, what do we need to know about hackle to tie classic Catskill flies?

"Let's start with the tail of the fly. You want long, stiff hackle fibers for tying the tails on these classic Catskills flies. Spade hackles, which are the feathers on the sides of dry-fly capes, are the best source of these fibers. With genetic hackle development, however, we've lost most of the spade feathers. I try to find old capes, like older Metz necks, that have good spade feathers for tying tails, but they're getting harder to find."

What do we need to know about selecting hackle for wrapping the collars of the flies?

"On the classic flies, you'll notice that the collars are always a little wider than on many contemporary dry flies. That's because really smaller hackles were hard to come by back then. Today we have a lot of small

Flight's Fancy
Hook: Dry fly, size 10.
Thread: Brown 8/0 (70 denier).
Tail: Ginger hackle fibers.
Body: Light fox fur.
Rib: Narrow gold tinsel.
Wings: Gray mallard.
Hackle: Ginger.

hackles. People say that the length of the fibers should equal one and one-half the width of the hook gap, but many times they were two times the width of the gap or even longer. So, I tend to use hackles with longer fibers to match the classic flies."

Do you use just one hackle per fly?

"That depends upon the water I'm fishing. If it's slow-moving water, the fly needs only one hackle; if it's heavier water, you might want a thicker collar. Even Theodore Gordon wrote—and these were his exact words—'Sometimes one hackle will do, but sometimes you need two.'

"On the other hand, Rube Cross's flies were very sparse. I think this was partly due to the fact that quality hackle was hard to find. Some original Rube Cross flies might be beefy with their hackle, but most of the time they are very delicate.

"The Dettes learned to tie from Rube Cross, you know. Walt told a story about how he went to Rube Cross and asked to learn to tie flies, and Cross told him to go to hell. So, Walt bought fifty dollars' worth of flies—this was back in the late 1920s—and the Dettes took them apart to see how they were made. The Dette style was really the Rube Cross style. In later years, however, some of their flies got a little beefier."

Why is that?

"I think some people asked for them that way. I also think that as they got older, their eyesight started to fail. Whenever you talk about the classic Catskill patterns and issues like sparseness and proportions, you have to ask who was the tyer and when did they tie the fly. You'll see that tyers made slight changes in their flies over their lives. My mantra has always been: What tyer and what era are you talking about?"

On average, how many wraps of hackle do you place on a fly?
"Like I said, my flies are usually pretty sparse. On average, maybe three wraps behind the wing and two in front.

"Now, look at the heads of my flies. See how I keep that small space for making a turle knot? This is something a lot of modern tyers fail to notice. Traditionally, a small space is left behind the hook eye to tie the fly to the leader using a turle knot."

I have your March Brown in my hand, and, yes, I can see a small bit of bare hook shank behind the eye.
"That space is for the turle knot. Rube Cross usually left a very profound amount of space for the turle knot. What happens sometimes, after wrapping the hackle, if I'm running out of space, I'll pinch the head of the fly and push the hackle back to create that space. Even the Dettes did this. In his writing, Theodore Gordon said that the turle knot was preferred for fishing dry flies.

"Walt showed me the trick about shoving the wrapped hackle back to create that space. I once asked him, 'But, Walt, your streamers and wet flies don't have this space; they have full heads. Why is that?' All he said was, 'Time for dinner.' I never did get an answer."

I suppose you use only natural hackle—no dyed feathers.
"I always try to use natural hackle. In the era in which I started tying, however, you couldn't find dun; if you could find those feathers, they were like gold. We had to use dyed dun."

One thing that strikes me about your flies is that they appear very erect.
"Yes, my flies tend to be a little high, and they go straight up. A lot of people say the wings should tilt slightly forward, but that's not exactly true; that usually

Queen of the Waters
Hook: Dry fly, size 10.
Thread: Tan 8/0 (70 denier).
Tail: Ginger hackle fibers.
Body: Orange silk thread.
Rib: Narrow gold tinsel.
Wing: Mallard-flank fibers.
Hackle: Ginger.

March Brown
Hook: Dry fly, size 10.
Thread: Brown 8/0 (70 denier).
Tail: Brown.
Body: Light fox fur.
Wing: Lemon wood-duck fibers.
Hackle: Brown and grizzly.

Pink Lady
Hook: Dry fly, size 10.
Thread: Tan 8/0 (70 denier).
Tail: Dark ginger hackle fibers.
Body: Pink floss.
Rib: Narrow gold tinsel.
Wing: Mallard-flank fibers.
Hackle: Dark ginger.

happens by accident. When you wrap the hackle behind the base of the wing, you have a tendency to push it forward. Even Preston Jennings wrote about this problem. But I tie my wings straight up, and I try to maintain this appearance when I wrap the hackle."

With respect to proportions, would you say that the tail about equals the length of the hook?
"Yes, or maybe it's a little longer. Even Walt sometimes tied a longer tail. Maybe it's an anachronistic approach—I think a fly might float better if the tail is actually a little shorter—but that's the way you tie the tails on these classic flies."

It also looks like the wings are about equal to the length of the hook.
"That's what I shoot for. I have a little gauge that I use, but I don't get anal over it if they're a little longer. Dave Brandt, who also ties the Catskill classics, ties shorter wings, which is more in the style of Art Flick."

The bodies of your flies are so slender and delicate; they're just lovely.
"Again, Rube Cross tied very slender bodies on his flies. I know I'm repeating myself, but if you look at early Dette flies, they also tied very slender bodies. Over time, however—I think because their eyes were failing—the bodies on their flies got beefier. Their flies from the mid-1980s are very different from their flies from the mid-1930s."

Even the dubbed body on the Cross Special is very slender.
"That's the way Cross tied it. That's light fox fur. I use only natural furs."

And the wings are wood-duck fibers.
"You use a lot of wood duck when you tie these patterns. It's one of the most common wing materials."

What's the state of these patterns? Is there still an interest in tying them?
"I still fish with them. I don't know: Maybe it's like the guys who drive old cars."

In mid-May I'll be on my home waters of Grand Lake Stream. The landlocked salmon will be rising to hendricksons, and I'll be fishing with a classic hendrickson dry fly. I've tried all the new dry-fly patterns, but that Light Hendrickson catches just as many fish, and it's so beautiful to tie.
"Let me tell you a true story about the Light Hendrickson. You know they tied the body of that fly using urine-stained red fox belly fur. When I was a kid, there was this furrier in town, and the owner gave me all the fur scraps I wanted. I found all these pieces of urine-burned fox, and the owner said he would trade the fur for some flies. He got mad at me because I gave him all Royal Coachmen—I didn't want to waste all of that fox fur. He was really kind of pissed off. But, hey, you can't just walk into the store and ask the clerk for urine-stained fox fur!"

Henryville Special
Hook: Dry fly, size 10.
Thread: Black 8/0 (70 denier).
Body: Olive floss.
Body hackle: Dun.
Wing: Mallard-flank fibers and slips of gray mallard.
Hackle: Brown.
Note: The Henryville Special is a pattern of Pennsylvania origin, but Mike Valla included it because it became very popular in the Catskills.

Chapter 20

Vince Wilcox:
"Fly Fishing and Tying Are Just in the Blood"

COURTESY OF VINCE WILCOX

One of the attributes of an accomplished fly tyer is that all of his patterns share common characteristics. You can usually tell that the same individual made all of them. They all fell from the same vise. Flip through the chapters of this book, and you'll see what I mean: Each collection of flies seems like a separate family. Every tyer has his preferences with respect to materials selection and proportions and how polished—or bedraggled and buggy—his finished flies look.

Vince Wilcox is a talented fly designer, an experienced guide, and a fly-shop owner. He is also a leader in using the latest materials to create better, fish-catching flies. At first some of his flies look a little wacky, but Vince doesn't have time for nonsense; as a guide, he must get his clients into fish, and he creates new patterns that achieve this goal.

You'll quickly recognize Vince's patterns as new—you might even say "newfangled"—designs. But there is nothing newfangled about his approach to the tying table or to what he wants to get out of his flies. Each pattern is well thought out and thoroughly tested; many evolved after several years of use on the water. Vince boldly uses new ingredients in unusual ways, and the ability of his flies to catch trout makes them best-sellers in his shop and through a commercial fly-tying outfit called Idylwilde Flies.

Vince is another accomplished angler and tyer who has fished his entire life. He learned both to fish and to tie flies from his father, who was a guide in New York's Adirondack Mountains.

"I'm originally from Saranac Lake, New York, right in the heart of the Adirondacks," Vince said. "Oh, yeah.

Vince Wilcox: "Fly Fishing and Tying Are Just in the Blood"

My dad was a fly fisherman, a tyer, and even a guide. Fly fishing and tying are just in the blood."

Vince knocked around the country for a while and eventually landed in Colorado. That move led to professional fly fishing.

"A friend of mine got married in Colorado, and I went to his wedding. I wasn't living in New York at the time—someplace else—and I didn't like where I was. But I liked Colorado, so I bought a new truck, packed it up, and moved there in 1995. I sold cars at a dealership for a while—it was a pretty good job—but then I started Wiley's Flies and ran a couple of different fly shops. Although I've fished my whole life, I really didn't get heavy into the commercial side of fly tying until about the year 2000."

A lot of us experience the same ebbs and flows with our fishing as we mature. We spend a lot time on the water when we're young, but then we start intimate relationships, establish families, and begin careers. We have less time to fish, and our tackle spends more time in the closet. Fortunately for Vince, the move to Colorado led to tying flies professionally and creating his own patterns.

"I started tying the type of flies I sent to you when I moved to Colorado. I was trying some of the flies I was finding in the local shops, and I wasn't getting the results I wanted, so I decided to start developing my own patterns. That's what spurred it on: I just wanted to catch a few more fish."

Vince returned to New York State a few years ago, built a new fly shop on Rainbow Lake, and established a guiding business. Living in the heart of the Adirondacks gives him a lot of options for fishing.

"I fish the Au Sable, the Saranac, the St. Regis, and the Salmon Rivers. But I also fish a lot of smaller streams for native brook trout. Only about 3 percent of the original brook trout range still exists in the Adirondacks, and a lot of that water happens to be within minutes of my shop. I get a lot of clients who

Foam Sally
Hook: Mustad C53S, sizes 16 to 10.
Thread: Light cahill 8/0 (70 denier).
Egg sac: Red Midge Diamond Braid.
Dorsal underbody: Dark brown Midge Diamond Braid.
Abdomen: Orange Micro Tubing.
Underwing: Medium brown cul de canard.
Wing: Yellow Wilcox's Foam Wing Sheets or a substitute.
Thorax: Tan UV Ice Dub.
Hackle: Grizzly dyed March brown.
Antennae: Brown speckled Centipede legs.

really want to fish for wild trout in small streams, so that's where I take them."

Vince's fly-tying philosophy seems about as varied as his fishing. All materials are fair game, and he quickly discovers what will help him catch more trout.

"I'm not stuck on any one type of material. I'll try just about anything if I can find a good application for it."

You've developed your own style of tying, haven't you?
"Many of my flies are a little bit different. I hope the style comes through. But each and every one catches fish."

We spent time reviewing Vince's collection of flies. I wanted to hear his thoughts about material selection and learn more about how he develops a new pattern. Throughout the interview, he kept using the word *fun*.

"The Foam Sally is a fun bug. There are a lot of sally stonefly dry-fly imitations out there, but a lot of them don't float the way I think they should, and you can't see them on the water very well. You can get away with using a yellow Elk-Hair Caddis—that'll serve the purpose to imitate an adult yellow sally—but I wanted to do something different."

What's different about the Foam Sally?
"For one thing, my Foam Sally has an egg sac. And there's an underbody of Midge Diamond Braid, and the body is Micro Tubing. I use that tubing on a lot of my nymphs and dry flies. It's a great, easy-to-use material. It's also transparent—even the colored varieties are transparent—so you can change the color or specific shade of the body by changing the color of tying thread or underbody."

When do you use this pattern?
"The Foam Sally is perfect for fishing in June and July to imitate a real sally stonefly, and it also works as a

golden stonefly imitation. I also use it as an attractor pattern throughout the fishing season."

Vince develops a lot of original ways to apply materials to his flies. The wing on the Foam Sally is a good example of his creativity.

"Look at Foam Sally from the bottom. I glue a piece of mottled Thin Skin to a sheet of foam using spray adhesive, then I cut out the wing. When looking up at the fly, the fish sees a natural-looking imitation, while the angler easily spots the top of the bright yellow wing on the water."

Vince is also a master at finding unusual names for his patterns. For example, take the terrestrial imitation he calls Herbie.

"That's named for *Herbie the Love Bug*. You know: from the movie! I tied that fly for fishing the Green River in Utah. It's a beetle, it's a cricket, it's a cicada—I use it to match all that stuff. It's a great bug, and it floats like a cork."

The Glo-Ant looks similar to the Herbie.

"To be honest, I don't know which fly came first: the Glo-Ant or Herbie. The night fishing on the North Park lakes up around Walden, Colorado, was absolutely fantastic. I started playing with GloYarn—the yarn on that fly is the UNI brand of GloYarn. I used it to make big ants—like size 8—and charge them up with a UV light. You'd cast the fly, and it was easy to see on the water. In fact, the first time I used it—it was around eleven o'clock at night—I couldn't see the ant. I quickly realized I couldn't see it because a fish had taken it! Then the light bulb went off: Set the hook when you no longer see the glowing yarn."

Herbie
Hook: Dai Rikki 280, sizes 12 to 8.
Thread: Orange 6/0 (140 denier).
Abdomen 1: Orange Midge Diamond Braid.
Abdomen 2: 2-millimeter-thick black foam.
Wing: 2-millimeter-thick black foam.
Hackle: Black.
Thorax: Orange Ice Dub.
Legs: Orange/yellow speckled Centipede legs.
Indicator: Wilcox's Psychedelic Foamicator.

Glo-Ant
Hook: Mustad C49S, sizes 16 to 12.
Thread: Orange 8/0 (70 denier).
Abdomen 1: 2-millimeter-thick black foam.
Abdomen 2: Red Midge Diamond Braid.
Hackle: Black.
Wing: UNI GloYarn.
Indicator: Wilcox's Psychedelic Foamicator.

VW Hopper
Hook: Dai Rikki 280, sizes 14 to 8.
Thread: Orange 6/0 (140 denier).
Abdomen 1: 2-millimeter-thick brown foam.
Abdomen 2: Chartreuse Midge Diamond
　　Braid.
Hackle: Furnace.
Abdomen 3: 2-millimeter-thick golden
　　stone foam.
Underwing: Pearl Krystal Flash.
Wing: Yearling elk.
Thorax: Chartreuse Ice Dub.
Legs: Yellow speckled Centipede Legs.
Eyes: Yellow dome eyes.
Indicator: Wilcox's Psychedelic Foamicator.

Do you use terrestrials in the Adirondacks?
"I have a tendency to fish terrestrial patterns later in the season, but I use this fly throughout the year as a big indicator dry fly and fish it with a nymph."

Tell me about some of your other terrestrials.
"The VW Hopper is another fun bug."

It must be unsinkable.
"It is, but it sits flush with the surface of the water. You see the wing and indicator, but the lower part of the abdomen sits in the water. The Chernobyl Ant was the inspiration for the VW Hopper. I tried different materials for the wing, but they twisted the leader. It looks nutty, but I designed that fly over several seasons."

This fly has very prominent eyes. You don't see a lot of terrestrial patterns with eyes. Are they necessary?
"I fished versions with and without eyes, and the ones with eyes just caught more fish. The eyes are a prominent feature on a grasshopper, and they must be important to the trout. I certainly have better results with hopper patterns that have eyes."

Vince Wilcox: "Fly Fishing and Tying Are Just in the Blood"

What's the origin of the JC Special?

"The JC Special is named for John Clark, my fishing partner in Colorado. He's a really nice guy and one of the best friends you could have. John is in his seventies, and he was having trouble seeing my AC Caddis and asked me to add the Hi-Vis parachute. Then he said he'd like the fly better if I threw some rubber legs on it, so I said I'd make a fly just for him. This pattern has become one of my best-sellers, and Idylwilde Flies is also having good luck selling it. I think they sell about one hundred thousand a year!"

You add egg sacs to a lot of your flies. How do you make them?

"I usually use Midge Diamond Braid for the egg sac. I melt the end with a cauterizing tool; if you don't seal the end, the material will fray when fishing."

Caddisflies are important throughout the United States, and you have several terrific imitations.

"The AC Caddis is my 'Anything Caddis.' I sent you the pheasant-tail version, and the antennae are just a couple pieces of elk hair pulled forward. I fish that fly during a caddis hatch, but I use larger versions to match stonefly hatches, and smaller ones work great during blue-winged olive mayfly hatches. Just change the sizes and colors to match different insects. I tie it in sizes 12 to 18. When I was designing that fly, it was about the only one I was fishing. It just gets it done."

JC Special
Hook: Mustad C49S, sizes 16 to 10.
Thread: Black 8/0 (70 denier).
Shuck: Dark brown Midge Diamond Braid.
Abdomen: Midge Tubing.
Underwing: Pearl Krystal Flash.
Wing: Elk hair.
Post: Float Vis.
Hackle: Furnace.
Legs: Speckled brown Centipede Legs.
Thorax: Olive brown Ice Dub.

AC Caddis
Hook: Mustad C49S, sizes 18 to 14.
Thread: Black 8/0 (70 denier).
Shuck: Dark brown Midge Diamond Braid.
Abdomen: Micro Tubing.
Underwing: Pearl Krystal Flash.
Wing: Elk hair.
Post: Elk-hair butts from the wing.
Thorax: Olive brown Ice Dub.
Hackle: Furnace.
Antennae: Elk-hair fibers pulled forward
    before trimming the post.

Para-Variant
Hook: Mustad 94840, sizes 18 to 10.
Thread: Black 8/0 (70 denier).
Tail: White Kip tail.
Abdomen: Midge Tubing.
Post: Float Vis.
Thorax: Olive brown Ice Dub.
Hackle: Furnace.

Micro Mayfly
Hook: Mustad C49S, sizes 20 to 16.
Thread: Olive 8/0 (70 denier).
Eyes: Wilcox's Nymph Tubing, black.
Abdomen: Olive Midge Tubing with
   Microfibbets.
Wing: Plastic packing material or raffia.
Hackle: Grizzly.
Thorax: Olive UV Ice Dub.

Vince continued our discussion by describing some of his other dry flies.

"The Para-Variant was one of the first dry flies on which I used Micro Tubing. The theory is that if you don't squeeze the tubing too tight, it holds a pocket of air that helps the fly to float. It is also more durable than a quill, is easy to work with, and it doesn't absorb water.

"I also use Micro Tubing to make extended bodies for mayflies. You can buy packaged extended bodies, but they end up costing about fifty cents apiece. I needed to come up with a simple way to create extended bodies, and Micro Tubing is the perfect ingredient. Jut slip a couple of Microfibbets into a short piece of tubing, and then tie the tubing to the hook to create the abdomen. That's how I make the abdomen on the Micro Mayfly."

Does the Micro Mayfly catch fish?

"You bet it's effective. I've used patterns tied that way to catch the most discriminate trout, even spring-creek trout. When there's an olive hatch on, and you've tried half a dozen flies and not caught a fish, this pattern will often produce."

In addition to terrestrials and dry flies, Vince creates original nymphs and emergers. Once again, he uses the newest materials to develop better patterns. And his flies are always evolving.

"The Big Thompson Special is a dummied-down nymph that has changed a lot over the years," he said. "It's based on the Copper Bob or Copper John—whatever you want to call it—and the original Sawyer Pheasant-Tail Nymph. I just dummied it down, and it still worked. Later on I switched to Diamond Braid for the abdomen and fine pearl chenille for the thorax. In addition to catching trout, the Big Thompson Special is a wicked steelhead fly."

The Big Thompson Special has a marabou tail. Do you fish it with a dead drift, or do you give it some action?

"I do both. I start with a dead-drift presentation, but if I catch nothing in an area where I know there are fish, I'll make it swim. I'll start the action maybe two feet in front of the strike zone just to move the fly a little bit and catch the attention of the trout. But the Big Thompson Special also works well on the swing like a regular wet fly."

The Superman is a really unusual pattern. Are people accepting it?

"Oh, yes. It's been around for a while, and people know that it catches fish. Initially people thought it was a little off, but then it was featured in *Fly Tyer* magazine, guys started tying and fishing it, and it really took off. I also sent free samples to people who ordered online from my shop, and they found out that it's not a novelty fly. I started getting stories from anglers who tried it, and they all talked about how well it works."

Big Thompson Special (B.T. Special)
Hook: Mustad 3906B, sizes 16 to 12.
Bead: Copper, brass, or tungsten.
Thread: Black 8/0 (70 denier).
Tail: Grizzly marabou dyed tan.
Abdomen: Rust Midge Diamond Braid.
Thorax: Fine black pearl chenille.
Collar: Rusty brown Ice Dub.

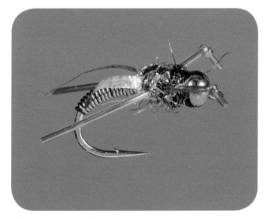

Pheasant-Tail Superman
Hook: Mustad C49S, sizes 18 to 10.
Bead: Gun metal, brass, or tungsten.
Thread: Black 8/0 (70 denier).
Abdomen: Copper brown Ultra Wire.
Wing: Fuchsia holographic tinsel.
Thorax: Olive brown Ice Dub.
Legs: Knotted Micro Tubing.
Wing case: Fuchsia holographic tinsel.
Collar: Black UV Ice Dub.

Olive Superman
Hook: Mustad C49S, sizes 18 to 10.
Bead: Gun metal, brass, or tungsten.
Thread: Olive 8/0 (70 denier).
Abdomen: Olive Ultra Wire.
Wing: Fuchsia holographic tinsel.
Thorax: Gray UV Ice Dub.
Legs and arms: Knotted olive Micro
   Tubing.
Wing case: Fuchsia holographic tinsel.
Collar: Black UV Ice Dub.

Ginger Snap
Hook: Mustad C49S, sizes 18 to 12.
Bead: Gun-metal brass.
Thread: Light cahill 8/0 (70 denier).
Abdomen: Light golden stone Micro Tubing.
Underbody: Dark brown Midge Diamond
   Braid.
Rib: Ginger Ultra Wire.
Hackle: Light ginger.
Thorax: Light yellow UV Ice Dub.
Collar: Olive brown Ice Dub.

Low Rider
Hook: Mustad C49S, size 18 or 16.
Thread: Olive 8/0 (140 denier).
Shuck: Olive Antron.
Abdomen: Olive Micro Tubing.
Underwing: Pearl Krystal Flash.
Wing: Medium dun cul de canard.
Post: Float Vis.
Hackle: Dun.
Thorax: Light olive UV Ice Dub.

"The Ginger Snap is also really catching on. It's a yellow sally or sulphur nymph. It's a great little subsurface fly tied with a dry-fly hackle. There's some logic behind making it that way. The folks at Idylwilde asked if I ran out of wet-fly hackle when I submitted this one, and I told them that I'd been experimenting with dry-fly feathers. Dry-fly hackle gives off small air bubbles in the water, and the fibers don't collapse around the fly. Also, even though it has a small tungsten bead head, if I grease the leader, I can fish the fly in the surface foam. I can fish the Ginger Snap deep when I have to, but I can also fish it just under the surface when the trout start to rise; there's no need to change flies."

We concluded our talk by discussing Vince's emerger imitation called the Low Rider.

"The Low Rider is a little emerging mayfly. It's sort of a Klinkhammer with a cul de canard trailing shuck; it's pretty dainty. It's available commercially in sizes 18 and 16, but I can tie that down to size 20. If I need to go larger or even smaller, I have some other flies I prefer, but within that size range—20 to 16—the Low Rider is perfect for matching an emerging mayfly. That's another pattern that is very visible on the water; the Low Rider is a good choice if you're having trouble seeing your fly, and you need to use a small pattern. It's my go-to small fly for anglers with failing eyesight."

Did you create these patterns in Colorado or New York?

"I designed most of those flies while living in Colorado, but this is what I try to explain to people: Fish are fish. I use the same flies from coast to coast. And I see this reflected in my online store. I have customers in every state except Hawaii and also in fourteen countries. Sizes and colors might change to match local conditions, but the same flies apply to most places. There is a lot of western influence in these flies, but these are the patterns I use in New York."

Chapter 21

Davy Wotton:
From Wales to the White River

We conclude our tour of the North American fly-fishing and fly-tying scene at the White River in Arkansas.

Fly fishers living in other parts of the country underestimate the quality of trout fishing in the South. From Appalachian freestone streams to a score of high-quality tailwater fisheries across the region, the South and lower Midwest offer thousands of miles of prime trout habitat. Couple this abundance of water with a moderate climate, and you can fly fish throughout the year. And southern tailwaters continue to produce the largest stream-bound trophy brown and rainbow trout in North America; the White River system has produced numerous fish weighing more than thirty pounds!

COURTESY OF DAVY WOTTON

Davy Wotton is a leading guide on the White River. Originally from Wales, Davy moved to the United States more than thirty years ago and moved to Arkansas to fish and guide. Davy has also participated in competitive fly fishing, and he has designed numerous fly-tying products.

Europe, especially the United Kingdom, has a rich fly-fishing tradition. Why, I wanted to know, did he decide to move to the United States?

"I first visited the United States in the 1970s to fish, and I came back and forth quite a lot. I've lived in Arkansas for twelve years, but I came to fish with Dave Whitlock before I moved here. I was living in Chicago before this; I needed to be there because I was constantly flying between the United States and the U.K. I had a factory manufacturing all the SLF Dubbing products.

Caddis Emerger
Hook: 2X-long wet-fly hooks, sizes 16 to 12.
Thread: Tan 6/0 (140 denier).
Bead: Gold.
Abdomen: Tan dubbing.
Wing: Tan Medallion Sheeting.
Legs: Teal-flank fibers.
Thorax: Tan Ice Dub.

Weighted Caddis Larva
Hook: Curved-shank caddis hook, sizes 18 to 14.
Thread: Gray 8/0 (70 denier).
Tail: Ostrich herl.
Abdomen: Cream or gray dubbing.
Back: Mallard.
Thorax: Dark gray dubbing.

"To be honest, the U.K. has some of the best trout fishing in the world, but it's more based toward still waters such as reservoirs and natural lakes. I did that for many years as a competitive fly fisherman, but I've always preferred fishing moving water. That was one of the main reasons I moved to the United States."

Do Americans appreciate the contributions the British and others made to fly fishing?

"You know, even though a lot of Americans don't realize it, a great deal of fly fishing was developed in the United Kingdom. They've been doing it over there for more than four hundred years. For me, being a professional fly tyer, which I started doing in the 1960s, my fundamental background was based on what occurred one hundred years ago in the United Kingdom. As a professional tyer, I was asked to make the patterns that were popular in that era, it didn't matter if they were dry flies or wet flies, or if they had been developed by Skues or Halford or whatever. That's what we were using at that time. A lot of Americans don't really understand the earlier origins of our sport."

Do you think European fishing methods are still influencing the North American fly-fishing scene?

"There's no doubt. In the last ten or fifteen years, there's been more of a European influence over here. Just look at the excitement over what they call 'European nymph-fishing methods and flies.' And today we have more means of communication where American and European anglers can exchange information."

You're well known for the SLF line of dubbing. What was involved in developing these materials?

"The majority of traditional U.K. flies incorporated seal fur for the bodies. There were a few exceptions with respect to natural furs, and those were primarily from species of animals that were indigenous to the United Kingdom, particularly hares, moles, and a few other animals. In the United States, you have a much wide population of animals that can provide furs for tying flies. In the United Kingdom, we were using mostly seal fur.

"When the use of seal fur was banned, we really didn't have an alternative. There is no other natural material that has the qualities of real seal fur, primarily its translucency and that fact that you can dye it any shade you wish. Close to where I lived, there was a factory that produced synthetic fibers that were being using in clothing. I knew a chemist who worked there, and he gave me some samples of the products they were making, and once I had those in my hands, I really got excited. I realized that if I could figure out different combinations of blends, and if it would dye easily, I could have a new fly-tying material."

So you were trying to imitate seal fur?

"Yes, that was it. If you take the term *SLF*, I originally marketed the product as 'Synthetic Living Fibre.' I produced a range of forty-eight standard colors, and then people asked for different combinations, and I ended up with 340 different blends. It took more than a year to figure out the blends to get the exact colors for the Dave Whitlock line of SLF Dubbing. You can't believe what's involved in doing this. Blending a custom dubbing in a coffee grinder is one thing, but figuring out how to produce a kilo of an exact color—and get the exact same color each and every time—is a whole different matter. And then I had to repeat this process to produce the Poul Jorgensen and Oliver Edwards Masterclass dubbing blends."

Whitetail Midge
Hook: Curved-shank emerger hook, sizes 20 to 14.
Thread: Black 8/0 (70 denier).
Bead: Silver.
Tail: White rabbit fur.
Abdomen: Tying thread.
Rib: Silver wire.
Thorax: Peacock Ice Dubbing.

Adult Midge
Hook: Regular dry-fly hook, sizes 22 to 18.
Thread: Black 8/0 (70 denier).
Body: Tying thread.
Rib: Silver wire.
Wing: Zelon.
Hackle: Light dun.

Badger and Silver Spider
Hook: Regular wet-fly hook, sizes 18 to 14.
Thread: Black 8/0 (70 denier).
Abdomen: Silver tinsel.
Rib: Silver wire.
Thorax: Tan UV Ice Dub.
Hackle: Grizzly hen.

Davy's Caddis
Hook: Regular dry-fly hook, size 16 or 14.
Thread: Tan 8/0 (70 denier).
Body: Hare's-ear dubbing.
Wing: Folded deer or elk hair.
Hackle: Dun, wrapped up a piece of thread
　　and folded over the top of the fly.

A lot of older fly recipes call for seal-fur dubbing. Which variety of SLF Dubbing best matches real seal fur?
"That's the SLF Standard dubbing. Real seal fur contains three different fibers: the long guard hairs, an underfur, and then an even finer underfur. SLF Standard dubbing is a combination of three different fibers, in the same quantities as real seal fur, to mimic the natural material. It took two years just to perfect that. Next, I had to work out how much dye to use to reproduce the exact shades I wanted. That's how much work goes into developing a really high-quality fly-tying product."

Today Wapsi Fly manufactures your line of dubbings, correct?
"Yes, I sold them my company, and they're still making the materials."

Let's talk about your guiding. How long have you been guiding on the White River?
"About eleven years. When I first moved here, I had to spend a lot of time learning the river, not so much about how to catch the fish, but I had to learn the river itself. There are one hundred miles in this river system."

What's the difference between fishing the White River and fishing other rivers across the country, especially free-flowing rivers?
"This tailwater system is a whole other wrinkle: Nothing remains constant. You can go from zero

water generation for several days, and then it can go to twenty-four thousand cfs. You have to learn how rising and falling water affects the fishery: what flies to use, when the fish will feed, and everything else. Understanding the impact of rising and falling water is the most important thing to successful fishing."

I used to live in Knoxville, Tennessee, and fished many of the tailwater rivers in that area. Southern tailwaters are extremely fertile, and the fish can grow quite large. But with quickly rising water levels, those rivers can also be quite dangerous. New anglers must be very safety conscious. Do you have any safety tips for anglers who are new to fishing the White and Norfork Rivers?

"The first thing is to never rely on the websites or Corps of Engineer phone numbers that give water-release schedules. This information can change at any time, and you should use it only as a guide."

From my experience, a wading angler should always have an exit strategy so he can leave the river quickly. By the time you're aware the water is rising, the path you took across the water might be too deep for wading, and the river will only continue rising. Surprisingly, once you get used to fishing one of these rivers, you can often hear and even see the water coming.

"You're absolutely correct: A wading angler should never, ever go to a place you can't quickly leave if the water starts rising."

HP Soft Hackle
Hook: Regular wet-fly hook, sizes 16 to 12.
Thread: Olive 8/0 (70 denier).
Tag: Tying thread.
Body: Hare's-ear dubbing or a substitute.
Rib: Round silver tinsel.
Hackle: Mottled hen or a substitute.

Skating Caddis
Hook: Regular dry-fly hook, sizes 16 to 12.
Thread: Brown 8/0 (70 denier).
Body: Orange dubbing.
Wing: Deer hair.
Legs: Teal-flank fibers.

White River Bugger
Hook: 4X-long streamer, sizes 6 to 2.
Bead: Gold.
Thread: Red 6/0 (140 denier).
Tail: Olive marabou and peacock herl.
Body: Olive chenille.
Hackle: Grizzly and olive grizzly.
Rib: Gold wire.

Sowbug
Hook: Curved-shank scud hook, size 16.
Thread: Gray 6/0 (140 denier).
Body: Gray dubbing.
Back: Dark gray Scud Back.

Your river is known for containing some huge trout.
"The White River has produced three world-record brown trout, and it holds a significant number of fish that weigh more than twenty pounds, which is exceptional for a river system. But this river also has an exceptional food base. A lot of issues affect how large fish will grow, including genetics and lifespan, but the availability of food is also critical. This river is full of smaller trout, sculpins, and crayfish. Big trout don't normally get that way eating midges and mayflies."

That's what surprised me with the flies you sent: You sent only one streamer, and the rest of the patterns are fairly small.
"Let me tell you an interesting thing about that. We'll catch the bulk of the big fish on small flies. One of the reasons is that they are vulnerable in low-water situations. First and foremost, they're in a small zone, but the river is also full of scuds and sowbugs.

"I caught my largest brown trout on the White River using a sowbug. The fish was just downstream of this little rivulet flowing into the river after high water had run for four or five days. Sowbugs were flowing into the river, and this fish was lying there and popping them off. That's when I caught him.

"Yes, a good number of large fish are caught using streamers, but the majority of big trout—I'm talking fish weighing between five and twelve pounds—are caught using small flies."

196

What are some of your other favorite big-fish flies?

"Worm patterns are also deadly for catching big brown trout on this river. When they run high water, the flow erodes the shoreline. The banks of this river are absolutely stuffed with worms, and they get washed into the water.

"Don't shy away from using small flies on this river, and be sure to have some imitations of aquatic worms. Those patterns are critical.

"You know, you can catch a lot of fish on the White River. Out west, even though you can catch a lot of trout, a good day might be twelve to twenty trout. On the White River, it's possible to catch eighty and even ninety fish in a day. The White River is a terrific fishery."

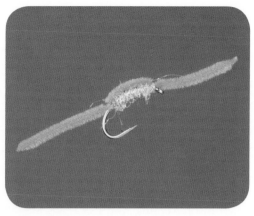

Prism Worm
Hook: Curved-shank scud hook, size 16.
Thread: Pink 8/0 (70 denier).
Underbody: Pink UV Dubbing.
Body: Pink chenille.

Bloodworm
Hook: Curved-shank scud hook, size 16.
Bead: Black.
Thread: Red 8/0 (70 denier).
Tail: Red craft fur.
Abdomen: Tying thread.
Thorax: Peacock Crystal Chenille or a
　　substitute.

Index

AC Caddis, 187
Adult Midge, 193
Amy's Ant, 51
anchor flies, 69
ants
  about: benefits of, 122; when to
    use, 114, 122, 149, 172
  Amy's Ant, 51
  Crimson Magma Ant, 123
  Glo-Ant, 185
  Gorilla Glue Ant, 152
  Mr. Rapidan Ant, 114
  Suspended Ant, 149
  Zelon Ant, 82
ARF flies. See Ritt, Al (flies)
Arkansas River, 50
Atherton No. 2, 176
Au Sable River, 116, 117, 118,
  123–24

Baby Boy Hopper, 35
Badger and Silver Spider, 194
Balanced Leech, 145
bamboo rods, 60
Bastian, Don, 13–20
  background/overview, 13–14,
    15–16
  commercial tying, 18
  first flies tied, 16–17
  home waters, 14–15
  photograph, 13
  professional guide, 14
  on *Trout* flies, 18–20
  tying all *Trout* flies, 18–19
  on tying wings, 17
  using duck/goose feathers, 17
  on wet-fly tying difficulty, 17
Bastian, Don (flies)
  Black and Silver, 15
  Black Gnat, 14

Blue Dun, 17
Gold-Ribbed Hare's Ear, 18
Governor, 13
Parmachene Belle, 16, 17, 20
Quill and Yellow, 17
Red Squirrel Picket Pin, 14
Royal Coachman, 15
Trout Fin, 20
Yellow Sally, 16, 17
Bead-Head Breadcrust, 55
Bead-Head Pheasant-Tail Nymph,
  159–60
Bead-Head Woolly Bugger, 105
Beatty, Al and Gretchen, 7–12
  background/overview, 7
  flies per year, 8
  fly-tying classes, 11–12
  home waters, 8–9
  photograph, 7
  tag-team approach, 7–8
Beatty, Al and Gretchen (flies)
  Bullethead Caddisfly, 9
  Bullethead Mayfly, 9
  Double Magic Royal Double
    Wing, 8
  Gray Wulff, 7
  H&L Variant, 10
  Muddle Mayfly, 10
  Regular Humpy, 12
  Royal Humpy, 12
  Royal Trude, 12
  Royal Wulff, 11
  Scuddle Muddle, 10–11
beetles
  about: when to use, 149, 172
  Double-Sided Beetle, 148
  Fat-Head Beetle, 122
  Murray's Fly Beetle, 113
  Suspended Beetle, 149
Big Thompson Special, 188–89

Black and Silver, 15
Black Ghost, 163
Black Gnat, 14
Black Holographic Chironomid
  Pupa, 25
Black Miracle Stonefly Nymph, 111
Black Rubber-Legged Biot
  Bug, 150
bloodworms
  Bloodworm, 197
  Rubber-Legged Bloodworm, 28
Blue Dun, 17
Blue Poison Tung, 39
Blue Ridge. See Murray, Harry
Blue River, 49
boat fishing, 37, 103, 138–39, 148,
  157, 158
boatman imitation, 29–30
Boise River, 8–9
Booby (Las Vegas Booby Leech),
  28–29
Bow River, 135, 137
British Columbia, 21–22, 24,
  27, 143
Brown Drakes, 93, 121–22
Brown X-Caddis, 100
Bullethead Caddisfly, 9
Bullethead Mayfly, 9

caddisfly imitations
  about: hatches and, 51, 70,
    77, 138, 154, 158–59, 160,
    168–69, 170, 187; larvae,
    103, 142
  AC Caddis, 187
  ARF Trailing Bubble Harey
    Caddis (Peacock), 130
  ARF Trailing Bubble Harey
    Caddis (Tan), 129
  Brown X-Caddis, 100

Index

Caddis Emerger, 192
Caddis Larva, 103
Caddistrophic Pupa, 36–37
CDC Caddis Pupa, 42
CDC Grannom Caddisfly, 168–69
Davy's Caddis, 194
Egg-Laying Caddis, 81–82
Elk-Hair Caddis, 57
Everfloat Caddis Emerger, 154
Gray Caddisfly, 160
Hi-Viz Caddisfly, 169
Iced Cased Caddis, 70
Improved Sunken Stone, 77
Iris Caddis, 76–77
JC Special, 187
Mercury Cased Caddis, 51
Missing Link Caddis, 94–96
Mr. Rapidan Delta-Wing Caddis, 110
Mugly Caddis, 35–36
October Caddis Soft Hackle, 169–70
Olive CDC Caddis, 159
Olive Magic Caddis Pupa, 115
Opal and Elk Caddis, 120
Parachute Caddis, 58
Peaking Caddis, 165–66
Pisco's Caddis Pupa, 45
Puterbaugh Caddis, 49
Stillwater Caddis Emerger, 25
Stillwater Caddis Pupa, 23
Tan X-Caddis, 161
TCO's Tan Adult Caddis, 44
Ultra Zug Free-Living Caddis, 150, 151
Weighted Caddis Larva, 192
West Branch Caddis, 103
X2 Caddis, 79
Cahill Quill, 175
Canadian prairies. See Rowley, Philip

Catskill Sulphur Spinner, 167–68
Catskill traditions
    book on classic patterns, 174–75
    Dettes and, 175–77, 178, 179
    richness of, 174
CDC Caddis Pupa, 42
CDC Grannom Caddisfly, 168–69
CDC Scud, 145
Chan, Brian, 21–30
    background/overview, 21–22
    on Booby imitation, 28–29
    on chironomids, 25–28
    photograph, 21
    Superfly International and, 135, 136
    See also Kamloops region
Chan, Brian (flies)
    Black Holographic Chironomid Pupa, 25
    Booby (Las Vegas Booby Leech), 28–29
    Chan's Chironomid, 27
    Lady McConnell, 28
    Red-Butt Black and Red Chironomid Pupa, 26
    Rubber-Legged Bloodworm, 28
    Ruby-Eyed Leech, 29
    Stillwater Boatman, 29–30
    Stillwater Caddis Emerger, 25
    Stillwater Caddis Pupa, 23
Chan's Chironomid, 27
Chaos Hopper, 83
Charlie Boy Hopper, 34–35
Charlie's flies. See Craven, Charlie (flies)
Chicken, The, 104, 105–6
chironomid imitations
    about: color of, 27; fishing with, 25–27, 144–45; getting no strikes, 26–27; importance of, 145; size of, 28

Black Holographic Chironomid Pupa, 25
Chan's Chironomid, 27
Jumbo Juju Chironomid, 33
Red-Butt Black and Red Chironomid Pupa, 26
Chromie, 144
Clark, John, 187
Clear Water Pupa, 136
Colorado home waters, 32, 49. See also Rocky Mountain National Park
Colorado River, 32, 49
competitive fishing
    answering objections to, 47
    camaraderie among teams, 46
    driving new development, 47–48
    European nymph-fishing methods and, 45
    George Daniel and, 40–43
    nature of, 43
    nymphs and, 44–45, 47
    strike indicators and, 45
    tying flies and, 46
    youth team, 45–46
Connecticut River (upper). See Savard, Lisa
Convertible Damselfly, 147–48
Copper Bead Poxyback Baetis, 90
Craven, Charlie, 31–39
    background/overview, 31–32
    commercial tying, 32
    home waters, 32
    photograph, 31
    on stillwater fishing, 32–33
    Umpqua Feather Merchants and, 33, 35
Craven, Charlie (flies)
    Baby Boy Hopper, 35
    Blue Poison Tung, 39
    Caddistrophic Pupa, 36–37
    Charlie Boy Hopper, 34–35

Index

Charlie's Mole Fly, 37
Charlie's Mysis, 38
Craven's Jujubaetis, 39
Craven's Soft-Hackle
    Emerger, 36
Go to Hell Variant, 32
Jumbo Juju Chironomid, 33
Mugly Caddis, 35–36
Two-Bit Hooker, 38–39
crayfish (crawfish) patterns, 132
    about: using for larger fish,
        119–20
    Mercer's Poxyback Crayfish, 86
    Ritt's Fighting Crawfish
        (Orange or Dirty Tan),
        132–33
Crimson Magma Ant, 123
Cross, Rube, 178, 180
Cross Special, 177
Crystal Killer, 42
Crystal Stone, 117

damselfly imitations
    about: dry fly, 133–34; hatches,
        134, 138; using, 133–34
    ARF Hi-Vis Damsel, 133
    ARF SlimFlash Damsel, 133
    Convertible Damselfly, 147–48
    Damselfly Nymph, 63
    Grizzly Damsel, 142
    Pearly Damsel, 141
    Swamp Monster, 148
Daniel, George, 40–48
    background/overview, 40–41
    on choosing flies for new water,
        43–44
    coaching youth fly-fishing team,
        45–46
    on competitive fishing, 41–43,
        46–47
    on competitors tying flies, 46
    on nymph fishing, 44–45

photograph, 40
on strike indicators, 45
Daniel, George (flies)
    CDC Caddis Pupa, 42
    Crystal Killer, 42
    Egan's Iron Lotus, 44
    GD's Czech Catnip, 41
    Hard-Bod Sow Bug, 41
    Pisco's Caddis Pupa, 45
    PT Cruncher, 43
    TCO's Tan Adult Caddis, 44
    William's Biot Nymph, 43
Dark Sulphur Nymph, 171
Dark Tungsten-Bead Soft
    Hackle, 116
Datum Glo-Brite, 69
Dave's Hopper, 60
Davy's Caddis, 194
Dette, Walt and Winnie, 175–77,
    178, 179
Devil's Doorman, ARF, 128–29
Dorsey, Pat, 49–55
    background/overview, 49
    on Colorado seasons, 49, 50, 51
    on glass beads, 52
    on hatches, 50
    home waters, 49
    photograph, 49
    on river characteristics, 49–51
    on using Tyvek, 54
Dorsey, Pat (flies)
    Amy's Ant, 51
    Bead-Head Breadcrust, 55
    Dorsey's Golden Stonefly, 54
    Dorsey's Hydropsyche, 51
    Dorsey's Medallion Midge, 52
    Matthew's Olive Sparkle
        Dun, 50
    Mercury Blood Midge, 52
    Paper Tiger, 54
    Puterbaugh Caddis, 49
    Sparkle Wing RS2, 52–53

Top Secret Midge, 50
UV Scud (Orange), 53
Double Magic Royal Double
    Wing, 8
Double-Sided Beetle, 148
Draggin, 140
dragonfly imitations
    about: making nymphs, 139–41;
        tying, 140–41
    Draggin, 140
    Grizzly Dragon, 139–41
Drake Foam Emerger, 78
drogues, 138–39
droppers, 27, 69, 71, 129, 159

Eagle River, 32
Egan's Iron Lotus, 44
Egg-Laying Caddis, 81–82
Elk-Hair Caddis, 57
Everything Emerger, 151

Fan Wing Coachman, 174
Fat-Head Beetle, 122
Favorite Flies (Marbury), 19
Fish Skulls, 131
Fishing Small Streams (Gierach),
    62–63
Flat-Water Spent Spinner
    (Sulphur), 168
Flavilinea, 60
Flight's Fancy, 178
Flush Floater Golden Stone, 95
With Fly, Plug, and Bait
    (Bergman), 18
Fly Beetle, 113
Fly Bugger, 119
Fly Craft Fullback-Flashback, 145
Fly Shop, 84–86
Fly Tyer magazine, 5, 7, 11, 57, 59,
    69, 146, 189
Foam Sally, 184–85
François, 68

Freeze Up event, 102–3

GD's Czech Catnip, 41
Gen-X Soft Hackle (Chartreuse), ARF, 128
Gen-X Soft Hackle (Copper), ARF, 127
Gen-X Soft Hackle (Hot Orange), ARF, 128
Giant Nature Stonefly Nymph, 80–81
Gierach, John, 56–63
  background/overview, 56–59
  on bamboo rods, 60
  coming to fly fishing, 58
  commercial tying, 57, 58
  photograph, 56
  writing and publications, 56, 57, 59–60, 61–63
Gierach, John (flies)
  Damselfly Nymph, 63
  Dave's Hopper, 60
  Elk-Hair Caddis, 57
  Flavilinea, 60
  Hare's-Ear Parachute, 59
  Hare's-Ear Soft Hackle, 61
  Hare's-Ear Stonefly Nymph, 62
  Olive Midge Emerger, 62
  Parachute Caddis, 58
  Pheasant-Tail Nymph, 59
gills on flies, 91–92
Ginger Snap, 190
glass beads, 52
Glo-Ant, 185
gnats
  Black Gnat, 14
  Griffith's Gnat, 105
Go to Hell Variant, 32
Gold Bead Poxyback PMD Nymph, 90
Golden Pheasant-Tail Soft Hackle, 169

Gold-Ribbed Hare's Ear, 18
Good Flies (Gierach), 61
Gorilla Glue Ant, 152
Gorilla Glue applications, 152–53
Governor, 13
Gray Caddisfly, 160
Gray Wulff, 7
Green Copper John, 104
Green River, 146, 185
Griffith's Gnat, 105
Grizzly Damsel, 142
Grizzly Dragon, 139–41
Grizzly Sedge Pupa, 142–43

H&L Variant, 10
hackle tips, 177–79, 180
Hard-Bod Sow Bug, 41
Hare and Copper, 72
Hare's-Ear Parachute, 59
Hare's-Ear Soft Hackle, 61
Hare's-Ear Stonefly Nymph, 62
Harey Caddis (Peacock), ARF Trailing Bubble, 130
Harey Caddis (Tan), ARF Trailing Bubble, 129
Harey Yellow Stone, ARF Trailing, 129–30
hatches
  Baetis, 50
  caddisfly, 51, 70, 77, 138, 154, 158–59, 160, 168–69, 170, 187
  damselfly, 134, 138
  Hex, 117–19, 120
  mayfly, 109, 117, 138, 167. See also Hex
  midge, 50, 52, 80, 171–72
  quill Gordon, 108–9, 110
  stonefly, 9, 114, 117
  Trico, 118
Hatching Pupa, 162
Henryville Special, 181
Herbie, 185

Herl May-Flashback, 135
Hex Dun, 105
Hi-Vis Damsel, 133
Hi-Viz Caddisfly, 169
Hi-Viz Klinkhammer, 73
Horse Hair Midge, 172
hot spots, 47, 68–69, 72, 121
Housefly, 112
How to Tie Flies (Gregg), 15, 19
HP Soft Hackle, 195
Humpies, 12
Humpulator, ARF, 129

I. C. Spinner, 118
Iced Cased Caddis, 70
Idaho home waters, 8
Improved Sunken Stone, 77
Inchworm, 113–14
Internet, fishing and, 97–98, 99–102
Iris Caddis, 76–77
Iron Lotus, 44
Irresistible, 161

Jasper, Aaron, 64–74
  on anchor flies, 70
  background/overview, 64–66
  on Datum Glo-Brite, 69
  on European nymph-fishing techniques, 66–67, 73
  guiding, 65–66
  on hot spots, 68–69
  learning fly-tying, 65
  on nymph and larvae imitations, 67–68, 69
  photograph, 64
  teaching new methods, 73
  on tying in colors, 71
  on wet flies with nymphs, 73–74
Jasper, Aaron (flies)
  François, 68
  Hare and Copper, 72
  Hi-Viz Klinkhammer, 73

Iced Cased Caddis, 70
Last Resort, 72
Leduc's Spiky Squirrel, 71
Pineapple Express, 69
Polish Woven Nymph, 70
Rabbit's Foot BWO, 71
Rocked Out, 66
Straight Up, 66
365 Nymph, 67
Triple Threat, 69
265 Nymph, 65
WMD, 68
J-Bug Nymph, 171
JC Special, 187
Jujubaetis, 39
Jumbo Juju Chironomid, 33
Just Fishing (Bergman), 18

Kamloops region, 21–30
  fishing opportunities, 21–23, 24
  lakes in, 23–24
  source of stocked fish, 24
  stocking fish in, 22–23, 24
  using chironomids in, 25–28
  See also Chan, Brian
Klinkhammers, 73, 170. *See also*
  Low Rider

Lady McConnell, 28
larvae
  about: caddis, 103, 142; hot spots
    on patterns, 68–69; increasing
    catch with, 67; size of, 69
  Caddis Larva, 103
  Weighted Caddis Larva, 192
  See also nymphs
Las Vegas Booby Leech, 28–29
Last Resort, 72
Leduc's Spiky Squirrel, 71
leech imitations
  Balanced Leech, 145
  Las Vegas Booby Leech, 28–29

Ruby-Eyed Leech, 29
Light Hendrickson, 181
lightning bug, 122
Lipstick Minnow, 153
literature, fly-fishing, 61–62
Low Rider, 190

Magog Smelt, 163–64
March Brown, 179
Matthews, Craig, 75–83
  background/overview, 75–76
  Blue Ribbon Flies shop, 82
  conservation efforts, 82–83
  photograph, 75
  on Zelon, 79–80
Matthews, Craig (flies)
  Chaos Hopper, 83
  Drake Foam Emerger, 78
  Egg-Laying Caddis, 81–82
  Giant Nature Stonefly Nymph,
    80–81
  Improved Sunken Stone, 77
  Iris Caddis, 76–77
  PMD Dun, 78
  PMD Foam Emerger, 78
  PMD Foam Spinner, 79
  Rusty Foam Spinner, 83
  Sunken Stone, 77
  X2 Caddis, 79
  Zelon Ant, 82
  Zelon Midge, 80
Matthew's Olive Sparkle Dun, 50
mayfly imitations
  about: hatches and, 109, 117,
    138, 167
  Catskill Sulphur Spinner,
    167–68
  Craven's Jujubaetis, 39
  Hex Dun, 105
  Low Rider, 190
  Micro Mayfly, 188
  Profile Spinner, Hexagenia, 88

Purple Soft Hackle, 167
Ruby Micro Mayfly Nymph, 91
Sparkle Wing RS2, 52–53
Sulphur Klinkhammer, 170
  See also chironomid imitations
McKay, Kevin, 97–106
  background/overview, 97–99
  Freeze Up event, 102–3
  guiding, 98, 100, 103
  Internet, website and, 97–98,
    99–102
  photograph, 97
  on spring fishing and flies,
    103–4
McKay, Kevin (flies)
  Bead-Head Woolly Bugger, 105
  Brown X-Caddis, 100
  Caddis Larva, 103
  The Chicken, 104, 105–6
  Green Copper John, 104
  Griffith's Gnat, 105
  Hex Dun, 105
  McKay Special, 99
  Secret Stone Nymph, 104, 105
  West Branch Caddis, 103
Mercer, Mike, 84–96
  background/overview, 84
  designing new patterns, 86–87,
    90–91
  Fly Shop and, 84–86
  on gills and legs, 91–92
  guiding, 87–88
  on nymph imitation, 88–89
  on parachutes, 92–94
  photograph, 84
  on Poxyback Nymphs, 88–89
  Umpqua Feather Merchants
    and, 96
Mercer, Mike (flies)
  Copper Bead Poxyback
    Baetis, 90
  Flush Floater Golden Stone, 95

Index

Flush Floater Salmonfly, 95
Gold Bead Poxyback PMD
    Nymph, 90
Mercer's PMD Trigger
    Nymph, 88
Mercer's Poxyback Crayfish, 86
Missing Link Caddis, 94–96
Poxyback Biot Golden Stone, 89
Poxyback Callibaetis Nymph, 87
Poxyback Green Drake
    Nymph, 84
Poxyback PMD Nymph, 89
Profile Spinner, Brown Drake, 93
Profile Spinner, BWO, 93
Profile Spinner, Foam Body
    Green Drake, 92
Profile Spinner, Hexagenia, 88
Profile Spinner, Pale Morning
    Dun, 92
Psycho Prince Nymph, 85
Ruby Micro Mayfly Nymph, 91
Mercury Blood Midge, 52
Mercury Cased Caddis, 51
Michigan fishing. See Potter,
    Dennis
Micro Mayfly, 188
midge imitations
    about: hatches and, 50, 52, 80,
        171–72; importance of, 52;
        winter fishing and, 80
    Adult Midge, 193
    ARF Midge Adult, 130
    ARF Midge Pupa, 126, 130
    Dorsey's Medallion Midge, 52
    Horse Hair Midge, 172
    Lady McConnell, 28
    Mercury Blood Midge, 52
    Mighty Midge, 81
    Olive Midge Emerger, 62
    Top Secret Midge, 50
    Whitetail Midge, 193
    Zelon Midge, 80

Mighty Midge, 81
minnows
    Lipstick Minnow, 153
    Waste Troll Minnow, 143–44
Missing Link Caddis, 94–96
Mole Fly, 37
moth, Potter's Moth, 122
Mr. Rapidan Ant, 114
Mr. Rapidan Bead-Head
    Nymph, 111
Mr. Rapidan Delta-Wing
    Caddis, 110
Muddle Mayfly, 10
Mugly Caddis, 35–36
Murray, Harry, 107–15
    background/overview, 107
    fishing Blue Ridge,
        Appalachians, 107, 108–10,
        111–15
    fly shop ownership, 107–8
    Mr. Rapidan patterns, 110
    photograph, 107
    on stoneflies, 112–13, 114
    on terrestrial patterns, 112, 113,
        114–15
Murray, Harry (flies)
    Black Miracle Stonefly
        Nymph, 111
    Mr. Rapidan Ant, 114
    Mr. Rapidan Bead-Head
        Nymph, 111
    Mr. Rapidan Delta-Wing
        Caddis, 110
    Murray's Fly Beetle, 113
    Murray's Housefly, 112
    Murray's Inchworm, 113–14
    Murray's Little Black Stonefly,
        112, 113
    Murray's Little Bronze
        Stonefly, 113
    Murray's Sulphur Dry Fly, 109
    Olive Magic Caddis Pupa, 115

Yellow Miracle Stonefly
    Nymph, 114
mysis shrimp imitation, 38

New Fly Fisher, The, 135, 139
New Hampshire. See Savard, Lisa
nymphs
    about: competitive fishing and,
        44–45, 47; European methods,
        45, 64, 66–67, 73, 192; extra-
        long rods for, 72; hot spots on
        patterns, 68–69; increasing
        catch with, 67; keys to imitat-
        ing, 88; prime times to use,
        111; size of, 69; wet flies in
        combination with, 73–74
    Bead-Head Pheasant-Tail
        Nymph, 159–60
    Big Thompson Special, 188–89
    Black Miracle Stonefly
        Nymph, 111
    Damselfly Nymph, 63
    Dark Sulphur Nymph, 171
    Giant Nature Stonefly Nymph,
        80–81
    Ginger Snap, 190
    Gold Bead Poxyback PMD
        Nymph, 90
    Grizzly Dragon, 139–41
    Hare's-Ear Stonefly Nymph, 62
    J-Bug Nymph, 171
    Mercer's PMD Trigger
        Nymph, 88
    Mr. Rapidan Bead-Head
        Nymph, 111
    Pheasant-Tail Nymph, 59
    Polish Woven Nymph, 70
    Poxyback Callibaetis Nymph, 87
    Poxyback Green Drake
        Nymph, 84
    Poxyback PMD Nymph, 89
    Prince Nymph, 159, 160

Psycho Prince Nymph, 85
Ruby Micro Mayfly Nymph, 91
Secret Stone Nymph, 104, 105
365 Nymph, 67
265 Nymph, 65
William's Biot Nymph, 43
Yellow Miracle Stonefly
    Nymph, 114
    See also larvae

October Caddis Soft Hackle,
    169–70
Olive CDC Caddis, 159
Olive Magic Caddis Pupa, 115
Olive Midge Emerger, 62
Olive Rubber-Legged Biot
    Bug, 150
Olive Superman, 189
opal tinsel, 120–21, 123
Opal Wulff, 121

Paper Tiger, 54
parachute patterns
    about: tails and wings, 93; tying,
        122; using, 92–94
    Hare's-Ear Parachute, 59
    Parachute Adams, 8
    Parachute Caddis, 58
    Potter's Brown Drake, 121–22
Para-Variant, 188
Parmachene Belle, 16, 17, 20
Peaking Caddis, 165–66
Pearly Damsel, 141
Pennsylvania home waters, 14–15
Pheasant-Tail Nymph, 59
Pheasant-Tail Superman, 189
pinch wrap, 17–18
Pineapple Express, 69
Pink Lady, 180
Pisco's Caddis Pupa, 45
PMD Dun, 78
PMD Foam Emerger, 78

PMD Foam Spinner, 79
Polish Woven Nymph, 70
Potter, Dennis, 116–24
    background/overview, 116
    on crayfish patterns, 119–20
    on hatches, 117–19
    on Michigan fishing season,
        116–17
    photograph, 116
    River House Fly Company,
        116, 124
    using opal tinsel, 120–21, 123
    using other new materials, 121
    video presentations events,
        123–24
Potter, Dennis (flies)
    Crimson Magma Ant, 123
    Crystal Stone, 117
    Dark Tungsten-Bead Soft
        Hackle, 116
    Fat-Head Beetle, 122
    Fly Bugger, 119
    I. C. Spinner, 118
    Opal and Elk Caddis, 120
    Opal Wulff, 121
    Potter's Brown Drake, 121–22
    Potter's Moth, 122
    Rivergod Emerger, Slate Wing
        Olive, 117
    Rubber Leg Lightning
        Bug, 122
Poxyback Biot Golden Stone, 89
Poxyback Callibaetis Nymph, 87
Poxyback Green Drake
    Nymph, 84
Poxyback PMD Nymph, 89
Prince Nymph, 159, 160
Prism Worm, 197
Profile Spinner, Brown Drake, 93
Profile Spinner, BWO, 93
Profile Spinner, Foam Body Green
    Drake, 92

Profile Spinner, Hexagenia, 88
Profile Spinner, Pale Morning
    Dun, 92
Psycho Prince Nymph, 85
PT Cruncher, 43
pupae
    ARF Midge Pupa, 126, 130
    Black Holographic Chironomid
        Pupa, 25
    Caddistrophic Pupa, 36–37
    CDC Caddis Pupa, 42
    Clear Water Pupa, 136
    Grizzly Sedge Pupa, 142–43
    Hatching Pupa, 162
    Olive Magic Caddis
        Pupa, 115
    Pisco's Caddis Pupa, 45
    Red-Butt Black and Red
        Chironomid Pupa, 26
    Stillwater Caddis Pupa, 23
Purple Soft Hackle, 167
Puterbaugh Caddis, 49
Putt's Favorite, 164

Queen of the Waters, 179
Quill and Yellow, 17
Quill Gordon, 175

Rabbit's Foot BWO, 71
Red Back Pheasant, 137
Red Copper John, 162
Red Squirrel Picket Pin, 14
Red-Butt Black and Red
    Chironomid Pupa, 26
Regular Humpy, 12
Ritt, Al, 125–34
    background/overview, 125
    color preferences, 127–28
    photograph, 125
    on Rocky Mountain National
        Park, 125–27
    on using Fish Skulls, 131

Ritt, Al (flies)
AFR Trailing Bubble Harey Yellow Stone, 129
ARF Devil's Doorman, 128–29
ARF Gen-X Soft Hackle (Chartreuse), 128
ARF Gen-X Soft Hackle (Copper), 127
ARF Gen-X Soft Hackle (Hot Orange), 128
ARF Hi-Vis Damsel, 133
ARF Humpulator, 129
ARF Midge Adult, 130
ARF Midge Pupa, 126
ARF Skulled Electric Zonker, 131
ARF SlimFlash Damsel, 133
ARF Trailing Bubble Harey Caddis (Peacock), 130
ARF Trailing Bubble Harey Caddis (Tan), 129
ARF Trailing Harey Yellow Stone, 129–30
ARF Tung-Syn Pheasant-Tail Soft, 127
Ritt's Fighting Crawfish (Orange or Dirty Tan), 132–33
River House Fly Company, 116, 124
Rivergod Emerger, Slate Wing Olive, 117
Rocked Out, 66
Rocky Mountain National Park, 125–27. See also Ritt, Al
rods
bamboo, 60
short, 111, 172
specialized, 72–73
Rowley, Philip, 135–45
on Alberta fishing, 135
background/overview, 135
on chironomids, 144–45
color preferences, 142

designing line of materials, 136
on fishing season, 138
on hatches, 138
photograph, 135
on stillwater fishing, 136–38
subsurface-pattern focus, 144
Superfly International and, 135, 136
Rowley, Philip (flies)
Balanced Leech, 145
CDC Scud, 145
Chromie, 144
Clear Water Pupa, 136
Draggin, 140
Fly Craft Fullback-Flashback, 145
Grizzly Damsel, 142
Grizzly Dragon, 139–41
Grizzly Sedge Pupa, 142–43
Herl May-Flashback, 135
Pearly Damsel, 141
Red Back Pheasant, 137
Stillwater Dun, 144
Waste Troll Minnow, 143–44
Royal Coachman, 15
Royal Humpy, 12
Royal Trude, 12
Royal Wulff, 11, 37, 113
Rubber Leg Lightning Bug, 122
Rubber-Legged Biot Bugs, 150
Rubber-Legged Bloodworm, 28
Ruby Micro Mayfly Nymph, 91
Ruby-Eyed Leech, 29
Rusty Foam Spinner, 83

salmonfly imitations, 80, 95
Salt River, 146
Sanchez, Scott, 146–55
on ants and beetles, 149
background/overview, 146
dry vs. subsurface preference, 154
on fishing season, 155

on Gorilla Glue applications, 152–53
guiding, 146
photograph, 146
rivers/streams fishing, 146–47
small-stream fly recommendation, 147
stillwater fishing, 148
time to design flies, 152
on tying with biot bodies, 150
Sanchez, Scott (flies)
Black Rubber-Legged Biot Bug, 150
Convertible Damselfly, 147–48
Double-Sided Beetle, 148–49
Everfloat Caddis Emerger, 154
Everything Emerger, 151
Gorilla Glue Ant, 152
Lipstick Minnow, 153
Olive Rubber-Legged Biot Bug, 150
Suspended Ant, 149
Suspended Beetle, 149
Swamp Monster, 148
Ultra Zug Free-Living Caddis, 150, 151
Savard, Lisa, 156–64
background/overview, 156
on Connecticut River hatches, 160
favorite nymph patterns, 159
on fishing season, 164
guiding, 156–57
photograph, 156
on size of trout, 159
on smelt, 163–64
on stillwater fishing, 158–59
on stoneflies, 160–61
using drift boats, 157, 158
using droppers, 159
on wade-fishing areas, 157
on water flows, 157–58

Savard, Lisa (flies)
  Bead-Head Pheasant-Tail
    Nymph, 159–60
  Black Ghost, 163
  Gray Caddisfly, 160
  Hatching Pupa, 162
  Irresistible, 161
  Magog Smelt, 163–64
  Olive CDC Caddis, 159
  Prince Nymph, 159, 160
  Putt's Favorite, 164
  Red Copper John, 162
  Stimulator, 160–61
  Tan X-Caddis, 161
  Woolly Bomber, 163
Scuddle Muddle, 10–11
scuds
  about: fishing with, 53
  CDC Scud, 145
  UV Scud (Orange), 53
Secret Stone Nymph, 104, 105
Shenandoah Valley. *See* Murray,
  Harry
Skating Caddis, 195
Skulled Electric Zonker,
  ARF, 131
SLF dubbing, about, 193–94
smelt, 163–64
Snake River, 146, 149, 155
South Platte River, 32, 49
sowbugs
  Hard-Bod Sow Bug, 41
  Sowbug, 196
Sparkle Wing RS2, 52–53
Stillwater Boatman, 29–30
Stillwater Caddis Emerger, 25
Stillwater Caddis Pupa, 23
Stillwater Dun, 144
stillwater fishing, 32–33, 34,
  133, 136–38, 145, 148,
  158–59
Stimulator, 160–61

stonefly imitations
  about: hatches and, 9, 114;
    importance of, 114
  AFR Trailing Bubble Harey
    Yellow Stone, 129
  ARF Trailing Harey Yellow
    Stone, 129–30
  Black Miracle Stonefly
    Nymph, 111
  Bullethead flies, 9
  Charlie Boy Hopper, 34–35
  Dorsey's Golden Stonefly, 54
  Flush Floater Golden Stone, 95
  Foam Sally, 184–85
  Giant Nature Stonefly Nymph,
    80–81
  Hare's-Ear Stonefly Nymph, 62
  Murray's Little Black Stonefly,
    112, 113
  Murray's Little Bronze
    Stonefly, 113
  for nymph fish, 104
  Paper Tiger, 54
  Poxyback Biot Golden Stone, 89
  Secret Stone Nymph, 104, 105
  Stimulator, 160–61
  Sunken Stone, 77
  Yellow Miracle Stonefly
    Nymph, 114
Straight Up, 66
strike indicators, 25–26, 27, 29,
  45, 71, 73
Stroup, Eric, 165–73
  background/overview, 165
  equipment tips, 172
  favorite summertime
    patterns, 172
  on fishing season, 170–71
  guide locations, 170
  influences on, 173
  photograph, 165
  on winter fishing, 170–71

Stroup, Eric (flies)
  Catskill Sulphur Spinner,
    167–68
  CDC Grannom Caddisfly,
    168–69
  Dark Sulphur Nymph, 171
  Flat-Water Spent Spinner
    (Sulphur), 168
  Golden Pheasant-Tail Soft
    Hackle, 169
  Hi-Viz Caddisfly, 169
  Horse Hair Midge, 172
  J-Bug Nymph, 171
  October Caddis Soft Hackle,
    169–70
  Peaking Caddis, 165–66
  Purple Soft Hackle, 167
  Sulphur Klinkhammer, 170
  Sulphur Soft Hackle, 170
  Walt's Worm, 166
Sulphur Klinkhammer, 170
Sulphur Soft Hackle, 170
Sunken Stone, 77
Superfly International, 135, 136
Superman, 189
Suspended Ant, 149
Suspended Beetle, 149
Swamp Monster, 148

Tan X-Caddis, 161
TCO's Tan Adult Caddis, 44
terrestrials, 112, 113, 114–15, 186.
  See also ants; beetles
Top Secret Midge, 50
Trailing Bubble Harey Caddis
  (Peacock), ARF, 130
Trailing Bubble Harey Caddis
  (Tan), ARF, 129
Trailing Harey Yellow Stone, ARF,
  129–30
Triple Threat, 69
Trout (Bergman), 15, 18–20

Trout Bum (Gierach), 56
Trout Fin, 20
Trudes, 11, 12, 120
Tung-Syn Pheasant-Tail Soft,
    ARF, 127
Two-Bit Hooker, 38–39
265 Nymph, 65
Tying Catskill-Style Dry Flies
    (Valla), 175
Tyvek, 54

Ultra Zug Free-Living Caddis,
    150, 151

Valla, Mike, 174–81
    background/overview, 174–75
    Dettes and, 175–77, 178, 179
    erect flies of, 179–80
    hackle tips, 177–79, 180
    photograph, 174
    slender bodies of flies, 180
    tying tips, 177–81
    wing-tying guidelines, 179–81
Valla, Mike (flies)
    Atherton No. 2, 176
    Cahill Quill, 175
    Cross Special, 177
    Fan Wing Coachman, 174
    Flight's Fancy, 178
    Henryville Special, 181
    March Brown, 179
    Pink Lady, 180
    Queen of the Waters, 179
    Quill Gordon, 175
VW Hopper, 186

Walt's Worm, 166
Waste Troll Minnow, 143–44
water boatman, 29–30
Waterman, Charlie, 63
Weighted Caddis Larva, 192
West Branch Caddis, 103

White River, 191, 194–95, 196, 197
White River Bugger, 196
Whitetail Midge, 193
Wilcox, Vince, 182–90
    background/overview, 182–84
    John Clark and, 187
    photograph, 182
    on terrestrial patterns, 186
    tying style, 184
Wilcox, Vince (flies)
    AC Caddis, 187
    Big Thompson Special, 188–89
    Foam Sally, 184–85
    Ginger Snap, 190
    Glo-Ant, 185
    Herbie, 185
    JC Special, 187
    Low Rider, 190
    Micro Mayfly, 188
    Olive Superman, 189
    Para-Variant, 188
    Pheasant-Tail Superman, 189
    VW Hopper, 186
William's Biot Nymph, 43
Williams Fork River, 49
wing-tying techniques
    duck or goose feathers, 17
    Flashabou wing stripes, 90, 91
    Glamour Madera thread, 53
    integrating other ideas with
        yours, 91, 147
    pearl braid, 53
    pinch wrap, 17–18
    squirrel-tail wings, 9
    Valla's guidelines, 179–81
    Wonder Wings, 10
WMD, 68
Wonder Wings, 10
Woolly Bomber, 163
Woolly Bugger, 105
worm patterns, 28, 113–14,
    166, 197

Wotton, Davy, 191–97
    background/overview, 191–92
    favorite big-fish flies, 197
    photograph, 191
    on size of flies, 196, 197
    SLF dubbing and, 193–94
    on U.K./European fishing, 192
    White River fishing, 191,
        194–95, 196, 197
Wotton, Davy (flies)
    Adult Midge, 193
    Badger and Silver Spider, 194
    Bloodworm, 197
    Caddis Emerger, 192
    Davy's Caddis, 194
    HP Soft Hackle, 195
    Prism Worm, 197
    Skating Caddis, 195
    Sowbug, 196
    Weighted Caddis Larva, 192
    White River Bugger, 196
    Whitetail Midge, 193
Wulffs
    Gray Wulff, 7
    Opal Wulff, 121
    Royal Wulff, 11, 37, 113
Wyoming. *See* Sanchez, Scott

X-Caddis flies, 79, 100, 120, 121,
    151, 161
X2 Caddis, 79

Yellow Miracle Stonefly
    Nymph, 114
Yellow Sally, 16, 17
Yellowstone River, 154

Zelon, about, 79–80, 81
Zelon Ant, 82
Zelon Midge, 80

About the Author

David Klausmeyer is editor of and photographer for *Fly Tyer* magazine. His articles and photography have appeared in many periodicals including *American Angler, Saltwater Fly Fishing, Fly Fisherman, Fly Rod & Reel,* and *Gray's Sporting Journal.* His books include *Trout Streams of Northern New England, Tying Contemporary Saltwater Flies, Tying Classic Freshwater Streamers, Rocky Mountain Trout Flies: A Postcard Book* (Lyons Press), *Unnaturals, Thunder Creek Streamers, with Keith Fulsher, Guide Flies,* and *Striped Bass Flies: Patterns of the Pros.*